EMPIRICAL ECONOMETRICS

Empirical Econometrics

J. S. CRAMER

University of Amsterdam

NORTH-HOLLAND PUBLISHING COMPANY – AMSTERDAM · LONDON

© NORTH-HOLLAND PUBLISHING COMPANY – 1971

All Rights Reserved. No part of this publication may be reproduced, stored in a retrieval system, or transmitted, in any form or by any means, electronic, mechanical, photocopying, recording or otherwise, without the prior permission of the Copyright owner.

Library of Congress Catalog Card Number 79-79722

ISBN North-Holland 0 7204 3050 X

PUBLISHERS:
NORTH-HOLLAND PUBLISHING COMPANY – AMSTERDAM
NORTH-HOLLAND PUBLISHING COMPANY – LONDON
SOLE DISTRIBUTORS FOR THE U.S.A. AND CANADA:

AMERICAN ELSEVIER PUBLISHING COMPANY, INC.
52 Vanderbilt Avenue
New York, N.Y. 10017

First printing 1969
Second printing 1971
Third printing 1973

PRINTED IN THE NETHERLANDS

Preface

Perhaps prefaces (like definitions) should be read at the very end of a book, and not at its beginning, so that the reader may have a proper appreciation of the writer's original intentions when they are finally revealed. But let me say that I have tried to provide a complement to the textbooks on econometric methods (as opposed to empirical applications) that are at present available. We now have several excellent texts that indicate the appropriate statistical procedure for a variety of situations or models. These models are however usually taken as given, and although any student of econometrics knows that their formulation must precede the application of statistical techniques he seldom knows how to set about it. A model does not spontaneously arise out of the continued contemplation of the problem at hand, but it must be deliberately created by the investigator. This process draws in varying proportions on economic theory, statistical conventions, experience and sheer inspiration, and it is not amenable to systematic treatment. I have therefore been content to bring together some examples from widely different fields of application. These examples do not constitute a complete catalogue of econometric models, but each chapter illustrates a certain type of approach, ranging from the direct and simple models of single stochastic phenomena to the highly abstract and indirect models of macro-economic relations. The selection of the actual examples is of course a matter of taste.

I wish to thank several people who have materially assisted me in completing this book. A.P.H. Saedt kept up a highly critical running commentary of the early chapters which I often found courage to disregard. C. R. Wichers and C. K. F. Nieuwenburg tracked down several examples of which I had lost all recognizable references. A. C. Kwak did the hard work of computation involved in the illustrative example of chapter 8. In the final stages H. Theil pointed out some errors that I had cherished until they appeared in the proofs. On behalf of the publishers, Mr. D. Philippo remade the figures and greatly added to their elegance. Miss N. Bouma was of great help in correcting the proofs. All remaining errors are mine alone.

The Amsterdamse Universiteits Vereniging gave financial support for the acquisition and processing of the German budget survey data used in section 125.

Amsterdam,
November 1968   J. S. CRAMER

The diligence of many readers and the magnanimity of the publishers have enabled me to correct a number of errors and mistakes in this second printing, notably on p. 133; I also rewrote part of p. 198 on my own initiative.

January 1971   J. S. C.

In this third printing I have corrected a glaring mistake in Figure 28 (p. 154) as well as a number of minor errors.

May 1973   J.S.C.

Contents

List of tables

List of figures

CHAPTER 1

Introduction

The nature of econometrics

1 Empirical econometrics, as opposed to econometric method, is not so much an academic discipline ˆas a practical pursuit, concerned with the quest for useful quantitative knowledge about economic phenomena and relations. Econometrics in this sense consists of a large volume of empirical research most of which has accumulated over the last thirty years. This vast and diffuse effort has drawn heavily on economics, mathematics and mathematical statistics, and at times it has taken its inspiration from biology and psychology as well. It is hard to think of a neat definition which would cover all cases, and we shall not attempt it ; the few common characteristics of this fairly succesful research effort are of more interest than the exact delimitation of what is econometrics and what is not.

2 Ideally, econometrics takes its models from economic theory and its methods from mathematical statistics. But in practice the situation is not so simple.

A *model* is an abstract representation of reality which brings out what is relevant to a particular question and neglects all other aspects. All sciences use models. A model reflects a definite *idea* about reality, and in most social sciences it does little more. *Economic models*, however, stand out favourably by being fairly exact and precise; they are usually elaborated in terms of well-defined variables and functions. Hence they are easily capable of a mathematical formulation, whether algebraic symbols are used or not.

Unfortunately economic theorists set great store by generality, and their models are therefore as a rule insufficiently specific to permit an empirical application. As a consequence, virtually all econometric studies add specific hypotheses of their own which are appropriate to the particular situation under review. These convenient approximations are dictated by the requirements of statistical estimation; they are based on common sense rather than on abstract economic theory.

3 Mathematical statistics provides, by design, a method of scientific inference from observed facts. This method should be used with great care. Many classic statistical techniques have been devised for experimental sciences like biology, and not all of them apply in the conditions of econometric research.

This holds in particular for statistical tests of hypotheses. The classical example of a situation which calls for such a test is Fisher's story of a lady who claims to be capable of detecting by taste alone in what order sugar and milk have been put in her tea[†]. This is hard to believe, and one may justifiably require some sort of proof before acknowledging such an extraordinary feat. Fisher accordingly sets out to devise a method of putting the lady's alleged powers to a test by allowing her full opportunities of exercising them on many cups of tea, prepared at random by the two alternative methods.

The situation is radically different when we consider an economic relationship like, say, the consumption function. There is an overwhelming case for the existence of this relation, and there is no point in testing a hypothesis that is not seriously questioned. We would moreover quite possibly have great difficulty in providing a statistical confirmation. Economic observations rarely constitute a fair experiment, and the unavoidable interference of other factors will often obscure the working of a particular relation. When this happens it is regrettable, but it is certainly not an argument for rejecting the existence of that relation; by itself, the available evidence does not permit us to conclude either way. The trouble with economic data is not so much that we have no means of experimental control over the variables, but that we are unable to achieve greater discriminating power by improving the experimental design.

In these conditions we must decide on other grounds whether to retain a particular hypothesis or not, and much will depend on its intuitive appeal or plausibility. At any rate the poor experimental quality of the processes which

---

[†] See FISHER (1935), p. 11.

generate economic observations does not justify the highly sceptical attitude which underlies the traditional statistical tests of significance. We must be far less exacting of economic data than of the outcome of a fair trial by experiments that are subject to control or at least to conscious design. As a rule economic evidence is equally compatible with a wide range of alternative hypotheses.

4 Since this is a common situation, econometrics is primarily concerned with the estimation of parameters rather than with the testing of hypotheses. But it frequently happens that economic observations are deficient even for this purpose and yield no results of any useful precision. In this case it would seem proper again to conclude that we cannot go further and that, at least for the time being, the information we seek is not available. One may, however, improve the apparent precision by adding to the a priori assumptions. This method of strengthening the model has become increasingly fashionable of late, and it may even take the form of establishing the numerical values of certain unknown coefficients on the basis of intuition. A variant of this method is to assign a fully specified prior probability distribution to the unknown parameters. This procedure, which raises many methodological questions, was first used in the calculus of probabilities by Bayes; the present-day estimation techniques which are based on the same principle are therefore known as Bayesian methods[†].

The validity of these methods, Bayesian and non-Bayesian alike, depends on the validity of the assumptions. At first sight it would seem incongruous that certain coefficients can be directly determined by the author's insight (tempered, it is true, by experience) while others remain to be laboriously estimated from data which are not particularly well suited for the purpose. But in the end this is a matter of degree and also of personal conviction.

Econometric models

5 The starting point of any econometric inquiry is the design of an *econometric model*. This term is here used in a definite technical meaning: it denotes a set of hypotheses that permits statistical inference from the

---

[†] The distinction between prior and posterior probabilities is put to use in Bayes' theorem, which dates back to Bayes (1763); but this source is rarely consulted by modern Bayesians engaged in econometrics.

particular data under review. As we have already seen the economic model must usually be adapted and strengthened to yield a definite and precise formulation of the economic processes at work; moreover the econometric model must specify the stochastic elements that are supposed to enter into the determination of the observations, so that the latter can be interpreted as a sample. On both counts the construction of econometric models is an art. It requires an understanding of what is relevant to the particular observations at hand far more than a wide knowledge of economic theory.

It is in keeping with this view that econometric models are often classified by the type of data involved. A common distinction is between *time series studies* on one hand and *cross-section analyses* on the other. Traditionally, time-series analyses are associated with the use of national aggregates, like national income and the price level of consumer goods. In most countries such data are now compiled annually as a matter of course, and as the records lengthen they provide a useful source of empirical evidence. Cross-section studies are usually based on surveys which yield direct information on the economic conditions of micro-economic units like households or firms at a given time. As Houthakker has pointed out, however, the distinction between time series and observations that refer to a single point in time is not necessarily related to the dichotomy of aggregates *versus* micro-economic data. A full classification by these two criteria yields four cases, not two, and we may add another pair to the two main types of data already named. The first of these consists of *panel data* or repeated surveys of a single sample which record the behaviour of individual micro-economic units over time. And the last case is filled by *international comparisons* of national aggregates of different countries (or other regional entities) observed at approximately the same time.

These are very broad classifications. Variations in the level of aggregation in particular are not restricted to the two extremes of national aggregates and individual micro-economic data; observations of particular markets or of particular industries occupy an intermediate position. It is a pity that data of this kind are relatively rare; they allow the use of simpler models than do micro-economic data while the analysis may come closer to a description of reality than in the case of macro-economic aggregates.

6 Econometric models come in different sizes. Some models can be summed up in a single equation while others consist of an impressive array of relations. The number of equations is of course an imperfect indication of the extent and detail of a model, but for present purposes it may serve as a rough measure of size. The point we wish to make is that there are two quite distinct considerations which dictate the choice in this matter.

If we consider an econometric model proper, viz. a set of hypotheses that permits statistical inference from a particular body of data, we have little freedom of action. Since empirical research is hard work we have an obvious interest in keeping the model as simple as is compatible with the process by which the observations are supposed to be generated. This involves a correct specification of the economic phenomena we wish to study as well as of the stochastic element that is supposed to have entered into the actual observations. The trouble is that economics abounds with interdependent relations which together simultaneously determine the course of events. This interdependence may affect the properties of the stochastic terms, and hence the probability distribution of the sample which the observations represent. In the interest of a correct specification we must take all relevant relations into account. Thus even if we wish to study only a single relation we may be forced to consider others as well because they have contributed to the determination of the observations at hand. We cannot ignore such relations at will; although opinions may differ, it is ultimately a question of fact and not of arbitrary personal choice what is the minimum number of relations that is necessary to describe properly in what manner the observations have been generated.

For the narrow purposes of statistical estimation there is no point in going beyond this minimum, but we may of course wish to extend the model for other reasons. New relations may be sketched in to relate the initial econometric model to the body of economic theory and to show where it fits in with a wider framework. Often a partial analysis of special aspects of an economic phenomenon is all that can be achieved on the basis of the available data; we may wish to put the results in a wider context to bring out more clearly what they mean.

In practice, model construction may also at times proceed in reverse order: the need for a reasonably complete description of the economic process for a particular purpose is the starting point, and the resulting structure or parts of it are then adapted to permit statistical estimation from particular data. The macro-economic models constructed by Tinbergen and Klein are a case in point[†]. These *policy models* are designed to serve

---

[†] The studies by TINBERGEN (1939) and KLEIN (1950) have set the example; several similar models of the American and of the British economy have since been published by these authors as well as by others.

economic policy and forecasting. They must therefore cover all relevant variables, i.e. all variables that are of interest as targets as well as those that are instrumental in shaping the course of events. This calls for a fairly comprehensive description of the national economy even at the simplest macro-economic level. Since almost all elaborations constitute an improvement, models of this type tend to grow in detail and extent, and apart from obvious limitations of time and money there is no reason why they should not continue to do so.

Policy models of this kind are often loosely called econometric models because they contain numerical coefficients which have been obtained by empirical research. But they provide a framework for the application of empirical knowledge rather than a means of obtaining it. Their structure is determined by the purpose they must serve rather than by the requirements of statistical estimation, and they have only one important link with econometric models proper: since there is only one single correct description of the interdependence of macro-economic variables, an econometric model for the analysis of aggregate time series cannot be at variance with the corresponding part of a policy model. But while the policy model must be complete, the econometric model need not be so: insofar as parts of the economy can be considered in isolation we may profitably do so for purposes of estimation.

7   At this point we may briefly raise the question of the connection between ends and means of econometric research. Econometrics has come into being in the early 1930's, partly in response to the need for numerical coefficients for the solution of practical problems. Much of the early work takes its themes from the pressing problems of the day and testifies to a sense of action and of impatience with the powerless generality of pure economic theory. These attitudes have disappeared. The opposition to theorizing generally and to economic theory in particular has vanished altogether, and much if not most research is at present undertaken with no immediately useful application of the results in mind. This is a normal sequel to any new departure in science and there is no reason to deplore it.

A subtler link between ends and means is implied by the arguments of *decision theory*. In principle and in the abstract there is a definite connection between the intended use of empirical estimates and the method of estimation. Statistical inference at best provides probability statements or estimates with certain stochastic properties. Neither of these can be considered by themselves: the use that will be made of the statistical information dictates what probability statements are required as well as what properties of the estimates are desirable.

This brief statement of the basic argument does little justice to decision theory. So far, however, it has made no appreciable difference to the practice of econometric research. It would seem that we are still a long way off from the advanced stage where these methodological refinements can usefully be introduced. For present purposes – that is, in writing this book – I have adopted the simple view that empirical knowledge is desirable in its own right. But this should be regarded as a working hypothesis rather than a firm methodological precept.

8   We return once more to a discussion of different types of models and examine more closely than before the nature of their probabilistic specification.

As we have already noted any *econometric model* must contain a stochastic element in order to permit statistical inference from the data. The usual procedure is to set up a model of varying degree of sophistication for the systematic description of the phenomenon under review and then to add, more or less as an afterthought, *disturbance terms* to which convenient probabilistic properties are ascribed. Thus linear systematic relations with additive disturbances lead up to the familiar regression model. In econometric models of this traditional type – linear and nonlinear alike – the disturbances represent all factors that are ignored in the systematic part of the model. These factors are seldom discussed, and it is rarely indicated by what arguments they may be supposed to imply the assumed properties of the disturbances. To insist on a justification of each model along these lines would be to call forth a stream of uniformly tedious and repetitive addenda to most econometric papers, so perhaps the present state of affairs where the regression model is simply taken for granted is preferable. Very often we can after all do no better than to use regression as a means of statistical analysis which brings out the main information contained in the data. In the case of aggregate data in particular there is little that can sensibly be said about the inherent characteristics of the disturbance term.

Yet there is an alternative approach which seems much more promising, at least where micro-economic data are concerned. This is to integrate the random element firmly with the economic model instead of adding it on reluctantly as a mere means of reconciling the theory with the data. On this view we should not distinguish between a systematic, "explained" part of the observed variation on one hand and a random "residual" part on the other, but we should aim at a model which ultimately specifies the distribution of the variables concerned and offers a reasonable argument in support of this specification. Insofar as economic relations reflect the behaviour of individuals which is necessarily erratic (though not entirely so), it would seem natural to introduce probabilistic considerations at the very outset into the model. Such *stochastic models* would "explain" the distribution and dispersion of the economic phenomena concerned just as much as the traditional models explain the systematic variation of their expected values.

So far very little progress has been made in this direction; the major part of current research still consists of an application of advanced methods of linear statistical analysis to highly aggregated data. But since I believe that stochastic models offer a promising line of research I have included them in this book.

The scope of this book

9   This book is about models and results. It is not concerned with the statistical methods of econometric research, for which several textbooks are now available. It is not concerned either with a complete catalogue of existing work. Instead I have set out to bring together selected examples from a few fields of application that illustrate accepted practices, and to show the type of results which they yield. At first, I meant to restrict the discussion to models and results which I regard as valid, but in the course of writing I have had so many fresh doubts on this point that I must leave the reader to judge for himself.

This reservation is no reflection on the quality of the research or on the honesty of the authors whose work I report; I am afraid that it is a symptom of the present state of econometrics. I have noticed that many writers of research papers resolve similar doubts by unduly submissive qualifications of results that were evidently intended. Apparently few authors really believe their results to hold good. Perhaps it is too early to start collecting empirical findings that are firmly established; occasionally I have been led to include subjects like the income distribution on which a great deal of work has been done without any satisfactory conclusion.

10   By its nature this book contains few original contributions; I have drawn freely and widely on the work of others. As a perusal of the table of contents will show I reported a number of distinct studies which show little unity. This is largely due to the inclusion of a few stochastic models of micro-economic phenomena of the type discussed above. In the latter part of the book we return to traditional regression analyses which at least employ a common statistical model. The order of presentation proceeds from the simple and direct approach of micro-economics to increasingly abstract and aggregative models.

While this book is not directly concerned with statistical technique the reader should have a fair working knowledge of statistics in general and of linear regression in particular. I could not bring myself to include yet another introductory chapter on probability, estimation, or, for that matter, matrix algebra when so many excellent systematic treatises of these subjects are available. At times temptation proved too strong and led me to include my own formulation of certain well-known results, as in chs 5 and 6. But this is meant as a mere reminder, and by no means as a substitute for the fuller treatment given by others elsewhere.

11   While this introductory chapter calls for no particular references we may indicate some books that can be profitably read in conjunction with (or perhaps as a substitute for) the present text. The first four titles listed below are advanced textbooks of the statistical methods used in traditional econometric work; Johnston's book is the simpler text, Goldberger's a workmanlike reference rather than a textbook, Theil's and Malinvaud's the most advanced of the set. The other three titles are concerned with econometric applications; they, too, are listed by increasing order of sophistication.

J. JOHNSTON, *Econometric methods*. New York: McGraw-Hill, 1963.
A. S. GOLDBERGER, *Econometric theory*. New York: Wiley, 1964.
H. THEIL, *Introduction to econometrics*. New York: Wiley, forthcoming.
E. MALINVAUD, *Statistical methods of econometrics*. Amsterdam: North-Holland, 1966.
J. TINBERGEN, *Econometrics*. London: Allen & Unwin, 1951.
L. R. KLEIN, *Introduction to econometrics*. Englewood Cliffs: Prentice Hall, 1962.
L. R. KLEIN, *A textbook of econometrics*. Evanston: Row, Peterson, 1953.

CHAPTER 2

Random arrivals and related events

The model

12   This chapter is concerned with a very simple yet fruitful model of the incidence of random and independent events in time. This model was first developed in 1909 by Erlang for the number of incoming telephone calls at a telephone exchange, but it is applicable to a wide class of similar events like traffic, the arrival of clients or again the failure of machines[†]. The importance of such phenomena in problems of capacity and production planning is obvious.

We consider the probability of exactly one *event* occurring during a brief time interval $(t, t + \Delta t)$ and assume that this probability is independent of t, the time at which the interval is situated, and that it is proportional to the length of the interval. The probability can then be represented as

$$\lambda \Delta t$$

where λ is a positive constant and Δt is at any rate sufficiently small to ensure the condition $\lambda \Delta t < 1$. The events under review are moreover assumed to occur independently of one another, so that the probability of more than one occurrence during the interval is given by

$$\lambda^2 \Delta t^2 + \lambda^3 \Delta t^3 + \dots$$

[†] See BROCKMEYER et al., (1948) for reprints of Erlang's articles which are otherwise inaccessible.

The accumulated number of events over the period extending from time zero up to time t is a random integer-valued variable $\underline{n}$.[†] Its discrete probability density obviously depends on t and will be denoted by

$$P(n,t) \qquad n = 0, 1, 2, \ldots$$

These probabilities change over time. From the earlier assumptions it follows that

$$P(n, t+\Delta t) = (1 - \lambda\Delta t - \lambda^2\Delta t^2 \ldots)P(n,t) + \lambda\Delta t\, P(n-1,t) \\ + \lambda^2\Delta t^2 P(n-2,t) + \ldots$$

or again

$$\frac{P(n, t+\Delta t) - P(n,t)}{\Delta t} = (-\lambda - \lambda^2\Delta t - \ldots)P(n,t) + \lambda P(n-1,t) \\ + \lambda^2 \Delta t P(n-2,t) + \ldots$$

Passage to the limit yields a differential equation

$$\frac{\mathrm{d}P(n,t)}{\mathrm{d}t} = P'(n,t) = \lambda P(n-1,t) - \lambda P(n,t) \tag{2.1}$$

which holds for all n with the reservation that negative values cannot occur so that $P(k,t) = 0$ for all $k < 0$. For $n = 0$ (2.1) therefore reduces to

$$P'(0,t) = -\lambda P(0,t),$$

and this equation is readily solved: the self-evident initial condition $P(0,0) = 1$ leads to

$$P(0,t) = \mathrm{e}^{-\lambda t}. \tag{2.2}$$

Substitution of this result in (2.1) for $n = 1$ yields a differential equation which is in turn solved for the initial condition $P(1,0) = 0$. Continuing in this manner we may find $P(n,t)$ for all $n = 0, 1, 2, \ldots$; it soon becomes apparent that the general expression is

$$P(n,t) = \frac{(\lambda t)^n}{n!}\mathrm{e}^{-\lambda t}, \tag{2.3}$$

and it can be proved by induction that this is indeed the solution of (2.1). Thus, for any period of finite length t the number of events $\underline{n} = 0, 1, 2, \ldots$ has a *Poisson distribution* with parameter (λt). We recall that both mean and

---

[†] We adopt the Dutch convention of underlining random variables. See HEMELRIJK (1966).

variance of $\underline{n}$ are equal to this parameter, which is a pure number since λ is a time rate and t is the length of a time period.

13   An alternative but equivalent formulation of this model is in terms of the probability distribution of the *waiting time until the first event*. This is a nonnegative continuous random variable $\underline{t}$; its distribution function $F(t)$ follows readily from the probability that a period of length t contains no events, as given by (2.2). We find

$$F(t) = P(\underline{t} \leqslant t) = 1 - P(\underline{t} > t) = 1 - e^{-\lambda t} \tag{2.4}$$

so that $\underline{t}$ has the *exponential distribution* with density

$$f(t) = \lambda e^{-\lambda t}.$$

The mean and standard deviation of $\underline{t}$ are both equal to $1/\lambda$, which is the inverse of a time rate or the length of a time period. Since we have imposed no conditions whatever on the choice of the time origin $t = 0$, the exponential distribution holds for the waiting time until the first event from any arbitrary moment onwards; in particular the distribution applies to the time interval between two successive events.

Examples in air traffic and shipping

14   Most of the economic phenomena that satisfy the conditions of this model, like the arrival of clients or the incidence of breakdowns in a machine shop, refer to a single firm. Such data are seldom disclosed. We therefore take our examples from incoming traffic by air and sea which offers a close analogy to the arrival of customers.

We begin by examining the waiting times between successive announcements of incoming aircraft at Schiphol Airport ground station[†]. The observations cover weekday afternoons during the winter months of 1950; this restriction ensures that they are homogeneous in the sense that they reflect a single constant traffic intensity λ. If $N(t)$ is the observed number of intervals $> t$, this should satisfy – by (2.4) – the relation

$$N(t) = N(0)e^{-\lambda t}. \tag{2.5}$$

[†] The data for this example, which was also used by THEIL et al., (1965), have been collected by the Dutch *Rijksluchtvaartdienst*. For an earlier application of the exponential distribution to air traffic see BOWEN and PEARCY (1948).

In fig. 1 $N(t)$ is plotted against t. The points conform closely to a declining exponential as shown by the fitted curve.

Fig. 1 gives a convincing picture of the agreement of observations and model. It must be borne in mind, however, that successive points are not at all independent, and that the cumulative character of $N(t)$ already ensures its steady decline with increasing t. Even so the agreement is remarkably good, the more so if we reflect that the data should meet the requirement that successive events are independent. Aircraft arrivals are subject to a schedule,

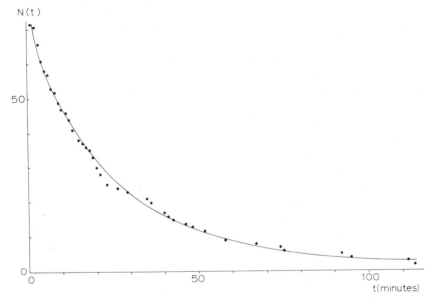

Fig. 1. Distribution of waiting times between successive arrivals of incoming aircraft (Schiphol airport, weekday afternoons, winter 1950; curve $N(0)e^{-\lambda t}$ drawn in). For notes see appendix B.

and if they behave in fact like random and independent events this is merely a sad reflection on the weather conditions of winter 1950.

15   Instead of the waiting times between successive arrivals we may of course equally well examine the number of arrivals in successive periods of given duration. We have done so for the daily number of incoming ships of various nationalities at the port of Amsterdam in 1963[†]. These data demonstrate the heterogeneity that results from variations in the arrival rate λ. If

---

[†]   Data collected by courtesy of the *Havenmeester van Amsterdam*.

λ were constant over the whole of the year, the daily arrivals during 1963 should by our model provide a sample of 365 observations from the Poisson distribution (2.3). Expressing λ as a daily arrival rate we may put $t = 1$ and obtain

$$P(n) = \frac{\lambda^n}{n!} e^{-\lambda} . \tag{2.6}$$

If, however, λ is subject to seasonal variation, the daily arrivals constitute a mixed sample in which various Poisson distributions with different parameters enter in unknown proportions. The familiar decomposition of the sample variation in variation within groups and variation between groups shows that heterogeneity in this sense tends to increase the sample variance. This provides a simple test. In the case of a homogeneous sample from a single Poisson distribution the sample mean and the sample variance should be approximately equal; if the sample variance far exceeds the mean this points to heterogeneity [†].

TABLE 1

Sample mean and variance of daily arrivals of shipping (Port of Amsterdam, 1963).

sample	sample mean	sample variance
Norwegian shipping, 365 daily records for 1963	1.22	1.17
All shipping, 365 daily records for 1963	23.40	33.74
All shipping, 30 daily records for June 1963	23.40	24.64

For notes see appendix A.

We illustrate these arguments by the three examples shown in table 1 and fig. 2. The first case refers to the daily arrival of Norwegian shipping during the full year 1963. Inspection of monthly arrivals by nationality suggested that Norwegian shipping would be free from seasonal variation, so that the full year's observations constitute a homogeneous sample from a single Poisson distribution. This is confirmed by the agreement of sample mean and sample variance in table 1, and also by fig. 2a which shows a typical Poisson distribution. Table 2, too, shows the close fit of the data to a Poisson distribution.

[†] For a proper test (in the technical sense) of Poisson distributions based on the ratio of sample mean to sample variance see HOEL (1947), p. 197.

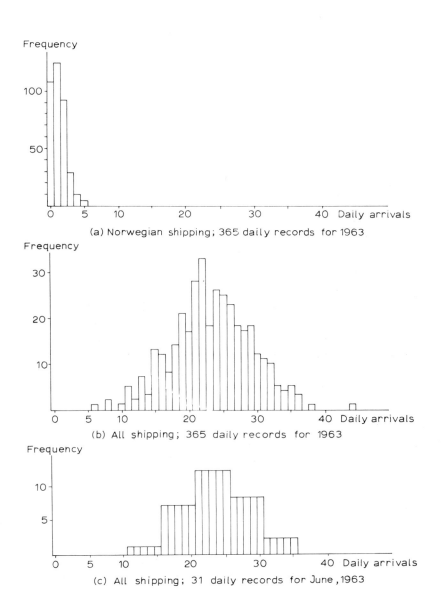

Fig. 2. Frequency distributions of daily arrivals of shipping (Amsterdam, 1963). For notes see appendix B.

TABLE 2

Observed and theoretical frequencies of daily arrivals of Norwegian shipping
(Port of Amsterdam, 1963).

| Number of | relative frequency | |
daily arrivals	observed	theoretical
0	.296	.295
1	.340	.360
2	.252	.220
3	.079	.089
4	.025	.027
5	.008	.007
6 and over	0	.002

For notes see appendix A.

In the second case we find evident heterogeneity. We consider the full year's daily arrivals of all shipping, regardless of nationality. If the arrivals of each nationality were Poisson distributed like Norwegian shipping, their sum would be Poisson distributed also, but with such a large value of λ that the result would be indistinguishable from a normal distribution – as indeed it is, according to fig. 2b. Even so, however, the equality of mean and variance should continue to hold, and the fact that the sample variance far exceeds the mean (as shown in table 1) is a clear indication of heterogeneity.

The third example shows that this heterogeneity is indeed due to seasonal variation, for it disappears if we restrict the sample to a single month. Since we again consider all shipping, regardless of nationality, λ is as large as in the preceding case and once more the distribution approaches normality, as shown in fig. 2c [†]. But this time table 1 shows the sample variance and sample mean to be approximately equal, so that we may confidently take this normal distribution to represent a Poisson distribution with a large parameter λ.

Purchases of floor polish

16   There is yet another kind of heterogeneity which we shall demonstrate by means of the data of table 3. This table shows the frequency distribution of the sales of a particular brand of floor polish recorded during 41 days in a department store [††]. Attempts at fitting a Poisson distribution to these data

---

[†] The equality of sample means in the second and third case is a mere coincidence.
[††] The example is taken from LEERGANG BESLISKUNDE (1963).

fall through; the excess of the sample variance over the sample mean—1.197 and .805 respectively—strongly suggests that the sample is not Poissonian, and it is clear that the trouble lies with the single day on which six sales were recorded. Closer examination brings out, however, that this observation refers to the sale of six units to a single customer. It will be clear that the Poisson model cannot account for this situation; it is concerned with single, indivisible events, and it does not allow for the possibility that these events come in different sizes.

TABLE 3

Frequency distribution of daily sales of floor polish.

daily sales	number of days
0	22
1	10
2	7
3	1
. . .	. . .
6	1
. . .	. . .
total	41

For notes see appendix A.

In the present case the error is easily corrected. The correct definition of an event is the arrival of a customer, irrespective of the extent of his purchases. If no other multiple sales have occurred apart from the single instance

TABLE 4

Observed and theoretical frequencies of daily number of floor polish customers.

daily number of customers	number of days	relative frequency observed	theoretical
0	22	.54	.50
1	11	.27	.34
2	7	.17	.12
3	1	.02	.03
4 and over	0	0	.01
total	41	1	1

For notes see appendix A.

already mentioned, the data for the number of customers are as shown in table 4, and in this form they closely fit a Poisson distribution.

The negative binomial distribution

17   Although the simple Poisson model is quite powerful and applicable to a wide range of phenomena we have already met two cases in which it is rendered useless by the presence of an additional source of variation. Since either case represents a common situation, considerable interest attaches to the distribution of the random variable that results from such more complex processes. There is of course no general answer to this question, as the outcome depends on the precise nature of the additional variation that is superimposed on the original model; as a matter of fact the problem does not permit of a solution but for a few special cases. Since their derivation is mainly a matter of mathematics, and lacks the immediate appeal of the simple Poisson model, we shall merely indicate the general argument involved and refer to other sources for details.

We first consider variations in the incidence rate of the events under review. The observations consist of numbers of events recorded during periods of equal length; each observation is distributed according to (2.6); but since the parameter λ varies, the data together constitute a heterogeneous sample from various Poisson distributions. In this case we may consider λ itself as a random variable with probability density $f(\lambda)$; the density of the number of events $\underline{n}$ is then given by

$$P(n) = \int_0^\infty \frac{\lambda^n}{n!} e^{-\lambda} f(\lambda) d\lambda. \tag{2.7}$$

The problem is of course to find a density $f(\lambda)$ which permits the evaluation of this integral. A density function which fits the case is the gamma distribution

$$f(\lambda) = \frac{1}{\alpha! \beta^{\alpha+1}} \lambda^\alpha e^{-\lambda/\beta}, \qquad \beta > 0, \; \alpha > -1. \tag{2.8}$$

Upon substituting this expression in (2.7) and relabelling the parameters we obtain the *negative binomial distribution*

$$P(n) = \binom{n+k-1}{n} p^k q^n \tag{2.9}$$

with

$$k = \alpha + 1, \quad p = 1/1 + \beta, \quad q = 1 - p.^{\dagger}$$

18　The second case, suggested by the floor polish example, is more involved. While events occur strictly according to the simple Poisson process the observations record some other random variable attached to each event. Suppose that we are interested in z, the number of units sold during a given period. The number of customers n is Poisson distributed as in (2.6), and the number of units bought by a customer is a random variable x with density $f(x)$. Then the total count z is the sum of a random number of random variables,

$$z = \sum_{i=1}^{n} x_i .$$

In this case it is difficult even to formulate by what expression the distribution of z is defined; it will be clear, however, that the solution depends on the choice of the density $f(x)$. A specification which does permit of a solution is the *logarithmic series distribution*

$$f(x) = \frac{-1}{\ln(1-\gamma)} \frac{\gamma^x}{x}, \qquad x = 1, 2, 3, \ldots, \qquad 0 < \gamma < 1, \qquad (2.10)$$

defined for positive integers alone; this is consistent with the view that a customer with zero purchases does not qualify as such. If the specification (2.10) holds, the distribution of z turns out to be once more the *negative binomial distribution*

$$P(z) = \binom{z+k-1}{z} p^k q^z$$

with

$$k = -\lambda/\ln(1-\gamma), \qquad p = 1-\gamma, \qquad q = \gamma.^{\dagger\dagger}$$

19　It would be idle to pretend that these complex models have not been prompted primarily by the mathematical feasibility of their derivation. There are some arguments, however, in support of the additional specifications that have been introduced. The gamma distribution (2.8) can be adapted

---

† See GREENWOOD and YULE (1920).
†† See QUENOUILLE (1949).

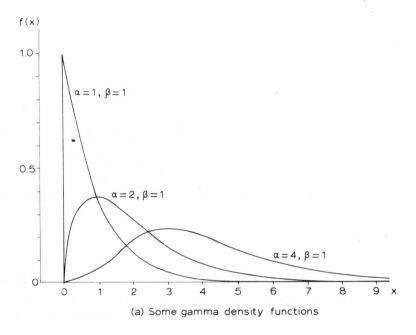

(a) Some gamma density functions

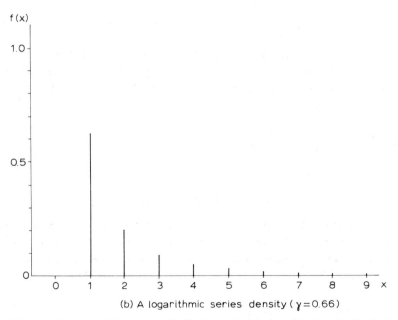

(b) A logarithmic series density ($\gamma = 0.66$)

Fig. 3. Density functions of the gamma distribution and of the logarithmic series distribution.

to a wide range of shapes by varying its two parameters, as is shown in fig. 3a. The logarithmic distribution (2.10), shown in fig. 3b, is not so flexible, but there is some evidence that the variable x, the number of units concerned in nonzero purchases, is in fact distributed in this manner[†].

We shall give no explanation for the fact that two quite different models both lead to the same negative binomial distribution. This is of course no mere coincidence, but it cannot be traced to any readily evident similarity. Likewise there is no way of constructing an analogy of either model with the classical negative binomial model which is concerned with the number of Bernoulli trials in order to accumulate exactly k successes.

20　A final argument in favour of the negative binomial distribution model is that it works. We illustrate this point by a few results due to EHRENBERG (1959), who has fitted the model (2.9) to the purchases of a large number of branded consumer goods recorded by some 2.000 households over periods of varying length. The parameters of the negative binomial distribution are established in a straightforward manner by observing that

$$P(\underline{z}=0)=p^k, \qquad E(\underline{z})=k(q/p).$$

These expressions are equated to the observed frequency of zero purchases and the sample mean respectively, and the resulting equations yield estimates of

$$m=k(q/p), \qquad a=q/p.$$

Ehrenberg writes (2.9) in terms of these parameters.

As fig. 4 shows, the negative binomial thus obtained gives an excellent fit to the data. As a further check on the model, Ehrenberg has compared the sample variance for some 180 products with its theoretical value, obtained by evaluating

$$\mathrm{var}(\underline{z})=k(q/p)(1/p)=m(1+a)$$

for the values of m and a derived in the manner just described. This comparison will bring out whether the relation between sample mean, sample variance and the sample frequency of zero observations agrees with the properties of the negative binomial distribution. Again the agreement

---

[†] I have matched the example of steel blooms given by WILLIAMSON and BRETHERTON (1964) by data from a department store, but these results have not yet been published.

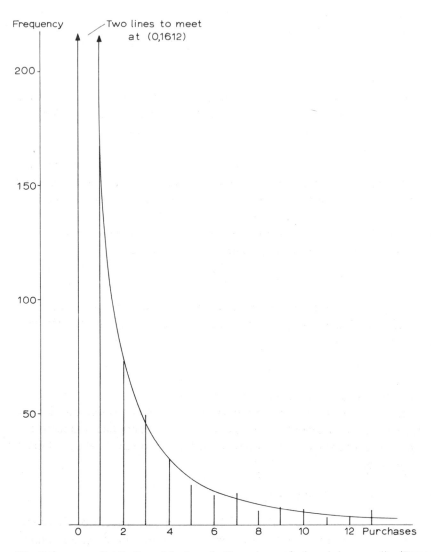

Fig. 4. Frequency distribution of the household purchases of a branded commodity (EHREN-BERG). For notes see appendix B.

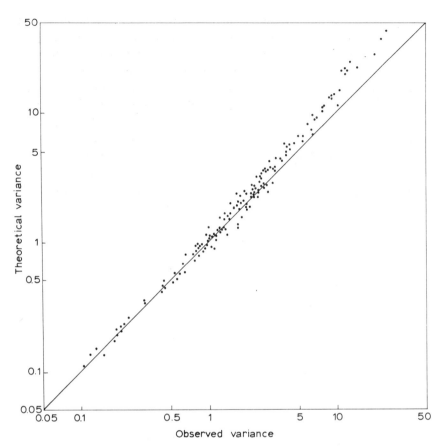

Fig. 5. Observed and theoretical variances of household purchases of branded commodities (EHRENBERG). For notes see appendix B.

between the theoretical value of the variance and its actual value, as shown in fig. 5, is good enough to inspire a fair degree of confidence in the negative binomial model [†].

Concluding remarks

21 We do not wish to dwell any longer on the models presented in the preceding sections, but a few remarks on method are in order. Throughout

---

[†] For further applications of this model see CHATFIELD et al. (1967).

the present chapter the traditional statistical methods of estimation, testing and curve-fitting have been abandoned in favour of simpler and more direct arguments. Parameters have been estimated by the simple expedient of equating sample statistics to their theoretical counterpart; the fit of distributions has been illustrated by graphical representation rather than by elaborate tests; finally, the specific properties of probability distributions have been singled out to provide a test of their applicability. The reader may compare our concern with the relation of sample variance to sample mean in alleged Poisson distributions with Ehrenberg's test of observed and theoretical variance in the negative binomial. Such methods are simple, straightforward and practical; whether they carry conviction the reader must decide for himself.

CHAPTER 3

Attributes of consumer behaviour

Introduction

22 *Consumer behaviour* is made up out of a variety of decisions and choices, and even when we keep to its economic aspects several distinct and separate phenomena may be singled out for analysis. In this chapter we are concerned only with those features that can be represented as a choice between two alternatives on the part of the individual consumer or household. The outcome of this choice is the presence (or absence) of a particular *attribute* of consumer behaviour in the household concerned.

We may of course reduce almost any situation to such a simple choice, but such drastic simplification makes more sense in some cases than in others. The ownership of major durable goods like motorcars or television sets is a good example of an attribute. There are two distinct arguments that may be advanced to explain why this is so. The first applies when these goods are recent innovations, so that there is little scope for quality variation and multiple ownership can be dismissed as a rare exception. In these conditions the main decision of the consumer is whether he will have a car or television or not, and the choice of vehicle or screen is of minor importance. When the commodity is no longer a novelty these particular conditions no longer hold; yet the ownership decision remains predominant because it affects the entire structure of the households demand. This is the second reason why the ownership of certain durable goods is a significant attribute of the individual households consumer behaviour. It applies to most major durables, and it explains why many econometric studies have been made of the ownership of cars but not of shoes or books. Physical durability has little to do with this distinction. In principle the notion of an attribute might indeed be extended to other fields of consumer demand ; ultimately, the participation in certain pastimes or the choice of a particular butcher may well affect the household's way of life in the same manner (although not to the same extent) as does car ownership.

We shall in fact return to this subject at a later stage – in section 120 – where we will establish a certain artificial hierarchy in the decisions of the consumer in respect of *any* commodity. The first decision is whether to adopt the commodity concerned, i.e. whether to consume it at all or not. This is a clear instance of an attribute, although for the reasons already given it is not always of sufficient interest to merit a separate analysis. The second choice bears on the amount consumed, and the third and final decision is concerned with quality. This approach is of course at variance with the pure theory of consumer behaviour, in which the individual is supposed to consider the whole continuum of all available alternatives simultaneously. We do not claim that our model is more realistic in the sense that the three choices that we have distinguished are actually made independently of one another in the order given; but we feel free to study them in isolation as if this were the case. This is at least a great help in bringing some order in our analyses.

We now turn to a discussion of the *lognormal* model which may be used to relate attributes of consumer behaviour to income and to prices and hence to yield Engel curves and demand curves of such attributes.

The lognormal Engel curve model

23 By an *Engel curve* we mean the relation of any characteristic of consumer behaviour to the consumer's income, *ceteris paribus*, or all other things (and prices in particular) being equal. Since a survey among households at approximately the same time is virtually the only source of data that meet the latter condition, Engel curves are specifically identified with the relations that emerge from the analysis of such surveys; traditionally, they refer to household expenditure and consumption of specific commodities, and they take their name from the German statistician Engel who used budget surveys in this manner as early as 1857 [†]. But there is no reason why we

---

[†] We discuss this type of analysis in ch. 7.

should not extend the term to cover other characteristics of household demand as well.

24 In the case of an attribute, say car ownership, the *individual* Engel curve is of the simple form depicted in fig. 6. It is completely determined by the

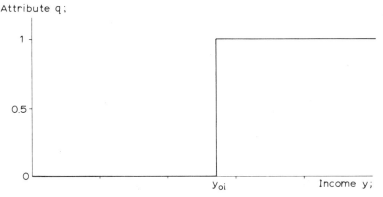

Fig. 6. Individual Engel curve for an attribute.

threshold income y_0 of the household concerned. The ith household will have the attribute if and only if its actual income y_i exceeds or equals its threshold income y_{0i}; denoting the attribute by a $(0, 1)$ variable q_i we write

$$q_i = 1 \quad \text{if} \quad y_i \geqslant y_{0i},$$
$$q_i = 0 \quad \text{otherwise}.$$
(3.1)

The value of the threshold income reflects the individual households preferences in respect of the attribute under consideration; since preferences vary from one household to another, so do the y_{0i}. We assume that the latter's frequency distribution is independent of the actual income of the households concerned. The crucial point is then the specification of this distribution. We assume that it is *lognormal*, i.e. that the (natural) logarithm of y_{0i} has a normal distribution. The distribution function of any variable $\underline{z}$ that is lognormally distributed with parameters μ, σ^2 is denoted by

$$\Lambda(z; \ \mu, \sigma^2)$$

and this is defined by

$$\Lambda(z; \ \mu, \sigma^2) = N(\log z; \ \mu, \sigma^2) = N\left\{ \frac{\log z - \mu}{\sigma}; \ 0, 1 \right\},$$
(3.2)

where the last expression stands for the standard normal distribution function

$$N(x;\ 0,1) = \int_{-\infty}^{x} \frac{1}{\sqrt{2\pi}}\, e^{-\frac{1}{2}t^2}\, \mathrm{d}t \ .$$

The shape of the lognormal distribution function as well as of the corresponding frequency distribution (or density function in the case of a random variable) are shown in fig. 7; it should be noted that the latter extends over the positive range only.

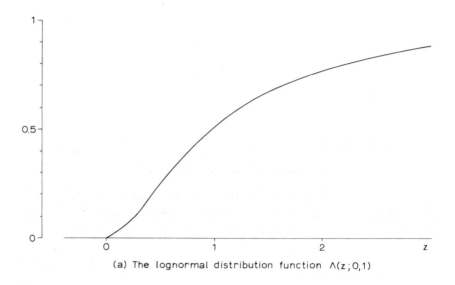

(a) The lognormal distribution function $\Lambda(z;0,1)$

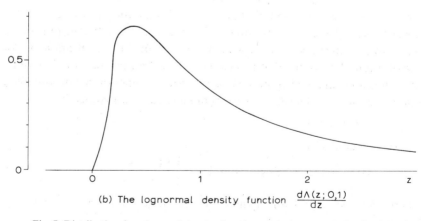

(b) The lognormal density function $\dfrac{\mathrm{d}\Lambda(z;0,1)}{\mathrm{d}z}$

Fig. 7. Distribution function and density function of the lognormal distribution.

25   Before we go on to discuss the assumption of a lognormal distribution of the y_{0i} we complete the model by deriving the Engel curve of an attribute like car ownership. In order to do so we consider the probability that the attribute occurs at a given income level y. The threshold income of a household taken at random from among all households with income y is itself a random variable, and the conditional probability of car ownership at the income level y follows immediately from (3.1) and (3.2); we have

$$P(\underline{q}_i = 1 \,|\, y_i = y) = P(\underline{y}_{0i} \leqslant y) = \Lambda(y;\ \mu, \sigma^2). \tag{3.3}$$

For simplicity we replace the probability by the expected frequency of the attribute, say $Q(y)$, and obtain

$$Q(y) = \Lambda(y;\ \mu, \sigma^2). \tag{3.4}$$

According to this model, then, the expected frequency of car ownership varies with income as a lognormal distribution function of the form shown in fig. 7a.

26   By (3.4) the expected frequency of the attribute increases monotonically with income and tends to unity as income continues to rise. In some cases, like the ownership of musical instruments (or even car ownership in urban areas) the attribute may fail to appeal to all consumers so that even at very high income levels the *saturation level S* is less than unity. In this case we may assign an infinitely large threshold income to a fraction $(1 - S)$ of all households, the lognormal specification being retained for the threshold incomes of the fraction S of potential consumers. It follows that in this variant of the main model the Engel curve is given by

$$Q(y) = S\Lambda(y;\ \mu, \sigma^2).$$

The logarithmic transformation

27   The lognormal distribution is highly versatile in that it may result from various basic assumptions, and we shall meet it in various guises[†]. The present specification of a lognormal distribution of threshold income levels

---

[†] The standard text is that of AITCHISON and BROWN (1957). This book gives a comprehensive treatment of the statistical properties of the distribution and of methods of estimation as well as an extensive survey of its application in economics and in other fields.

is a direct translation into economics of a wide class of biological models which deal with the response to physical stimuli like the concentration of active agents in insecticides. Once we accept the notion of an individual *tolerance level* which determines the response, it makes little difference whether we consider a positive stimulus like income or a negative stimulus like price, which will be examined shortly. In either case it will be readily conceded that individual tolerance levels vary; whether they are in fact determinate constants or should best be regarded as random variables even at the individual level is immaterial.

Now it will be shown that this variation is adequately described by a lognormal distribution. Again the normal character of the distribution does not call for much discussion. After all many individual traits follow a normal distribution, and we usually refer to the Central Limit Theorem for an explanation of this fact. As for the logarithmic transformation, however, while we cannot of course *explain* it, some comment is in order.

28   In the present case the main argument is of course a matter of fact: the lognormal distribution adequately describes the observations but the normal distribution does not. For physical stimuli the hypothesis that their intensity as perceived by the individual should be measured on a logarithmic scale has been formulated long ago in the celebrated *Weber-Fechner law*[†]; there is no reason why it should not equally apply to economic stimuli. In the case of economic variables the idea has indeed a strong intuitive appeal: whenever we wish to compare incomes or prices we use *relative* differences (usually on a percentage base) as a matter of course. The transformation of economic variables to a logarithmic scale is at any rate an ancient tradition; Bernoulli expressed the utility of a sum of money by its logarithm in order to solve the Petersburg paradox as early as in 1738[††].

29   A less romantic line of argument in support of the logarithmic transformation of economic variables like incomes and prices is that they are by their very nature restricted to the positive range, barring some pathological exceptions. Unless the mean is quite large relatively to the standard deviation this rules out the normal distribution; and if we impose the restric-

---

[†] This law holds that the reaction to physiological stimuli is proportional to the logarithm of the stimulus; it takes its name from Weber's work in the early 19th century and Fechner's towards the end of that century.
[††] See BERNOULLI (1738).

tion to positive values on a process which would lead to a normal distribution if it were to proceed unhampered, it may well result in a skew distribution of the lognormal type. The Central Limit Theorem leads to a normal distribution whenever the value of a variable is determined by a large number of *additive* independent random shocks; the simplest analogous model which excludes negative and zero values consists of a large number of nonnegative independent random shocks that have *multiplicative* effects. Since the latters' logarithms again satisfy the additive model this will lead to the lognormal distribution.

30　　The use of the logarithmic transformation of economic variables is not restricted to the lognormal distribution, and we shall meet it in many other instances. If an economic relationship is formulated in terms of logarithms, the derivatives turn of course into *elasticities* since

$$\frac{d \log X}{d \log Y} = \frac{Y}{X} \frac{dX}{dY} = \frac{dX}{X} \Big/ \frac{dY}{Y} .$$

Insofar as elasticities are introduced as a means of relating *relative* changes in cause and effect, the same intuitive arguments set out above can be invoked. The main practical advantage is of course that, as a measure of economic relationships, elasticities have the dimension of a pure number so that we can dispense with the conversion of units of measurement when it comes to a comparison of coefficients from different countries or from different periods. Since there exists no fixed standard of comparison for the money values usually involved, the choice of a rate of conversion is a real problem.

　　Finally, the logarithmic transformation may offer distinct technical advantages in regression analysis, namely in the case of heteroskedasticity. We return to this argument in section 68.

Examples of lognormal Engel curves

31　　We demonstrate the lognormal Engel curve model by a series of examples in which the incidence of various attributes in different income classes agrees reasonably well with equation (3.4). To treat all households in a given income class as if they all had the same income – usually represented by the class mean – is an approximation with obvious limitations and defects; its major advantage is that it permits a quick graphical presentation, which is impossible if we insist on using the individual household data.

Fig. 8 shows the fit of a lognormal curve to the incidence of motor vehicle use in nine income classes. The parameters of the fitted curve have been estimated from the nine observations by fairly advanced numerical methods[†]; but the data might almost equally well been set out on lognormal graph paper, a straight line then being fitted by eye. The horizontal axis of this graph paper has a logarithmic or ratio scale, and the vertical has a probability scale which represents fractions by equidistant standard normal deviates according to the normal distribution function. This grid transforms

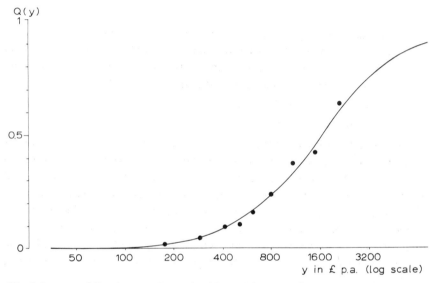

Fig. 8. Lognormal Engel curve of motoring (Great Britain, 1953). For notes see appendix B.

a lognormal curve as shown in figs. 7a and 8 into a straight line. Once a straight line has been fitted to the data set out on such paper we may read off the values of y that correspond to the 16%, 50% and 84% percentage points. From equations (3.4), (3.1), (3.2) and a table of the normal distribution we find that

$$Q = 0.16 \quad \text{for} \quad \log y = \mu - \sigma ,$$
$$Q = 0.50 \quad \text{for} \quad \log y = \mu ,$$
$$Q = 0.84 \quad \text{for} \quad \log y = \mu + \sigma ,$$

[†] In fact maximum likelihood estimates have been obtained by the scoring method or probit analysis. See AITCHISON and BROWN (1957), especially ch. 7.

so that estimates of μ and σ are obtained by taking

$$m = \log(y_{.50}),$$
$$s = \tfrac{1}{2}\{\log(y_{.50}/y_{.16}) + \log(y_{.84}/y_{.50})\}.$$

(3.5)

The use of lognormal paper provides a quick check on lognormal curves and yields fairly reliable estimates of their parameters. In the case of Engel curves it may however occasionally suffer from the fact that the probability scale is very sensitive to small deviations when Q approaches zero or unity.

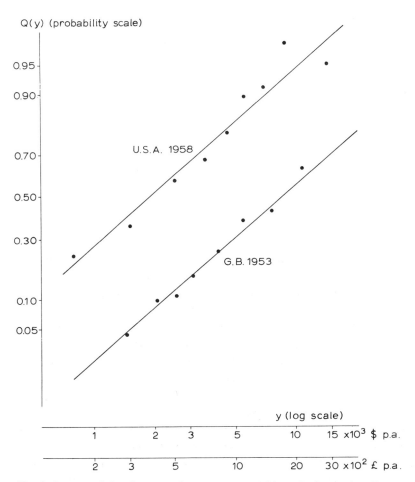

Fig. 9. Lognormal Engel curves of motorcar ownership and of motoring. For notes see appendix B.

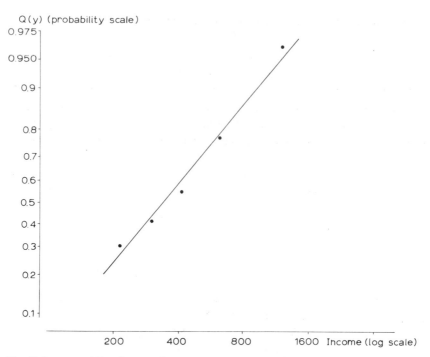

Fig. 10. Lognormal Engel curve of butter consumption, considered as an attribute (Holland, 1935–1936). For notes see appendix B.

If such values occur at all they are usually situated in the extreme income classes on either side, which often contain only a limited number of house-holds so that little weight can be attached to the observed incidence rate. This point is easily overlooked in visual inspection of the graph.

The properties of lognormal paper are illustrated in fig. 9, which shows the same data as fig. 8 along with American data on motorcar ownership. In fig. 10 we give an example of an altogether different attribute, viz. the consumption of butter (as opposed to margarine).

32   The parameter μ or its estimate m indicate, by (3.5), the logarithm of the median tolerance income or, always in logs, the income level at which the degree of penetration of the durable goods concerned equals 50%. This measures how far acceptation of a new durable good has advanced, and it can be a quite revealing parameter when comparisons between different durable goods, different periods or different countries are in order. But even so the value of μ is mainly of historical interest, and it tells us little about the character of consumer behaviour.

The standard deviation σ or its estimate s, on the other hand, indicates the dispersion of tolerance income levels and provides a measure of the spread of individual preferences among the households concerned. It stands to reason that individual tolerance levels for a particular attribute will vary systematically (if imperfectly) according to the circumstances of the household. In the case of refrigerators and washing machines, ownership preferences may be expected to depend on family size, and in the case of motorcar ownership is *ceteris paribus* less attractive in urban areas than in the countryside. Fig. 11 illustrates the latter example. It follows that the dispersion of tolerance income levels, σ, varies with the heterogeneity of the population under review in respect of the relevant conditions; indeed σ *is a*

TABLE 5

Estimates of σ for various lognormal Engel curves.

attribute	s	note
motoring		
Great Britain, 1953	.98	1
Cambridgeshire, rural/urban areas, 1954	.84	1
motorcar ownership		
U.S.A. 1958	.97	2
Great Britain, 1953	.99	3
Great Britain, 1964	.84	4
France, 1949	.70	5
France, 1956	.77	5
France, 1960	.99	6
Holland, 1957	.70	7
Holland, 1962	.63	7
Holland, 1965	.55	7
Holland, 1965–66	.74	8
refrigerator ownership		
Great Britain, 1953	1.01	3
Great Britain, 1964	1.22	4
Holland, 1962	.66	7
Holland, 1965	.74	7
Holland, 1965–66	1.06	8
miscellaneous		
having bathroom or shower, Holland 1965–66	.88	8
taking holidays abroad, Holland 1965–66	1.13	8
butter consumption, Holland 1935–36	.84	9

For notes see appendix A.

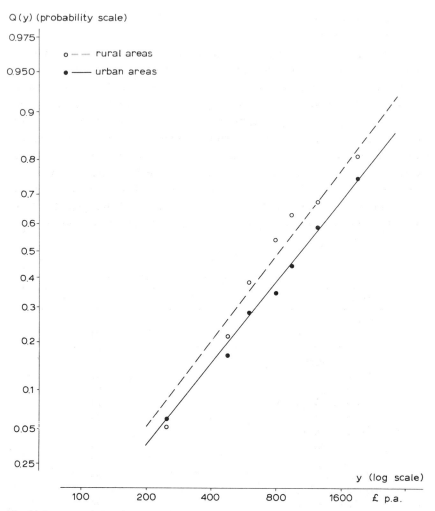

Fig. 11. Lognormal Engel curves of motoring in rural and in urban areas (Cambridgeshire, 1954). For notes see appendix B.

measure of the heterogeneity of the population concerned. In principle it should be possible to vary *s* at will by controlling the composition of the sample; the dispersion might possibly be reduced to zero by restricting the sample to households that by profound psycho-sociological investigations are found to be perfectly similar.

It follows from the above argument that *s*, the estimate of σ, will vary according to the heterogeneity of the sample. Table 5 shows some empirical results. The value of s, expressed in natural logarithms, varies between .6 and 1; in most cases no specific control has been exercised to render the sample data homogeneous in respect of family size, age or similar criteria. Even so sample designs vary considerably and a further analysis of the data collection methods would no doubt explain some of the differences that occur in the table.

Aggregation of lognormal Engel curves

33 Equation (3.4) and the various Engel curves shown above determine the incidence of an attribute at any particular income level. Market research apart, it is the aggregate or average incidence rate over a given population with varying incomes which is of more practical interest. This calls for aggregation of the income-specific incidence rates over the income distribution concerned. The aggregate incidence rate $\bar{Q}$ can be defined as the probability of a consumer taken at random from this population possessing the attribute, i.e. of his actual income exceeding his threshold income. Quite generally the threshold income y_0 is a random variable with distribution function $F_{y_0}(y_0)$, and the income of a consumer taken at random is another random variable y with a distribution function $F_y(y)$ determined by the income distribution of the population under review. Since we assume the tolerance income level to be independent of actual income we may write the joint density of these two variates as the product of their marginal densities, or

$$\bar{Q} = P(\underline{y}_0 < \underline{y}) = \iint_{y_0 < y} f_{y_0}(y_0) f_{\underline{y}}(y) \mathrm{d}y_0 \, \mathrm{d}y$$

or again

$$\bar{Q} = \int_0^\infty \left\{ \int_0^y f_{y_0}(y_0) \mathrm{d}y_0 \right\} f_{\underline{y}}(y) \mathrm{d}y = \int_0^\infty F_{y_0}(y) \mathrm{d}F_{\underline{y}}(y).$$

Upon substitution of the lognormal distribution (3.4) of the threshold incomes we obtain

$$\bar{Q} = \int_0^\infty \Lambda(y; \mu, \sigma^2) \mathrm{d}F_{\underline{y}}(y). \tag{3.6}$$

This representation would not be superior over the tedious procedure of numerical aggregation – the computation of a weighted average of $Q(y)$ over income classes – unless there were an acceptable specification of $F_y(y)$ that permits the integration (3.6) to be carried out. There is such a specification: it is the lognormal income distribution

$$F_y(y) = \Lambda(y;\ \mu_y, \sigma_y^2) \tag{3.7}$$

This model is further discussed in the next chapter, sections 56 to 58, where it is shown to be at least approximatively valid as a description of the income distribution. For present purposes this is enough.

In itself the lognormal *income distribution* (3.7) has nothing to do with the lognormal distribution of *tolerance income levels* for a particular attribute given by (3.4); nor is there any link between the two sets of parameters (μ, σ^2) and (μ_y, σ_y^2); (3.7) is introduced here because it provides for a general solution of (3.6). Upon substitution we obtain

$$\bar{Q} = \int_0^\infty \Lambda(y;\ \mu, \sigma^2)\, d\Lambda(y;\ \mu_y, \sigma_y^2) \tag{3.8}$$

and by the *convolution property* of normal distributions this can be written as[†]

$$\bar{Q} = \Lambda\{1,\ (\mu - \mu_y),\ (\sigma^2 + \sigma_y^2)\}, \tag{3.9}$$

or, what comes to the same thing, as

$$\bar{Q} = \Lambda\{\exp(\mu_y);\ \mu,\ (\sigma^2 + \sigma_y^2)\}. \tag{3.10}$$

34   If we regard μ, σ^2 and σ_y^2 as constants, equation (3.10) relates the aggregate frequency of an attribute to $\exp(\mu_y)$, which is the geometric mean income of the population under review; as this income increases, $\bar{Q}$ moves along a lognormal curve as shown in fig. 7a. In the abstract this is a plausible way of examining the effect of income variation; it assumes that tolerance income levels are independent of the actual income distribution, and that changes in aggregate income take the form of proportionate changes in all incomes. The first of these assumptions fixes μ and σ^2 as constants, and the latter does so for σ_y^2. As a description of the actual course of events when income increases over time these assumptions are inaccurate. While σ^2 and σ_y^2 are fairly stable parameters in fact, μ is not: it often shows a definite

---

[†] For the convolution theorem used in the passage from (3.8) to (3.9) see CRAMÈR (1945), p. 190, and AITCHISON and BROWN (1957), p. 11, p. 139.

trend-like movement in time. The best example is the downward shift of μ for ownership curves of durable goods that are still in the process of becoming established and widely accepted amenities. Even in such cases, however, it is clearly desirable to separate the effect of income changes from the autonomous variation of consumer preferences reflected by changes in μ.

By taking μ, σ^2 and σ_y^2 to be constant we thus turn (3.10) into an aggregate consumption function for the attribute concerned which holds only under rather stringent *ceteris paribus* conditions. The sensitivity of $\bar{Q}$ to changes in income is then measured by its elasticity in respect of aggregate or average income, say $\bar{y}$, defined as

$$\eta_{\bar{Q}} = \frac{\mathrm{d} \log \bar{Q}}{\mathrm{d} \log \bar{y}}.$$

In the conditions given above $\bar{y}$ is proportional to $\exp(\mu_y)$, and we may write

$$\eta_{\bar{Q}} = \frac{\mathrm{d} \log \bar{Q}}{\mathrm{d}\mu_y} = \frac{1}{\bar{Q}} \frac{\mathrm{d}\bar{Q}}{\mathrm{d}\mu_y}. \tag{3.11}$$

In order to evaluate this expression we return to equation (3.10) and translate it in terms of the standard normal distribution by introducing

$$t = \frac{\mu_y - \mu}{\sqrt{\sigma_y^2 + \sigma^2}}.$$

By (3.2) we may now write (3.10) as

$$\bar{Q} = N(t;\ 0, 1), \tag{3.12}$$

so that, upon substitution into (3.11), we obtain

$$\eta_{\bar{Q}} = \frac{1}{\sqrt{\sigma^2 + \sigma_y^2}} \frac{n(t;0,1)}{N(t;0,1)} \tag{3.13}$$

with

$$n(t;0,1) = \frac{\mathrm{d}N(t;0,1)}{\mathrm{d}t} = \frac{1}{\sqrt{2\pi}} \mathrm{e}^{-\frac{1}{2}t^2}.$$

Equation (3.13) is well worth the trouble of deriving, for it permits a quick and easy evaluation of $\eta_{\bar{Q}}$. As a rule $\bar{Q}$, the aggregate incidence of an attribute like, say, motorcar ownership, is known. By (3.12) $\bar{Q}$ equals $N(t;0,1)$ and thus determines t; this in turn determines $n(t;0,1)$. The quotient in (3.13) can thus be derived from tables of the normal distribution [†].

[†] It has been tabulated by AITCHISON and BROWN (1957), appendix A 5.

The multiplicative constant remains to be determined. As we have seen above, σ^2 varies between .6 and 1; as we shall see in the next chapter, σ_y^2 is generally between .5 and .6. Thus $\sigma_y^2 + \sigma^2$ varies from 1.1 to 1.6, and the first term in (3.13) from say .8 to .95. These are of course not universal constants, but reasonable approximate values; they permit us to tabulate the income elasticity $\eta_{\bar{Q}}$ as a function of $\bar{Q}$, and this has been done in table 6. By the

TABLE 6

Income elasticity of an attribute at various aggregate incidence rates.

aggregate incidence rate $\bar{Q}$	income elasticity η	
	$\sigma^2 = 1$	$\sigma^2 = .6$
.05	1.66	1.98
.10	1.41	1.67
.20	1.12	1.33
.30	.92	1.10
.40	.77	.92
.50	.64	.76
.60	.52	.61
.70	.40	.47
.80	.28	.33
.90	.16	.19
.95	.09	.10

For notes see appendix A.

argument of section 32 the second column, i.e. with the lesser value of σ^2, applies in the case of the more homogeneous markets. The result shows clearly how in either case the income elasticity steadily declines as the incidence of the attribute approaches saturation (i.e. unity) with increasing income.

Lognormal demand curves

35 Attributes of consumer behaviour may be related to price in exactly the same manner as they have been related to income; it suffices to repeat the argument of sections 24 and 25 in terms of (maximum) threshold prices instead of (minimum) threshold incomes. Denoting the *tolerance price level* of the ith household by p_{0i}, and the actual market price by p, the individual demand curve is described by

$$q_i = 1 \quad \text{if} \quad p_{0i} \geqslant p \, ,$$
$$q_i = 0 \quad \text{otherwise} \, , \tag{3.14}$$

which is the analogue of (3.1). Assuming a lognormal distribution of the p_{0i}, with parameters μ_p, σ_p^2, we have for a consumer i taken at random from among potential consumers

$$P(\underline{q}_i = 1 | p) = P(\underline{p}_{0i} \geqslant p) = 1 - \Lambda(p; \, \mu_p, \sigma_p^2) \, . \tag{3.15}$$

Again writing Q for the (expected) proportion of buyers in a given market we have

$$Q(p) = 1 - \Lambda(p; \, \mu_p, \sigma_p^2) = \Lambda(1/p; \, -\mu_p, \sigma_p^2). \tag{3.16}$$

The shape of this demand curve for an attribute is shown in fig. 12.

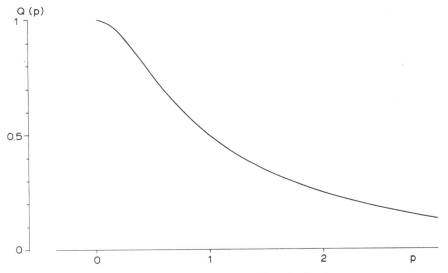

Fig. 12. A lognormal demand curve $(\mu_p = 0, \, \sigma_p^2 = 1)$.

36   In practice it is virtually impossible to observe the behaviour of consumers at different prices under anything approaching *ceteris paribus* conditions; in contrast to lognormal Engel curves, examples of demand curves are hard to find. Apart from the ingenious examples of VAN DE WOESTIJNE (1953)–like the collectors' valuation of stamps originally issued in different numbers–the surveys reported by ADAM (1958) are virtually the only data relating to the demand curve (3.16). In these surveys consumers are asked to quote two limiting prices for a specimen which is submitted to their examination. These two prices are (i) the least price at which the respondent would consider the item too expensive, and (ii) the highest price at which he would dismiss it as a shoddy article of inferior quality. But for the infinitesimal adjustment of turning (3.14) into a strict inequality–i.e. replacing $p_{0i} \geqslant p$ by $p_{0i} > p$–the first of these prices corresponds to the threshold price p_{0i}, and the recorded values may serve to illustrate the present model. Insofar as the goods concerned in Adam's surveys–refrigerator,

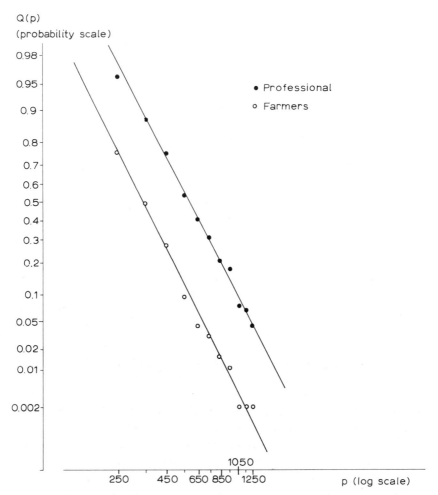

Fig. 13. Lognormal demand curves for a refrigerator of professional people and farmers (France, circa 1950). For notes see appendix B.

cigarette lighter, children's shoes – are seldom bought in quantity, the number of prospective buyers equals the number of putative sales, so that the demand curve for the attribute comes close to the classical quantity demand curve.

By (3.14) we may identify the fraction of respondents quoting a threshold price exceeding a given price p with $Q(p)$; if $Q(p)$ is plotted against p on lognormal graph paper, we should by (3.16) obtain a downward sloping straight line (since $\log 1/p$ equals $-\log p$). This is precisely what has been done by Adam; we reproduce some of his results in fig. 13. The results inspire a fair degree of confidence in the model. It should be noted, however, that successive values of $Q(p)$ are in fact constructed by cumulation, so that the observations are not independent: by its definition the observed value of $Q(p)$ declines with increasing p. This favours the neatness of the graphs but it is in itself no confirmation of the model.

37   In either type of consumer survey considered in this chapter incomes vary from one household to another, but prices do not. Consequently the problem of aggregation over the income distribution does not arise for demand curves, provided the samples from which they are derived reflect at least approximately the income distribution of the population. Income variation within the sample should make for heterogeneity and add to the dispersion of the tolerance prices, just as social differences (or, for that matter, prices differences if there were any) do in the case of lognormal Engel curves. As a matter of fact Adam does distinguish several roughly homogeneous groups in the analysis of his survey results, as can be seen from the example reproduced in fig. 13. In those cases where it is possible to compare the results for separate groups with the overall demand curve for all respondents together, homogeneity does not appear to reduce the variance σ_p^2 very much; still, rigorous homogeneity in respect of the really relevant conditions must be expected to lead to a lesser dispersion.

The parameters μ_p and σ_p^2 may be estimated from graphs in the same manner as in the case of Engel curves, and the estimates bear much the same interpretation. In table 7 we give estimates of σ_p from Adam's data together with a few examples from other sources. The American data, due to PESSE-MIER (1963), refer to repeated experimental shopping trips, the prices of well-known brands of toothpaste and toilet soap being adjusted at each trip. These price changes start off from the current nonexperimental price, and while the lognormal demand curve does describe the two branches that result from price increases and price reductions respectively, there is a sharp discontinuity at the current price. The French housing example is taken from a large-scale survey in which those households wishing to move were asked to put a limit on the rent or the purchase price they would be willing to pay for a given type of apartment. Altogether the estimates of table 7 suggest that the dispersion of threshold prices varies considerably from one product to another, and that it is much less for routine purchases involving moderate expenditure than for the far weightier items like refrigerators or housing. Even so, however, the standard deviations of threshold prices are much smaller than those of threshold incomes shown in table 5. (Since both are expressed in natural logarithms they are fully comparable.) Now threshold incomes and threshold prices differ in two respects. On the one hand there is the effect of income differences within the sample, which may increase the dispersion of individual tolerance prices; on the other hand the

TABLE 7

Estimates of σ_p for various lognormal demand curves.

product	s_p	sample	note
toothpaste	.19–.27 ⎫	random sample of 320	1
toilet soap	.33–.40 ⎭	consumers in one town	
children's shoes	.15–.22	675 housewives classified into 4 town size strata	2
slip	.20–.30	900 women classified into 3 income strata	2
men's shirt	.26–.29	650 men and women classified into 3 income strata	2
stockings	.37	450 women	2
lighter	.35–.42	300 men and women classified into 2 income strata	2
refrigerator	.40–.45	2143 housewives classified into 6 occupational strata	2
apartment (to let)	.48 ⎫	1055 and 1098 housholds	3
apartment (for sale)	.57 ⎭	respectively who wish to move	

For notes see appendix A.

belief that prices should be uniform, as well as the competitive effect of known market prices, will reduce this dispersion. Apparently, the latter factor is the stronger of the two.

Finally we may derive the price elasticity along the lognormal demand curve for an attribute by the method of section 34. From the definition of this price elasticity as

$$\pi = \frac{d \log Q(p)}{d \log p}$$

we obtain, from equation (3.16),

$$\pi = -\frac{1}{\sigma_p} \frac{n(v; 0, 1)}{N(v; 0, 1)} \qquad (3.17)$$

with

$$v = \frac{\mu_p - \log p}{\sigma_p}. \qquad (3.18)$$

Taking σ_p equal to .2 respectively .4, on the evidence of table 7, we may again tabulate the elasticity as a function of $Q(p)$, the proportion of buyers in a given market or the degree of market penetration. The result is given in table 8.

TABLE 8

Price elasticity of an attribute at various market penetration rates.

market penetration rate $Q(p)$	price elasticity π	
	$\sigma_p = .4$	$\sigma_p = .2$
.05	− 5.2	− 10.4
.10	− 4.4	− 8.8
.20	− 3.5	− 7.0
.30	− 2.9	− 5.8
.40	− 2.4	− 4.8
.50	− 2.0	− 4.0
.60	− 1.61	− 3.2
.70	− 1.24	− 2.49
.80	− .88	− 1.75
.90	− .49	− .98
.95	− .27	− .54

For notes see appendix A.

CHAPTER 4

The distribution of personal incomes
and other size distributions

An unsolved problem

38 The size distribution of personal incomes is skew and persistently exhibits the same characteristics for different countries and different epochs. It is one of the earliest economic phenomena for which a mathematical description was attempted, and ever since the introduction of income tax returns there is an ample supply of statistical data. Yet, in spite of these favourable conditions, the subject is still highly controversial, and we have no single generally acceptable model to account for the striking regularities that have been observed. There are two rival functions for the description of the income distribution – Pareto's law and the lognormal distribution – and their relative qualities arouse strong feelings. Moreover there are many other variables like personal wealth, market shares, output and manpower of firms or of industrial establishments, which have a similar size distribution as personal incomes so that they can be described by the same functions; and in other fields the distributions of cities by size, of authors by number of publications, of words by frequency of occurrence and of biological genera by the number of species have similar characteristics. As matters stand a number of models have been put forward for particular instances of the Pareto and the lognormal distribution, but I think that it is fair to say that no satisfactory explanation of either description of the size distribution of economic variables has so far been given.

Although by the many institutional factors involved the case of the income distribution is probably harder than that of several other size distributions, we shall still take it as our main example. It is the case that has attracted most attention, and it is of particular interest precisely because it shows a fairly stable and regular distribution in spite of the many complicating factors that are known to operate. We shall first discuss these particular characteristics of income, and then present Pareto's law and the lognormal distribution, each being followed by a brief review of the relevant models. Applications to other size distributions are noted as we go along.

39 A major obstacle to the explanation of the form of the observed income distribution is the fact that the individual incomes which make up the distribution may be delimited in different ways. These alternative definitions are not just technically distinct, but they refer to different magnitudes which are determined by different factors.

The first definition is the income of an individual household or, more technically, of a *spending unit*. A single income in this sense consists of all income that is submitted to a common set of decisions about its disposal, regardless of its sources. It is the distribution of these incomes that is at issue in discussions of the degree of income inequality and in the aggregation of micro-economic relations. For social reform and market research alike a mere mathematical description of this income distribution is all that is needed; both Pareto's law and the lognormal distribution–although each within its own limitations–can be used to this end, for they describe the income distribution over spending units fairly well.

As soon as we inquire into the processes which govern these distributions, however, we are led to consider the incomes of *earning units* rather than of spending units. When we attempt an economic analysis and treat income determination as a special case of price formation, an individual income is the reward of an individual productive agent performing a specific function. Now in practice a single person may of course receive income in several distinct capacities. We can pool all earnings of a single individual when we change over from a purely economic analysis to a statistical model; in the latter there is no need to distinguish between, say, property income, bonuses and overtime earnings that are being added to the principal income of an individual. But even then any intelligent discussion of income formation, however abstract, inevitably turns to earning units rather than spending units.

When we wish to pass on to spending units several difficulties arise. A minor problem is that many spending units comprise several earners who pool their incomes; a major complication is the fact that a fair proportion of spending units receive income transfers. If there is a State old-page pension scheme, for example, the incomes of many spending units are determined by administrative rules which are incapable of any intelligent interpretation in terms of a statistical model, let alone of economic analysis. Apart from old-age pensions, social security schemes provide unemployment benefits and family allowances; the earnings of particular categories, such as married women and young employees, are often affected by administrative action; and collective bargaining adds another element not easily amenable to mathematical representation. The express purpose of all these institutions is to remedy the ill effects of the free operation of the economic process; the social needs of spending units are their first consideration. Most of the abstract models of income determination, on the other hand, must leave these institutional constraints out of account; they appear to refer exclusively to active earners, employed in conditions that have virtually ceased to exist in modern society.

In these circumstances it is probably vain to hope for a model that explains in simple mathematical terms how the overall income distribution over spending units (or, for that matter, over earning units) comes about. The best course for empirical work is probably to concentrate on smaller, homogeneous sections of the population where the process of income determination is reasonably clear, and to leave the larger problem unsolved.

40   Another empirical point that must not be overlooked is the fact that the apparent stability of the income distribution conceals a considerable turnover of earning units and spending units alike. We shall meet several models that take a stochastic process over time as their starting-point. For firms, products or even personal fortunes it may be a legitimate approximation to assume that the observed size distribution arises out of individual movements within a given population without entry or exit. In the case of incomes, however, replacement is too rapid to be altogether ignored: as a rough estimate we may put the proportion of active earners dropping out through retirement and death at some 3 to 5% per annum. Since it cannot be assumed that new entrants have at all the same incomes as those departing, some provision must be made for these changes in the composition of the population. This is difficult because exits and entries are naturally connected with age and not with income, the variable under consideration. The disappearance of a firm or a product may be thought to follow upon the decline of output or market share towards zero, and new entrants may be assumed to start in on the same ground level; in the case of incomes, however, births and deaths are very much related to the genuine physiological phenomena, and have little to do with the income level of the individual concerned. It is hard to allow for such an alien element in the model.

Some empirical income distributions

41   We shall now briefly present some empirical income distributions which will serve as illustrations of the subsequent models. The first couple of examples is taken from Dutch income tax returns for 1959. These data refer to individual taxpayers, but since the Dutch administration at the time added the income of married women to that of their husbands the concept approaches the income of a spending unit. Apart from the distribution of total taxable income, however, separate tabulations have been made on the basis of the *principal income* of the taxpayer. This comes close to the income of an earning unit, even by the standards of economic analysis. In addition, the use of narrow income class intervals and the provision of cross-classification by age, family composition and profession make this a good source of empirical income distributions; we quote two examples.

The first is the overall distribution of taxpayers by total taxable income, shown in fig. 14. These data cover 94 % of all households, the remaining 6 % consisting mainly of old-age pensioners with no additional income apart from the state pension. The narrow income class intervals bring out that the overall distribution, shown in fig. 14a, is markedly bimodal; as fig. 14b shows, this can be attributed to heterogeneity in respect of age. When we separate apprentices and young employees from the adult population two fairly well-behaved distributions are obtained.

This example shows to what extent the social characteristics of the population condition the income distribution. A full analysis would require further classifications by several criteria other than age, such as occupational status and the number of earners per household[†]. We omit the intermediate stages of such an investigation and go on at once to a small and homogeneous group. This is the distribution of the self-employed engaged in commerce and trade by their principal income alone. This distribution, shown in fig. 15, comes close to the income distribution among active earners under conditions approaching those of the economic model.

[†]   As an example see the analyses along these lines of United States data by MILLER (1955, 1966).

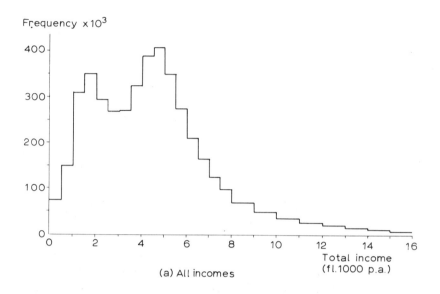

(a) All incomes

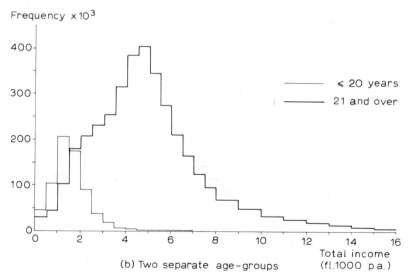

(b) Two separate age-groups

Fig. 14. Frequency distribution of total incomes (Holland, 1959). For notes see appendix B.

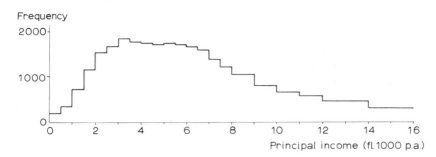

Fig. 15. Frequency distribution of principal incomes of the self-employed in commerce and trade (Holland, 1959). For notes see appendix B.

42 The next examples refer to the United States in 1949 and 1951. The data have been obtained by special sample surveys in connection with the Census and they are therefore free from the defects of fiscal definitions that affect tax return statistics. The first distribution, shown in fig. 16a, refers to the total money income of all households, i.e. families and unrelated individuals; it corresponds to the overall income distribution among spending units. Again the overall distribution shows bimodality which disappears when we separate families and individuals, as in fig. 16b. For contrast we add once more an example of the individual earnings of a homogeneous group, viz. of male, experienced pharmacists having worked at least 50 weeks during the year considered. The restriction to such a very homogeneous group considerably reduces the skewness of the distribution; as fig. 17 shows it is almost symmetrical.

Pareto's law

43 We write

$$N(y) = \text{the number of incomes} > y$$

and consider the relation

$$N(y) = \beta y^{-\alpha}. \qquad (4.1)$$

This is Pareto's law, first stated by its author in 1897[†]. The simplest way of

---

[†] See PARETO (1897, 1964), para. 957–961.

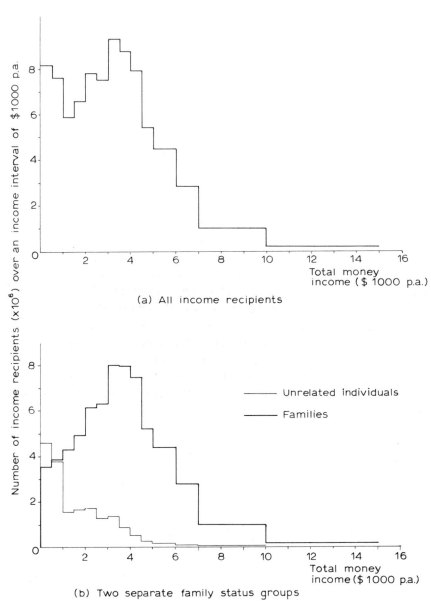

(a) All income recipients

(b) Two separate family status groups

Fig. 16. Frequency distribution of total money incomes (U.S.A., 1951). For notes see appendix B.

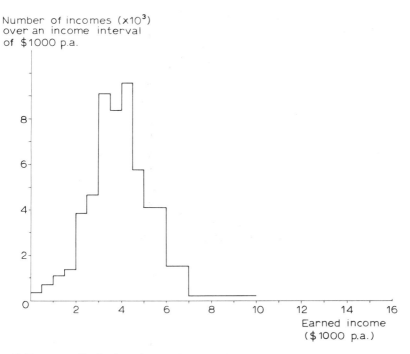

Fig. 17. Frequency distribution of earned incomes of experienced pharmacists (U.S.A., 1949). For notes see appendix B.

demonstrating it is to plot $N(y)$ against y on graph paper with a logarithmic scale on either axis, and to see whether the points thus plotted lie on the straight line

$$\log N(y) = \log \beta - \alpha \log y . \qquad (4.2)$$

This has been done for the four empirical distributions under review in figs. 18, 19 and 20. Since the $N(y)$ are cumulative figures, successive points in these graphs are not independent, and the representation that has been adopted suggests a better fit than is in fact the case; $N(y)$ will by its definition decrease monotonically with increasing y. Even so the agreement of the observed distributions with Pareto's law is striking indeed, provided we limit the latter's operation to the higher income levels. Since we do so we need not be concerned over the bimodality of the overall distributions of figs. 14a and 16a, which occurs among the lower income ranges; cumulation and logarithmic transformation anyhow remove all traces of this irregularity, as can be seen in figs. 18 and 19.

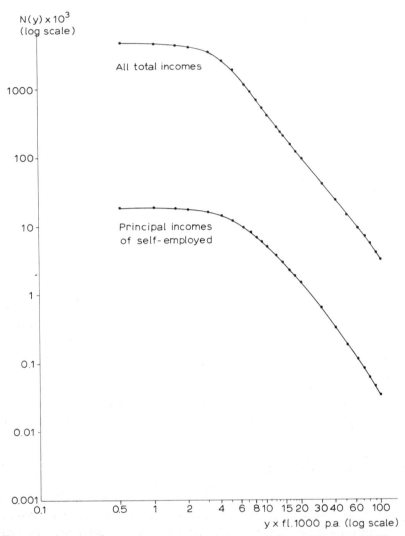

Fig. 18. Pareto representation of Dutch income distributions (data of figs. 14a and 15).

The restriction of Pareto's law to incomes exceeding a certain lower limit y^0 is nowadays universally accepted, but it was not made by Pareto himself for the reason that his statistics did not extend to the lower income groups. Such was income tax in the nineteenth century. It should be noted that the limitation is quite severe. The lower limit does not correspond to a minimum income in any sense, but it indicates an income level slightly exceeding the

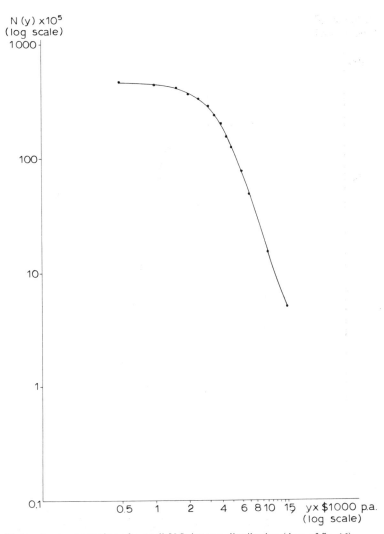

Fig. 19. Pareto representation of overall U.S. income distribution (data of fig. 16).

mode of the income distribution. Pareto's law is capable only of describing frequencies that decrease towards the right, and in most empirical distributions it applies to less than half of all income recipients.

In spite of this limitation Pareto's law is widely accepted without much questioning, and a great deal of play has been made of estimating α – Pareto's constant – from the slope of the straight line segment in graphs like figs. 18

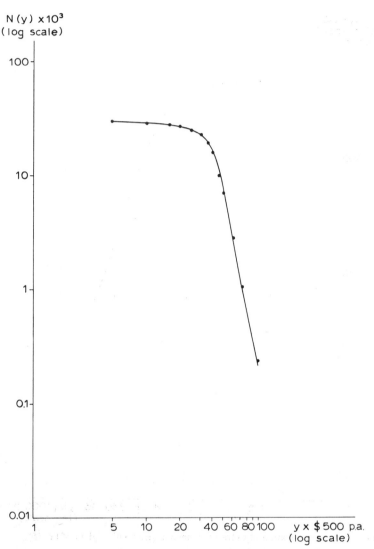

Fig. 20. Pareto representation of income distribution of U.S. pharmacists (data of fig. 17).

to 20[†]. This value is regarded as a measure of the inequality of income; a high value of α corresponds to a steeper decline of $N(y)$ with increasing y, and thus in some sense to a greater degree of income equality. Although this

---

[†] CLARK (1951) lists over a hundred and fifty estimates for different countries and different years.

interpretation is open to discussion, it is gratifying to find that the value of α has increased from between 1.6 and 1.8 in the nineteenth century to between 1.9 and 2.1 in developed countries at the present time. It should be borne in mind, however, that such analyses are based exclusively on the upper tail of the income distribution alone.

44 Pareto's law has some interesting mathematical properties but when we try to turn it into a probability distribution we run into difficulties. Let us first introduce the restriction of Pareto's law to higher incomes and explicitly state the condition that α be positive by rewriting (4.1) as

$$N(y) = \beta y^{-\alpha} \quad \text{for} \quad y > y^0; \ \alpha > 0. \tag{4.3}$$

We next express all incomes as multiples of the lower limit y^0 by introducing

$$y^* = \frac{y}{y^0}.$$

The probability distribution of an income taken at random from Pareto's law (4.3) is obtained from

$$F(y) = P(\underline{y} \leqslant y) = 1 - \frac{N(y)}{N(y^0)},$$

and this yields

$$F(y^*) = 1 - y^{*-\alpha}, \qquad y^* \geqslant 1; \ \alpha > 0,$$

with density function

$$f(y^*) = \alpha y^{*-(1+\alpha)}. \tag{4.4}$$

Provided $\alpha > 1$ the mean of this distribution is

$$E(\underline{y}^*) = \int_1^\infty \alpha y^{*-\alpha} dy^* = \frac{\alpha}{\alpha-1}, \tag{4.5}$$

and mean income in the original money units is

$$E(\underline{y}) = y^0 \frac{\alpha}{\alpha-1}. \tag{4.6}$$

In empirical work we shall usually put y^0 equal to the lowest income beyond which Pareto's law applies, but the formulae given above of course continue to hold if we shift y^0 upwards. It follows therefore from (4.6) that the average of all incomes exceeding a given value in the Pareto range is proportional to that value[†].

If the condition $\alpha > 1$ is not met, the integral in (4.5) does not converge and no finite mean exists; but since in practice α always well exceeds unity, this case can be safely dismissed. For the second moment of $\underline{y}^*$,

$$E\left(\underline{y}^{*2}\right) = \int_1^\infty \alpha y^{*1-\alpha} \, dy^* \,, \tag{4.7}$$

convergence of the integral similarly requires that $\alpha > 2$. If this condition is met we have

$$E\left(\underline{y}^{*2}\right) = \frac{\alpha}{\alpha - 2}$$

and hence the variance

$$D^2\left(\underline{y}^*\right) = \frac{\alpha}{(\alpha - 2)(\alpha - 1)^2} \,.$$

For $\alpha < 2$, however, (4.7) does not converge and the income distribution has no finite variance.

This condition for a finite variance is a little awkward because the observed values of α do in fact fluctuate around the critical value $\alpha = 2$. Of course this does not mean that social progress is immeasurably advanced when α increases beyond 2 and we pass from an infinite income variance to a finite value; as long as incomes themselves are finite, any observed income distribution has a finite variance which can easily be ascertained, if necessary by direct computation. While we need not worry about the sample, the question remains whether it comes from a distribution with a finite variance or not; and this can have some bearing on the choice of a model.

45   Since Pareto's law applies to higher incomes only it is natural that the models leading to it concentrate on the limiting behaviour of certain distributions for large values of the variate concerned. This allows for a number of different approaches. Most models are fairly complicated, and they often make use of advanced mathematical results. Our brief review is mainly concerned with the underlying ideas; for the full technical details the reader should turn to the original publications.

[†] See ALLEN (1937), p. 408.

Mandelbrot's model

46 A highly abstract model of Pareto's law with infinite variance has been advocated by Mandelbrot [†]. The author starts from the observation (which may be granted although it is not strictly substantiated) that the upper tails of observed income distributions all tend to Pareto's law, regardless of the precise definition of income employed. Moreover the various income concepts are related to one another by addition: thus, for example, total income of an earning unit is obtained by adding income from various sources, and income of a spending unit is again obtained by further summation (see section 39). In Mandelbrot's view all income variables should therefore be considered as sums of independent random variables with varying domains of summation. Since all these sums have the same type of distribution as their constituent parts (i.e. a distribution approaching Pareto's law) we should turn to the class of *stable distributions*. Consider the sum of n independent random variables

$$U_n = \underline{u}_1 + \underline{u}_2 + \dots + \underline{u}_n,$$

where all $\underline{u}_i$ have the same distribution up to a linear transformation of their scale, so that there exist coefficients $a_i > 0$ and b_i such that

$$a_1 \underline{u}_1 + b_1, \; a_2 \underline{u}_2 + b_2, \; \dots, \; a_n \underline{u}_n + b_n,$$

all have the same probability distribution, say $F(z)$. If now the sum U_n has the same distribution, again up to a linear transformation, so that there exist some $A_n > 0$, B_n such that

$$A_n U_n + B_n$$

has the probability distribution $F(z)$, the distribution $F(z)$ is *stable*. The simplest example of a stable distribution is the normal distribution since it stands up to linear transformation of the variate as well as to the addition of independent variates.

The subject of stable distributions belongs to mathematics rather than to textbook statistics; it has been studied by Lévy and by few others[††]. Apart from the normal distribution, which apparently is the only stable distribution with a finite variance, there are others as well. Mandelbrot for obvious

---

[†] We here follow the simpler representation of MANDELBROT (1960), but the theory has been further developed in MANDELBROT (1961).
[††] See LÉVY (1925, 1937) and FELLER (1966). ch. 6.

reasons considers the case of a distribution which has (i) finite mean, (ii) infinite variance and (iii) maximum skewness towards the right. There is a single stable distribution which meets these requirements, and he names it the Pareto-Lévy distribution.

Unfortunately the distribution function nor the density of the Pareto-Lévy distribution can be written in simple analytic form, and in order to represent it one must have recourse to a Laplace transform or to its characteristic function. We do not copy these impressive formulae but merely record that Mandelbrot infers from the former that Pareto's law holds asymptotically for large values of the random variable concerned, that is for large $\underline{u}_i$ or $\underline{U}_n$ (but *not* necessarily large *n*). And this is of course exactly what is required of the model.

A stochastic process: Champernowne's model

47 Apart from Mandelbrot's model of Pareto's law all others are concerned with the operation of a stochastic process over time. We begin with a brief review of the model of CHAMPERNOWNE (1953), which is the only one specifically designed for the income distribution. Once more we keep to the simplest version of the model and omit its generalisations.

Champernowne first introduces a minimum income, say y_{min}, below which incomes cannot possibly fall. This should not be confused with y^0, the lower end of the income range over which Pareto's law applies (see section 43); y^0 is of course much larger than y_{min}. Starting off from y_{min}, an infinite number of successive income classes $j, j = 1, 2, ...$ are marked off by class limits that are equidistant on a logarithmic scale; if their width on such a scale is h the jth income class refers to the income interval

$$y_{min} e^{h(j-1)}, \quad y_{min} e^{hj} . \tag{4.8}$$

We now consider the movement across these income classes from one discrete time period to the next. An individual income recipient who at time t belongs to income class r may move to income class s at time $(t+1)$; the probability of this move is denoted as the *transition probability*

$$p(r, s, t) .$$

If $P(r, t)$ denotes the probability of an individual income belonging to income class r at time t, we obviously have

$$P(s, t+1) = \sum_r p(r, s, t) P(r, t) . \tag{4.9}$$

This equation brings out that the behaviour of the probability density $P(s,t)$ over time is determined by the transition probabilities $p(r,s,t)$.

Champernowne makes a number of assumptions about these transition probabilities; some of these assumptions are justified only for large values of s and r, i.e. among the higher incomes, and this is where the restriction of his model to the upper tail of the income distribution comes in. We shall here ignore (but Champernowne does not) what goes on among the lower incomes.

There are three assumptions that drastically simplify (4.9). First, the $p(r,s,t)$ are constants, independent of time; secondly, they are equally independent of the income levels r and s, and determined fully by $u=s-r$, the number of income-classes income moves in a single period. Since the income class limits are equidistant on a logarithmic scale, this specification corresponds to the assumption that any given *proportionate* income change is equiprobable at all (higher) income levels (see sections 28 and 29). Finally, u is restricted to the interval $(-k, 1)$ so that income may at most move one class up or k classes down. It follows from these assumptions that we may write the transition probabilities $p(r,s,t)$ as $p(u)$, where $u=s-r$ and $p(u)=0$ for $u>1$ or $u<-k$, and that we can replace (4.9) by

$$P(s,\ t+1) = \sum_{u=-k}^{1} p(u)P(s-u,t). \tag{4.10}$$

48   At this stage it is perhaps helpful to refer to the usual representation of a stochastic process of this type in terms of a vector $\boldsymbol{P}(t)$, with elements $P(s,t)$, and of a *transition matrix* $\boldsymbol{A}(t)$ with elements $p(r,s,t)$. In this notation (4.9) is written as

$$\boldsymbol{P}(t+1) = \boldsymbol{A}(t)\boldsymbol{P}(t) \tag{4.11}$$

Since the transition probabilities $p(r,s,t)$ apply to any income recipient who is in income class r at time t, regardless of his former history (i.e. the state of his income at $t-1$, $t-2$, ...), the process is known as a *Markov chain*; if, as is the case here, the transition probabilities are moreover constants, independent of time, it is called *homogeneous*. In this case we may denote the transition matrix by $\boldsymbol{A}$, deleting the time index, and it is easily seen from (4.11) that the probability distribution $\boldsymbol{P}(t)$ which is generated by the repeated application of the process to a given initial frequency distribution $\boldsymbol{P}(0)$ is given by

$$\boldsymbol{P}(t) = \boldsymbol{A}^t \boldsymbol{P}(0). \tag{4.12}$$

In Champernowne's model both vector and matrix are of infinite order, and apart from an oblique reference to a general theorem no use will be made of the matrix formulation in what follows. For what it is worth we show part

TABLE 9

Transition matrix of Champernowne's model of the generation of the income distribution.

income class	income class								
	0	1	2	3	... $i-2$	$i-1$	i	$i+1$	...
0	$1-p(1)$	$p(1)$	0	0	... 0	0	0	0	...
1	$1-p(1)-p(0)$	$p(0)$	$p(1)$	0	... 0	0	0	0	...
2	$p(-2)$	$p(-1)$	$p(0)$	$p(1)$	... 0	0	0	0	...
3	0	$p(-2)$	$p(-1)$	$p(0)$	... 0	0	0	0	...
...	...	...	...	...	... ...	...	...	...	...
i	0	0	0	0	... $p(-2)$	$p(-1)$	$p(0)$	$p(1)$	...
$i+1$	0	0	0	0	... 0	$p(-2)$	$p(-1)$	$p(0)$	...
...	...	...	...	...	... ...	...	...	...	...

For notes see appendix A.

of the matrix A' as defined by Champernowne's assumptions in table 9; we have taken $k=2$, but this is a mere typographical restriction[†].

49 Apart from the three assumptions made so far the transition probabilities are subject to further restrictions. Since they are probabilities we have

$$p(u) \geqslant 0 \quad \text{for all } u \qquad (4.13)$$

and

$$\sum_{u=-k}^{+1} p(u) = 1 . \qquad (4.14)$$

Champernowne finally assumes that

$$\sum_{u=-k}^{1} up(u) < 0 , \qquad (4.15)$$

which means that the expected income change is negative. This assumption is needed to prevent the model from implying an ever-increasing dispersion of incomes. Before forming an opinion on this assumption the reader should remember that we are here dealing with the higher incomes alone.

50 For the standard case of a homogeneous Markov chain with a finite number of states it can be shown that the continued operation of the process

---

[†] Note that table 9 refers to the transpose of A, not to A itself.

will, under certain conditions, ultimately lead to an equilibrium distribution. When we recall (4.12) this statement can be made more precise: we assert the existence, under certain conditions, of a unique limiting distribution P^* which is independent of the initial distribution $P(0)$, or

$$P^* = \lim_{t \to \infty} P(t) = \lim_{t \to \infty} A^t P(0) \quad \text{for all } P(0).$$

Moreover this limiting distribution is the *steady state distribution* which satisfies

$$P^* = AP^* \tag{4.16}$$

and it can be determined by solving this equation.

Champernowne states that the process defined for an infinite number of states by his model has the same property. Through the operation of his process the income distribution will therefore tend to a limiting distribution $P^*(s)$. By analogy to (4.16) it follows from (4.10) that $P^*(s)$ must satisfy

$$P^*(s) = \sum_{u=-k}^{1} p(u)P^*(s-u) \quad \text{for all } s. \tag{4.17}$$

It now only remains to determine $P^*(s)$ by finding a unique solution of (4.17). To this end we substitute $P^*(s) = cz^s$, where c is an arbitrary constant; the resulting equation in z is

$$g(z) = \sum_{u=-k}^{1} p(u)z^{1-u} - z = 0, \tag{4.18}$$

where $g(z)$ is a polynomial of degree $(k+1)$ in z. By (4.13), all coefficients are positive, but for the linear term. Obviously $g(0) = p(1)$; by (4.14) $g(1) = 0$; and from (4.14) and (4.15) $g'(1) > 0$. Together these conditions ensure that (4.18) has a unique root between 0 and 1, say b. Hence

$$P^*(s) = cb^s, \qquad 0 < b < 1, \tag{4.19}$$

is a solution of (4.17), and it is the only one which meets the requirements that the $P^*(s)$ are positive and decrease for increasing s. The constant c can be adjusted at will so as to make the probabilities sum to unity over all admissible values of s.

The last link is that between (4.19) and Pareto's law. Consider the lower limit of income class s, say y_s. By (4.8)

$$y_s = y_{\min} e^{h(s-1)}$$

so that $\log y_s$ is linear in s with a positive slope coefficient h. The probability that an income taken at random y exceeds y_s is, by (4.19),

$$P(\underline{y} > y_s) = \sum_{j=s}^{\infty} P^*(j) = \sum_{j=s}^{\infty} cb^s = \frac{c}{1-b} b^s ,$$

and the logarithm of this probability is linear in s with a negative slope $\log b$ $(0 < b < 1)$. Hence, if we vary s, $\log P(\underline{y} > y_s)$ and $\log y_s$ are linearly related with a negative slope

$$\frac{\log b}{h} = -\alpha , \tag{4.20}$$

where α is Pareto's constant. But for the substitution of probabilities for frequencies this is Pareto's law as given in (4.2).

51   Champernowne's theory is one of the simpler stochastic process models, and its simplicity is in part due to the use of discrete income intervals of some arbitrary proportionate width. The implications of this convention have however been insufficiently explored, and it appears that it does in fact introduce some degree of arbitrariness in the basic assumptions about income variation. The argument runs as follows : clearly, Pareto's constant α should be independent of the arbitrary width of the income intervals h that is adopted. By (4.20) this should be accomplished by varying b as a function of h. Since b is defined as a particular root of (4.18), the coefficients of this equation should be adjusted to variations in h, and these coefficients are the initial transition probabilities. In itself this is what we would expect, for it is obvious that there must be some connection between the transition probabilities and the width of the income intervals if a given real probability distribution of income variation is to be described in terms of the latter. It is not clear, however, what is the precise relation between the $p(u)$ and h that is imposed by the requirement that α is invariant under changes in h, nor is it at all certain that this relation agrees with the condition that the same income variation is in some sense consistently described by the transition probabilities that correspond to varying values of h.

Other stochastic processes

52   There are several other stochastic processes that lead to Pareto's law. We refer to the theories of SIMON (1955) and of STEINDL (1965). Both authors consider a discrete random variable $\underline{i}$ having a steady-state distribution with a Pareto tail. There are no specific assumptions about the behaviour of large $\underline{i}$ in particular, and the restriction to the upper tail is a matter of approximation; the models determine the full distribution of i for $i = 1, 2, \ldots$, but this happens to conform to Pareto's law only for large values.

Both writers freely use results from the general theory of stochastic processes. We confine ourselves to a very brief sketch of their main line of argument and then raise the question what economic size variables may be expected to meet their assumptions. Neither model is specifically designed for the income distribution.

53 In Steindl's model i stands for the number of customers, but it may be identified equally well with any other discrete measure of a firms' size by sales, output or assets. The behaviour of this random variable over continuous time is described in similar terms as were used in Poisson process of section 12, but the situation is somewhat more complicated. In a brief time interval Δt i may grow from i to $(i+1)$ with probability

$$\lambda i \Delta t \; ;$$

it may remain the same; or it may decline to $(i-1)$ with probability

$$\mu i \Delta t \; .$$

We have omitted terms of smaller order in Δt which are bound to disappear. These assumptions determine the growth or decline of an individual firm by what is known as a *birth and death process* from the application of similar assumptions to biological populations. As in section 12 the assumptions lead to an equation

$$\begin{aligned} P(i, \ t+\Delta t) = &(1-(\mu+\lambda)i\,\Delta t)P(i,t) \\ &+\lambda(i-1)\Delta t P(i-1,t) \\ &+\mu(i+1)\Delta t P(i+1,t) \end{aligned}$$

which yields a differential equation for $P(i,t)$ upon passage to the limit for $\Delta t \to 0$. Solving this equation for the initial condition

$$P(1,0) = 1$$

we obtain the probability distribution at time t of the size i of a firm that starts off with unit size at time zero. When it is assumed that all firms come into being with unit size this is equivalent to the size distribution of firms of age t. Since firms of zero size are taken to have ceased to exist, Steindl simultaneously obtains (i) the cumulative mortality as a function of age, and (ii) the size distribution of surviving firms of age t, $P(i,t)$, for $i > 0$.

The exit or death of firms having thus been determined, allowance is made for the birth or entry of new firms, all of unit size, by additional assumptions.

These state that the probability of one new firm arising in the brief time interval $(t, t + \Delta t)$ is proportional to the number of firms in existence at time t. When we postulate an initial population of N_0 firms at time zero the probability of a birth is therefore

$$\eta(1 - P(0, t)) N_0 \Delta t$$

where η is a constant. Together, the probabilities of exit and entry determine a second birth and death process *for firms* which governs their number as well as their distribution by age.

Steindl now assumes that the age-distribution of firms is in steady-state equilibrium while at the same time the total number of firms is growing. The overall distribution of i may then be obtained by aggregating the age-specific size distribution obtained earlier over the age distribution for a steady state. This procedure is quite similar to that employed in another context in section 33. The resulting distribution of i has a Pareto tail, provided the parameters λ, μ and η meet certain conditions. First, λ/μ must not be close to unity, so that the expected change in an individual firms' size $(\lambda - \mu)i$ must not be zero: on the average, all existing firms must be either growing or declining indefinitely in size. Secondly, η must in either case be sufficiently large to ensure that the total number of firms is increasing.

54 In Simon's model the discrete measure of firm size i should preferably be identified with a stock variable like assets rather than with flows such as sales or output [†]. This is because Simon assumes a continued accumulation of units to take place: in each discrete time period a single unit is added to the total already in existence. Hence if we put total assets at time zero at zero, the total at time t equals t, i.e. the number distributed so far, and this is distributed over firms of size i occurring with frequency (not probability) $f(i, t)$. For all t, therefore,

$$\sum_i i f(i, t) = t \ .$$

[†] Applications of the model to firms' assets are discussed in SIMON and BONINI (1958) and IJIRI and SIMON (1964); but these papers do not contain a detailed derivation of the model, and for this the reader is referrred to SIMON (1955). Since the latter paper is primarily concerned with the distribution of words by their frequency of occurrence in a text, some difficulties of interpretation are bound to arise. We here discuss the basic model; there is a variant which does not postulate indefinite accumulation, but it appears to be hardly applicable to economic phenomena since it requires that in the event of a transition of i from i to $i - 1$ the individual entity concerned disappears altogether.

This means either that total assets accumulate at a constant unit rate (in real time), or that time is measured by the accumulation of units (operational time).

The behaviour of the $f(i, t)$ is wholly determined by two assumptions about the attribution of the additional unit that is introduced by the passage from t to $(t+1)$. First, there is a constant probability – say η – that this unit gives rise to a new firm (of unit size). Second, the probability that it goes to an existing firm of size i is proportional to $if(i)$, i.e. to the total assets of all firms of that size. The factor of proportionality ensures that these probabilities sum to $(1-\eta)$. If we were to add the further restriction that all firms of the same size have equal chances of growth, the second assumption would imply that any firm's chances in this respect are proportional to its size. But this further specification is not necessary, and Simon's model allows for any variation in the probabilities of growth among the $f(i)$ firms of size i.

As a matter of arithmetic we cannot define a steady-state distribution by the condition that the *relative* frequencies (or probabilities)

$$\frac{f(i, t)}{\sum_i f(i, t)}$$

are constant, irrespective of t; on the assumptions made it is impossible that *all* frequencies $f(i, t)$ increase in the same proportion to $f(i, t+1)$ as t increases to $(t+1)$. Simon does however find a distribution that is similar to a steady-state solution in the sense that any deviations from it tend to be corrected by the operation of the process. This is the so-called Yule distribution which approaches asymptotically (for large i) to Pareto's law. The value of Pareto's constant α depends of course on the single parameter of Simon's model, η, the rate of entry of new firms.

55   Neither Steindl's nor Simon's model have been designed for the income distribution nor do they seem applicable to this variable, if only because of the treatment of entry and exit (if any) of the individual entities concerned. Either model might conceivably refer to personal wealth, if individual fortunes were assumed to preserve their identity even upon succession (which they do not)[†]. When it comes to the size distribution of firms, the

---

[†] But Pareto's law may be obtained from yet another stochastic process which is based precisely on the assumption that a steady growth of personal fortunes is interrrupted over and again by their equal division among k inheritors upon the holders' death. See WOLD and WHITTLE (1957).

scope of either model has already been indicated. Steindl's assumptions would seem to apply equally well to almost any measure of a firm's size, Simon's model is restricted to assets as a stock variable permitting steady accumulation.

A much more restrictive characteristic of both models is that they both consider steady-state distributions which occur while otherwise persistent and definite changes are continuing indefinitely. These stable distributions do not arise by leaving a closed population to itself but by leaving a *process* to itself. Simon's model implies a continued and indefinite growth of total "size"; in Steindl's model the occurrence of a Pareto tail depends on the numerical values of the three parameters λ, μ and η – the expected growth of individual firms must not be zero, and the rate of entry must ensure a net increase of their number.

The lognormal distribution

56 The main contender of Pareto's law is the lognormal income distribution

$$F(y) = \Lambda(y; \; \mu_0, \sigma_0^2) \, . \tag{4.21}$$

In figs. 21 and 22 the same data earlier used to illustrate Pareto's law are plotted on lognormal graph paper (see section 31). Once more the cumulative character of the point ordinates suggests a better fit than is in fact the case. But even so the agreement is not very good. Both overall distributions show distinct curvature, even though we have removed the initial bimodality by eliminating the young from the Dutch data and the unrelated individuals from the American figures. Among the homogeneous occupational groups the Dutch self-employed show a satisfactory fit, but the income distribution of American pharmacists is not nearly as skew as is required by the lognormal. We have already noticed before the symmetry of this distribution (see fig. 15).

In the present examples we have on purpose used tabulations with an exceptional fine income classification, and as a result the marked departures from the lognormal form are clearly brought out. The overall American income distribution of fig. 22 is typical in that the discrepancies occur in the two tails of the distribution. In this respect the lognormal is often contrasted with the Pareto distribution; while the latter applies to a minority of high incomes alone, the lognormal does better over the middle income brackets

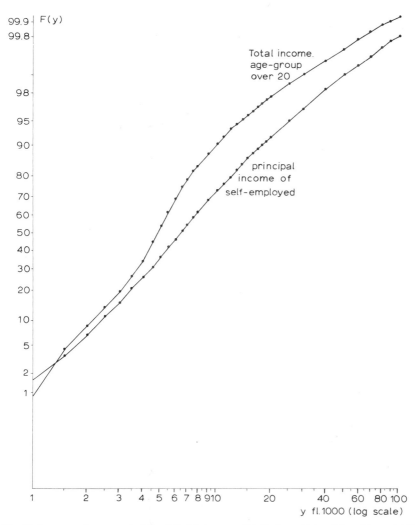

Fig. 21. Lognormal representation of Dutch income distributions (data of figs. 14a and 15).

which, in the case of fig. 22, comprise over 60 % of all families. If a convenient approximation is required, the choice between the two distributions depends on these considerations; the Pareto distribution fits the rich, but the lognormal is in order if we wish to consider the full income range. This is the justification for the use of the lognormal in the aggregation of Engel curves in section 33.

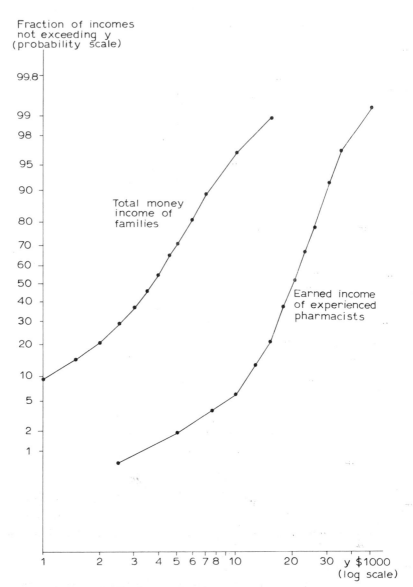

Fig. 22. Lognormal representation of U.S. income distributions (data of figs. 16b and 17).

57   When the lognormal distribution is adopted, its parameter σ_0 replaces Pareto's α as the natural measure of the dispersion or inequality of incomes. The relation between the two parameters of these two distinct models can be approximately established by equating Pareto's constant $-\alpha$ to the corresponding elasticity

$$\frac{\text{d} \log(1-F(y))}{\text{d} \log y}$$

of a lognormal distribution, evaluated at some convenient point in the upper income ranges of which the Pareto slope is representative. As we have shown in section 34 this elasticity along a lognormal curve is

$$-\frac{1}{\sigma_0} \frac{n(s;\ 0,1)}{1-N(s;\ 0,1)} \tag{4.22}$$

with

$$s = \frac{\log y - \mu_0}{\sigma_0}.$$

We equate the slopes of the two income distributions at the income level

$$y = e^{\mu_0 + \sigma_0},$$

which corresponds to the upper 84 % point of the income distribution. Upon evaluating (4.22) at this point (where $s = +1$) and putting the result equal to the elasticity of the Pareto curve which is $-\alpha$ everywhere, we obtain

$$\alpha = \frac{1}{\sigma_0} 1.525$$

or

$$\alpha\sigma_0 = 1.525$$

As an approximation to the correspondence between α and σ_0 this expression works well. An α of 2 is equivalent to a σ_0 of .75 with a variance of the logarithms of income of .5.

58 The lognormal distribution has been applied to income and to many other size variables by GIBRAT (1931), who assumes that the values taken by these variables are affected by a great many independent random factors (of finite variance) that operate in multiplicative rather than in additive fashion. The latter qualification is known as Gibrat's law of proportionate effect. When this is adopted a straightforward application of the Central Limit Theorem to the logarithms of the random elements involved leads to the lognormal as the limiting distribution.

Gibrat's law is of course just another example of the general presumption in favour of the logarithmic transformation of economic variables that was discussed in sections 28 and 29. Since this is largely a matter of intuitive appeal there is no point in prolonging the argument. But the lognormal model still allows of two alternative interpretations. The simpler model holds that the random factors that determine an individual income (or indeed any other size variable) operate simultaneously at any given time. A particular example of this is the multiple classification of items by several independent criteria[†], which would seem to apply to the market shares of individual products in conditions of monopolistic competition and product differentiation. If the customer selects a particular brand by the successive application of various criteria, the market share of any single brand is correspondingly derived from the total market by many successive sub-divisions, i.e. by repeated multiplication by proper fractions. If the latter are many, random and independent, a lognormal size distribution of market shares will result.

59 A slightly more sophisticated interpretation of the lognormal model is to assume a stochastic process whereby $z = \log y$ is exposed to *consecutive* independent random shocks,

$$z(t+1) = z(t) + u(t),$$

so that

$$z(t) = z(0) + \sum_{i}^{t-1} u(i)$$

with

$$\mu_0(t) = E(z(t)) = E(z(0)) + \sum_{i}^{t-1} E(u(i)),$$

$$\sigma_0^2(t) = \text{var}(z(t)) = \text{var}(z(0)) + \sum_{i}^{t-1} \text{var}(u(i)). \tag{4.23}$$

If the $u(i)$ have finite variance the distribution of $y(t)$ will tend to the log-normal for $t \to \infty$; it may also be assumed (and often is assumed) that $z(0)$ and all $u(i)$ are normal so that $y(t)$ is lognormal for all t.

This random walk of $\log y$ raises the question of the stability or otherwise of the parameters $\mu_0(t)$ and $\sigma_0^2(t)$ over time. The mean $\mu_0(t)$ may be set constant by assuming that all $u(i)$ have zero expectation, but the variance cannot be stabilized in this manner and by (4.23) it will increase inde-

---

[†] See AITCHISON and BROWN (1955), especially ch. 27.

finitely with t. In some cases this is quite acceptable; in the case of firm size, for example, the evidence does often suggest an increase in dispersion over time which is known as the tendency towards concentration or towards greater inequality. The observed income distributions, on the other hand, show no increase in variance over time, so that the model must be amended. One way of doing so is to assume that the shocks $\underline{u}(t)$ are not independent of the prevailing income level $\underline{y}(t)$, but that there is a negative correlation between the two which keeps $\sigma_0^2(t)$ constant. This assumption, used by KALECKI (1945), is convenient but questionable: as a matter of fact the variance of income *does* increase with time if we consider a closed population, as becomes apparent when we examine the income distribution of different age groups: up to the age of retirement the dispersion of log income invariably increases with age. Hence the stability of the income distribution over all age groups taken together must be brought about by the continuous replacement, upon retirement and death, of highly dispersed incomes by the much more uniform incomes of the retired and of new entrants. This factor

TABLE 10

Measures of inequality of various size distributions.

	a, Pareto	s, lognormal	note
Private incomes			
Augsburg 1471	1.43		1
U.S.A. 1864	1.46		2
England 1867	1.47		3
India 1960		.94	4
U.S.A. 1950		.64	5
England 1957	2.09		6
Holland 1958	2.15		7
Private wealth			
Sweden 1959	1.72		8
Holland 1959	1.44		7
Business size			
Germany 1896: profits		.99	9
England 1950: corporations, market value		1.40	10
U.S.A. 1959: corporations, assets	.83		8
Austria 1957: corporations, assets		1.75	8
Germany 1959: retail trade, turnover	1.08		8

For notes see appendix A.

has been introduced in a lognormal model by RUTHERFORD (1955), who assumes that new generations enter with a lognormal income distribution. As time proceeds its variance increases, but the number of incomes of a given generation steadily declines through death and retirement. This ensures that the overall income distribution is lognormal with a constant variance.

Other size distributions

60   In the course of this chapter we have repeatedly referred to other size variables than income, such as personal wealth and various measures of

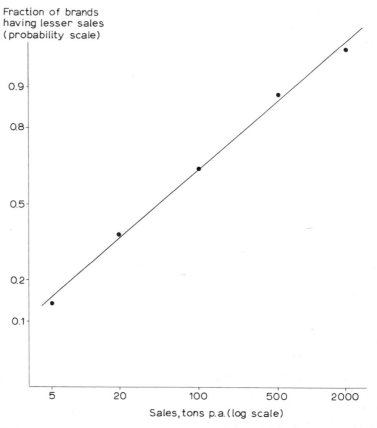

Fig. 23. Lognormal distribution of sales of cigarette brands (France, 1958). For notes see appendix B.

firm size. For the choice of a model it may make a considerable difference whether the population concerned has a rapid turnover (as in the case of individuals) or not (as with firms), and again whether it refers to a stock variable (assets, wealth) or to flows (income, output, sales). The empirical distributions are however all very much the same and vary mainly in the range of observation, the observation of individual wealth and firm size being usually restricted to the upper ranges. Size distributions of all types have been described by Pareto's law and by the lognormal distribution. A single example is given in fig. 23, which illustrates an application of the lognormal multiple classification model of section 58 to the market shares of branded products. A sample of results from other empirical studies is shown in table 10, which includes a few typical estimates of Pareto's constant and the lognormal standard deviation for income distributions. The reader may convert these alternative measures of inequality into one another by the approximate formula of section 57.

CHAPTER 5

The linear regression model

The basic argument

61 At this stage we turn to a type of econometric model that is radically different from the complete stochastic models of the preceding chapters. We begin by recalling the distinctive characteristics of either model, already briefly touched upon in section 8.

So far we have been dealing with models that completely specify the probability distribution of the economic phenomenon concerned. Such models leave room for sampling variation but in principle they permit no other cause for disagreement between theory and observations. Suppose that we have observed several series of waiting times that may be expected to conform to the model of section 13. We may perform a goodness-of-fit test to see whether this is in fact the case; we may estimate the parameter in each sample and assess the variance of the estimators employed; finally we may, by the appropriate statistical test, decide whether the differences between various samples can be attributed to sampling variation alone or must be taken as evidence of differences between the underlying distributions. In all these operations we acknowledge no other source of variation but sampling variation. Within any single set of observations no distinction can be made between systematic variations, allowed for by the model, on one hand, and random or irrelevant variations on the other: the very terms are meaningless in this type of model.

Models of this kind are rare, and most econometric work is based on a different approach. Very briefly the argument runs as follows: economic theory presupposes the existence of many relations such as are partially depicted in the usual textbook diagrams. We wish to give empirical substance to these curves by assessing their actual slope and shape. Since by their very nature and design economic relations constitute abstractions from reality, we will never observe data that exactly fit the economic model. The best we can do then is to set up a statistical model which permits us to separate the relevant economic relation from other, disturbing, factors. A simple and convenient statistical model that meets this requirement is the *linear regression model*.

This model is at the basis of by far the major part of all econometric research. We assume that the reader is familiar with the statistical technique of least-squares regression which is the appropriate method of estimation [†]. In this chapter we wish to retrace with some care the arguments that lead up to the linear regression hypothesis as it is usually stated at the outset of the estimation problem. We shall then briefly recall the elements of least-squares regression and review some of its properties which substantially affect the formulation of the economic models to which it is applied. The problems raised by economic models that consist of a set of simultaneous equations are discussed in the next chapter.

62 The income elasticity of consumer demand for beef is a concept freely used in economic theory. This does not mean that, even in economics, income is the sole or principal determinant of the demand for beef; it simply means that at a certain stage of the economic argument it is convenient to consider the relation of beef demand to income *ceteris paribus*. Consumers' expenditure on beef may indeed be a function of any variables one may wish to suggest; in certain situations it is of interest to isolate the effect of income alone. The *ceteris paribus* condition means that we consider the partial derivative in respect of one particular variable by holding all others constant.

We may try to approximate this ideal relation between expenditure on beef and income by examining the values taken by the former variable for households of varying income. Fig. 24 shows a scatter diagram obtained by plotting these two variables for 65 households that took part in the Dutch budget survey of 1935[††]. These observations at first sight largely meet the

---

[†] We have already referred to the treatises of JOHNSTON (1963), GOLDBERGER (1964), THEIL (forthcoming) and MALINVAUD (1966) in section 11.

[††] Data from HUISHOUDREKENINGEN (1937). Each household has provided detailed records of its expenditure during a full year; although this may have unfavourably affected the composition of the sample, errors of observation are negligible.

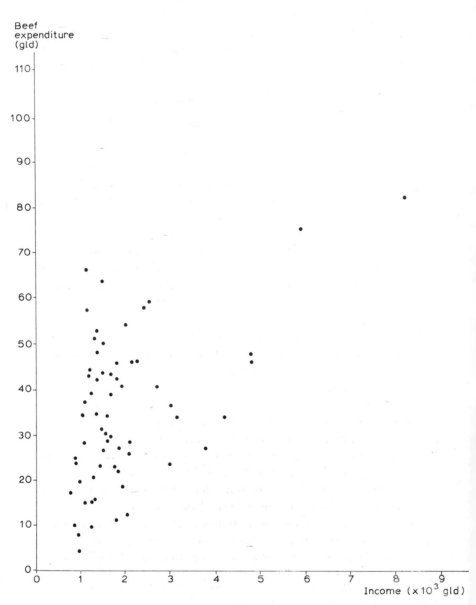

Fig. 24. Income and expenditure on beef of 65 households (Holland, 1935–1936). For notes see appendix B.

requirement that, apart from income, most factors likely to affect beef consumption are constant, or nearly so. All households confront similar prices (hence the equivalence of expenditure and demand) and the same general economic environment; moreover, while individual characteristics inevitably persist, we have removed two major distinctions–age and family size–by restricting the sample under consideration to households consisting of a couple with one child under 16.

The scatter diagram of fig. 24 shows a vague tendency of the two variables to move together but nothing like a clear functional relation. The crucial step in the argument is the interpretation of this state of affairs as if there does exist a systematic functional relation which, in the observations at hand, has been affected by disturbances that can be treated as random variables. The latter assumption does not mean that these disturbances are not capable of further explanation. As a matter of fact there is no intrinsic difference between stochastic and deterministic phenomena; even dice behave according to the laws of mechanics. A variable is random merely because we chose, as a matter of convenience, to describe its behaviour by a probability distribution. In the case under review there is equally no doubt that consumer expenditure on beef is determinate; the deviations from the income curve simply indicate that we have not succeeded in holding all other factors constant. There are definite reasons for each individual deviation from the relation with income, and these reasons can in principle be detected. But since we merely wish to determine the income elasticity of demand it is not profitable to do so. The fundamental reason why we prefer to treat the effect of all neglected factors as a random disturbance is that we believe them to be irrelevant to the economic relation under review.

63 We repeat the argument in a more precise form. We start off from the basic premise that all phenomena are completely determined by causal relationships. Any economic variable Y is determined by w variables X_j, $j = 1, 2, ..., w$, which together exhaust all possible determinants of Y; some of these variables are considered in economic theory, many are not. In order to stress the causal character of this relation we shall at times write

$$Y := \phi(X_1, X_2, ..., X_w),$$

(5.1)

which of course implies that Y satisfies the equation

$$Y = \phi(X_1, X_2, ..., X_w).$$

(5.2)

Suppose now, for the sake of the argument, that we have a set of n observations that each give the values of *all* w X_j as well as the corresponding value of Y. We denote individual observations by the index i, $i = 1, 2, ..., n$. By assumption each observation

$$Y_i, X_{1i}, X_{2i}, ..., X_{wi}$$

satisfies (5.2), or

$$Y_i = \phi(X_{1i}, X_{2i}, ..., X_{wi}) \quad \text{for} \quad i = 1, 2, ..., n. \tag{5.3}$$

We replace the right-hand side of this expression by the expansion of ϕ in a Taylor series around the point

$$Y_0, \bar{X}_1, \bar{X}_2, ..., \bar{X}_w$$

where the X_j assume their mean observed value,

$$\bar{X}_j = \frac{1}{n} \sum_i^n X_{ji} \quad \text{for } j = 1, 2, ..., w, \tag{5.4}$$

and

$$Y_0 = \phi(\bar{X}_1, \bar{X}_2, ..., \bar{X}_w). \tag{5.5}$$

By Taylor's theorem (5.3) can be written as

$$Y_i = Y_0 + \frac{\partial \phi}{\partial X_1}(X_{1i} - \bar{X}_1) + \frac{\partial \phi}{\partial X_2}(X_{2i} - \bar{X}_2) + ... \frac{\partial \phi}{\partial X_w}(X_{wi} - \bar{X}_w)$$

$$+ \frac{1}{2!}\left\{ \frac{\partial^2 \phi}{\partial X_1^2}(X_{1i} - \bar{X}_1)^2 + 2\frac{\partial^2 \phi}{\partial X_1 \partial X_2}(X_{1i} - \bar{X}_1)(X_{2i} - \bar{X}_2) + ...\right\}$$

$$+ ... \quad \text{for } i = 1, 2, ..., n.$$

Since the w variables X_j by assumption contain all possible determinants of Y it is quite likely that a fair number of them, say $(w - v)$, is constant among the observations in hand. We suppose that these are the last $(w - v)$ variables listed, or

$$\text{for } j = v+1, \ v+2, ..., w: \quad X_{ji} = \bar{X}_j, X_{ji} - \bar{X}_j = 0 \text{ for all } i.$$

Clearly all terms of the Taylor series involving any of these variables vanish. We omit these zero terms and retain only the first v variables that do vary in the sample data. Hence all observations satisfy

$$Y_i = Y_0 + \frac{\partial \phi}{\partial X_1}(X_{1i} - \bar{X}_1) + \frac{\partial \phi}{\partial X_2}(X_{2i} - \bar{X}_2) + ... \frac{\partial \phi}{\partial X_v}(X_{vi} - \bar{X}_v)$$

$$+ \frac{1}{2!}\left\{ \frac{\partial^2 \phi}{\partial X_1^2}(X_{1i} - \bar{X}_1)^2 + 2\frac{\partial^2 \phi}{\partial X_1 \partial X_2}(X_{1i} - \bar{X}_1)(X_{2i} - \bar{X}_2)...\right\}$$

$$+ ... \quad \text{for } i = 1, 2, ..., n. \tag{5.6}$$

If it were asked in what way the observed Y_i have arisen the answer would be that they have been determined according to

$$Y_i := Y_0 + \frac{\partial \phi}{\partial X_1}(X_{1i} - \bar{X}_1) + \ldots \tag{5.7}$$

where the right-hand side is the same as in (5.6).

64   Suppose now that among the v variables X_j that occur in (5.6) the first k variables X_j with $j = 1, 2, \ldots, k$ are of interest to economic theory, and that we wish to assess their effect on Y. Since these effects are usually defined in economics under the *ceteris paribus* condition this amounts to the determination of the first k partial derivatives

$$\frac{\partial \phi}{\partial X_1}, \frac{\partial \phi}{\partial X_2}, \ldots, \frac{\partial \phi}{\partial X_k}.$$

The statistical model that is used in the estimation of these partial derivatives assumes that the observations satisfy

$$Y_i = Y_0 + \frac{\partial \phi}{\partial X_1}(X_{1i} - \bar{X}_1) + \frac{\partial \phi}{\partial X_2}(X_{2i} - \bar{X}_2)\ldots$$
$$+ \frac{\partial \phi}{\partial X_k}(X_{ki} - \bar{X}_k) + U_i \tag{5.8}$$

where U_i is the value taken by a random disturbance term $\underline{U}_i$. Usually, of course, the model is written in a simpler notation. The first-order partial derivatives that occur in (5.8) are the same as in (5.6); since these are understood to be evaluated at the point

$$Y_0, \bar{X}_1, \bar{X}_2, \ldots, \bar{X}_w$$

they take the same value for all i. We may therefore replace these partial derivatives by constant coefficients β, writing

$$\frac{\partial \phi}{\partial X_j} = \beta_j \quad \text{for } j = 1, 2, \ldots, k.$$

Moreover we introduce

$$\beta_0 = Y_0 - \sum_{j=1}^{k} \beta_j \bar{X}_j. \tag{5.9}$$

Upon these changes in notation (5.8) can be written as

$$Y_i = \beta_0 + \beta_1 X_{1i} + \beta_2 X_{2i} \ldots + \beta_k X_{ki} + U_i \,. \tag{5.10}$$

If it is now asked how the observed Y_i arise according to *this* model the answer must be that they are random variables generated by

$$\underline{Y}_i := \beta_0 + \beta_1 X_{1i} + \beta_2 X_{2i} \ldots + \beta_k X_{ki} + \underline{U}_i \,, \tag{5.11}$$

where $\underline{U}_i$ is a random variable with certain specified properties which we shall discuss presently.

This is the linear regression model. It depends exclusively on the passage from (5.6) or (5.7) to (5.10) or (5.11) respectively: several terms of the former expansion are dropped and a disturbance term $\underline{U}_i$ is added in their stead. The essential assumptions of the regression model are those involved in this transition; we shall therefore examine it somewhat more closely.

65   The expression on the right-hand side of (5.6) contains partial derivatives of first and higher order of ϕ in respect of v variables X_j. The terms involving the first order derivatives in respect of the first k of these variables are retained unchanged in (5.10). Among the other terms we distinguish three categories.

First, the partial derivatives of higher order in respect of the k retained variables are downright neglected. This is the *linearity hypothesis*. It is assumed either that these derivatives of higher order vanish–i.e. that ϕ is linear in the first k variables X_j–or that the deviations from the sample mean

$$(X_{ji} - \overline{X}_j)$$

are sufficiently small to justify the neglect of the terms involving squares, products and higher powers of these deviations: ϕ is represented by a linear approximation over the observed domain. The linearity hypothesis may of course apply to transformed variables. If we wish to estimate partial elasticities rather than partial derivatives (as is often the case), Y and the X_j are defined at the outset as the logarithms of the economic magnitudes concerned; the argument is not affected.

The second group of terms of (5.6) which does not reappear in (5.10) consists of the derivatives of any order in respect of the $(v-k)$ omitted variables. These terms are summarized in the random disturbance term $\underline{U}_i$. We repeat that this does not mean that the omitted variables operate in a different manner from the k variables that are retained, nor that they are in any sense unimportant or have little effect on Y; the joint effect of these omitted variables on the observed Y_i may well be substantial. If this is the case we must presumably attribute a large variance to U_i; but the linear regression model does not require that it is small.

We do however assume that the omitted variables are irrelevant to the relation between Y and the retained variables, i.e. that the cross partial derivatives in respect of variables from the retained and the omitted set respectively vanish. This accounts for the third and final group of terms of (5.6) that are absent from (5.10). It corresponds to the fundamental statistical assumption of the linear regression model that the disturbance U_i is independent of the X_{ji} with $j = 1, 2, ..., k$.

Throughout this discussion we have maintained the patently unrealistic assumption (introduced at the outset) that the observations cover all w possible determinants of Y. After elimination of those X_j that are constant among the observations, the remaining variables were divided into retained and omitted variables on the basis of their economic interest. In practice we cannot proceed in this order, and our choice is restricted by the fact that we observe only a limited number of the determinants of Y. All others must .necessarily be relegated to the set of omitted variables. If any of the observed variables are constant they are eliminated as before, and we are only then free to select the retained variables from the remainder. This choice depends on the object of the analysis, i.e. on our interests, but it is also affected by certain statistical considerations to which we return in section 77.

Properties of the random disturbances

66   The linear regression model is incomplete without assumptions about the properties of the U_i. Since the reader is supposed to be already familiar with the matter, he should know that there are various alternative specifications which are all compatible with the estimation of the β_j by the method of least squares. We here employ the set of assumptions that seems best suited to econometric applications.

So far we have treated the X_{ji} as given constants without any stochastic connotation, so that U_i is the sole random variable of the model. We may however equally well consider the X_{ji} as random variables too; the estimates of the β_j that we obtain must then be regarded as being conditional upon the observed sample values X_{ji} of the X_{ji}. Since it facilitates the discussion of the asymptotic properties of the estimates we shall take this course.

The first assumption of the regression model is that the X_{ji} and the U_i are unrelated. This now refers to a pair of random variables which are independent, or, more generally, have zero covariance [†].

assumption 1

$$\text{covar}(\underline{X}_{ji}, \underline{U}_i) = 0 \qquad \text{for } j = 1, 2, ..., k \text{ and } i = 1, 2, ..., n. \qquad (5.12)$$

This is the major assumption of regression analysis and the only one that cannot be abandoned without destroying the whole edifice of estimation by least squares. Unfortunately it is often inappropriate to simple economic relations; we discuss this problem in the next chapter.

67 The other three assumptions are of minor importance. To begin with we have

assumption 2

$$E(\underline{U}_i) = 0 \text{ for } i = 1, 2, ..., n. \qquad (5.13)$$

If the X_{ji} are treated as nonstochastic constants the former assumption follows from this one, since in that case (5.13) implies $E(X_{ji}\underline{U}_i) = 0$. In the present formulation, however, (5.12) stands on its own and (5.13) is of little importance. We shall see below that it serves only for the estimation of the constant term β_0 of (5.10); when we take no interest in this coefficient we may put the expected value of $\underline{U}_i$ at any constant we please, and need not assume that it is zero.

Although this freedom in specifying $E(\underline{U}_i)$ is never exercised, lack of interest in β_0 is quite common; it is often not estimated, or its estimate is not reported, or it is reported without an indication of its standard error. There are good reasons for this neglect. As we have argued, the economic reaction coefficients defined under *ceteris paribus* conditions correspond to partial derivatives; hence our interest in estimating the β_j for $j = 1, 2, ..., k$. But in general β_0 has no particular meaning in economic theory. It first appears in (5.10), where it serves to simplify the formula; by (5.9) and (5.5) it can be expressed in terms of the initial deterministic model as

---

[†] In the sequel we shall often refer loosely to the independence of two variables when in fact the operative assumption is that they have zero covariance. Since independence is defined for a pair of random variables only, and follows from zero covariance for normal variates alone, the assumption of independence is in these cases by strict standards unnecessarily restrictive. We feel little qualms in using it, however, since the justification of zero covariance would invariably turn on the view that the variables concerned are independent in the sense that they have nothing in common.

$$\beta_0 = \phi(\bar{X}_1, \bar{X}_2, ..., \bar{X}_w) - \sum_j^k \beta_j \bar{X}_j \; .$$

The point is that the index j has different ranges in the two terms on the right-hand side: the first term includes *all* w possible determinants of Y, the second refers to the subset of variables that are observed, not constant, and retained in the analysis because of their economic interest. The value of β_0 hence depends largely on variables left out of consideration or even unobserved; but for certain special cases it is a descriptive constant of the sample under review which is of no consequence.

68   The next assumption is the *homoskedasticity condition*
assumption 3

$$\text{var}(\underline{U}_i) = \sigma^2 \qquad \text{for } i = 1, 2, ..., n \; . \tag{5.14}$$

This may be read as the hypothesis that the $\underline{Y}_i$ – always conditional upon the values X_{ji} taken by the $\underline{X}_{ji}$ – have constant variance, irrespective of i and hence irrespective of the X_{ji} and of $\underline{Y}_i$'s expected value.

Assumption 3 can easily be replaced by the somewhat more general assumption of

$$\text{heteroskedasticity} \qquad \text{var}(\underline{U}_i) = \lambda_i \sigma^2 \; , \tag{5.15}$$

where the λ_i are positive constants that are supposed to be known, if only up to a multiplicative factor which can be arbitrarily varied by inverse adjustment of the numerical value of σ^2. In this case the standard prescription is to modify the least-squares procedure by *reweighting* the observations, i.e. by attaching multiplicative weights that are inversely proportional to $\sqrt{\lambda_i}$ to all observed magnitudes pertaining to the ith observation. This is equivalent to a transformation of the observations. Suppose we believe the relation between

$$\underline{Y}', X'_1, X'_2, ..., X'_k$$

to be heteroskedastic, so that for the disturbance term

$$\underline{U}'_i = \underline{Y}'_i - \beta_0 - \beta_1 X'_{1i} - \beta_2 X'_{2i} ... - \beta_k X'_{ki} \tag{5.16}$$

we have

$$\text{var}(\underline{U}'_i) = \lambda_i \sigma^2 \tag{5.17}$$

where the λ_i are known constants. We now transform the ith observed values into

$$\underline{Y}_i = \underline{Y}'_i/\sqrt{\lambda_i}, \ X_{ji} = X'_{ji}/\sqrt{\lambda_i} \qquad \text{for } j = 1, 2, ..., k \ .$$

After dividing both sides of (5.16) by $\sqrt{\lambda_i}$ substitution of the transformed variables yields

$$\underline{U}'_i/\sqrt{\lambda_i} = \underline{Y}_i - \beta_0/\sqrt{\lambda_i} - \beta_1 X_{1i} - \beta_2 X_{2i} ... - \beta_k X_{ki}$$

Hence the disturbance of the regression equation in the transformed variables, say $\underline{U}_i$, is

$$\underline{U}_i = \underline{U}'_i/\sqrt{\lambda_i}$$

and by (5.17) again satisfies the homoskedasticity condition (5.16). Thus, upon the appropriate transformation of the observations, the original assumption once more holds, but for a change in the constant term which we shall however continue to neglect [†].

In economic applications it is often believed that it is the coefficient of variation rather than the variance of $\underline{Y}_i$ that is constant. Since the variance of $\underline{Y}_i$ (always conditional upon the X_{ji}) equals var $(\underline{U}_i)$ it is the latter that must be taken to vary with the expected value of $\underline{Y}_i$. This can be treated as a special case of heteroskedasticity with the λ_i of (5.15) defined as a function of the X_{ji}. This type of heteroskedasticity in respect of an economic magnitude Y' is however approximately removed if the regression equation applies to its logarithm, that is if

$$\underline{Y}_i = \log \underline{Y}'_i$$

enters into

$$\underline{Y}_i = \beta_0 + \beta_1 X_{1i} + \beta_2 X_{2i} ... + \beta_k X_{ki} + \underline{U}_i \ .$$

It is immaterial whether the X_j of this linear relation are also logarithms of "natural" magnitudes or not; in either case the original variable Y' satisfies

$$\underline{Y}'_i = \exp(\beta_0 + \beta_1 X_{1i} ... + \beta_k X_{ki}) \cdot \exp(\underline{U}_i) \ . \tag{5.18}$$

We now simply maintain the homoskedasticity assumption (5.14) and attribute a constant variance to the $\underline{U}_i$; by (5.18), the variance of $\underline{Y}'_i$ (always conditional upon the X_{ji}) will still be roughly proportional [††] to the square of

---

[†] The problem is resolved if we think of β_0 as the multiplicative coefficient of a dummy variable that is identically equal to 1 for all i; in the heteroskedastic case it is transformed to $1/\sqrt{\lambda_i}$ along with the other variables.

[††] Not quite: since (5.18) is nonlinear in U, the usual arithmetic of expectations does not apply.

its expected value, and its coefficient of variation will be nearly constant as required.

69   The last property attributed to the $\underline{U}_i$ is that they are independent of one another, or

assumption 4

$$\text{covar}(\underline{U}_i, \underline{U}_j) = 0 \quad \text{for all } i \neq j. \tag{5.19}$$

Like the preceding assumption this one again is often inappropriate to econometric analysis, particularly so when the observations consist of *economic time series*. In this case the observed Y_i, X_{ji} usually refer to macro-economic aggregates like national income, investment or the price level in a series of consecutive years. We take it that the indices $i = 1, 2, ..., n$ in their natural order denote successive periods. It is often found that adjoining disturbance terms (which refer to consecutive periods) are no longer independent but positively related, so that assumption 4 should be replaced by

$$(serial\ correlation) \qquad \text{covar}(\underline{U}_i, \underline{U}_{i-1}) = \rho\sigma^2, \qquad 0 < \rho < 1, \tag{5.20}$$

where ρ is the (first order) serial correlation coefficient of the disturbances [†].

The positive serial correlation of the disturbances is primarily due to the positive serial correlation of economic time series in general, which is well established [††]. After all, the disturbance terms represent the joint effect of omitted variables, and in any time series analysis these are bound to consist largely of economic time series too. The positive autocorrelation of economic time series in turn reflects the prevalence of trends and cycles which extend over a number of years. It may also be attributed to the fact that economic agents are often slow in adapting their behaviour to changes in their circumstances; we shall illustrate this for the consumption function in ch. 8. The fact that several economic variables react to some or all of their determinants with a definite time lag, coupled with the existence of many causal relations among *all* macro-economic variables, makes all aggregate time series move smoothly and in unison. Hence almost any pair of economic time series will show a sizeable correlation, whether they are directly causally related or not,

---

[†] A test for detecting significant deviations from the serial independence assumption (5.19) has been designed by Durbin and Watson (1950), (1951); for a variant see Theil and Nagar (1961). Here as elsewhere the additional assumption that the disturbances are normally distributed is required as we pass from estimation to testing.

[††] See Orcutt (1948).

and almost any economic time series will show a positive serial correlation. These two characteristics together amount to the business cycle[†]. The consequences of the interrelations among all macro-economic time series will be further explored in section 80 below; here we merely wish to quote their smooth movement in time as an explanation of the serial correlation of disturbances in time series analyses.

Once more the usual procedure in the case of serial correlation is to remove the complicating factor (if only approximately) by a transformation of the observations. Suppose that we have a regression equation in

$$Y', X'_1, X'_2, ..., X'_k$$

and that the disturbances

$$\underline{U}'_i = \underline{Y}'_i - \beta_0 - \beta_1 X'_{1i} - \beta_2 X'_{2i} ... - \beta_k X'_{ki} \tag{5.21}$$

are serially correlated, or–as in (5.20)–

$$\text{covar}(\underline{U}'_i, \underline{U}'_{i-1}) = \rho\sigma^2 , \qquad 0 < \rho < 1 .$$

It is easily shown that this corresponds to the generation of the $\underline{U}'_i$ by an autoregressive scheme of the form

$$\underline{U}'_i = \rho\underline{U}'_{i-1} + \underline{V}_i$$

where the $\underline{V}_i$ *are* serially independent (i.e. satisfy (5.19)) and are moreover independent of $\underline{U}'_{i-1}$. Hence

$$\underline{V}_i = \underline{U}'_i - \rho\underline{U}'_{i-1} \tag{5.22}$$

meets the standard assumptions, and the problem is to transform the observed values $\underline{Y}'_i, X'_{1i}, X'_{2i}, ..., X'_{ki}$ in such a manner that a regression equation in the transformed variables has $\underline{V}_i$ instead of $\underline{U}'_i$ as its disturbance term. It follows from (5.21) and (5.22) that a transformation to

$$(\underline{Y}'_i - \rho\underline{Y}'_{i-1}), \ (X'_{1i} - \rho X'_{1(i-1)}), \ ...$$

would meet the case; but since ρ is unknown this is hardly practicable. If there is a strong serial correlation one may however transform the observations to *first differences*, or

$$Y_i = \Delta Y'_i = Y'_i - Y'_{i-1} ,$$

$$X_{ji} = \Delta X'_{ji} = X'_{ji} - X'_{j(i-1)} , \quad \text{for } j = 1, 2, ..., k .$$

[†] They do not, of course, amount to a theory or explanation of the business cycle.

Clearly, the disturbance of a regression equation in these variables,

$$\underline{U}_i = \underline{Y}_i - \beta_1 X_{1i} - \beta_2 X_{2i} \ldots - \beta_k X_{ki} , \tag{5.23}$$

satisfies, by (5.21),

$$\underline{U}_i = \underline{U}'_i - \underline{U}'_{i-1} .$$

Upon comparing this with (5.22) we find that $\underline{U}_i$ is not equal to $\underline{V}_i$ and does not satisfy (5.19); indeed, since the $\underline{V}_i$ are serially independent by assumption, the $\underline{U}_i$ have a negative autocorrelation,

$$\text{covar}(\underline{U}_i, \underline{U}_{i-1}) = -(1-\rho)^2 \sigma^2, \quad 0 < \rho < 1 .$$

When the original autocorrelation is strong, however, ρ approaches 1 and the autocorrelation of the disturbances of the first difference equation tends to zero, so that assumption 4 (5.19) very nearly applies. The transformation to first differences may therefore serve to deal with the worst cases of serially correlated disturbances.

Observant readers may have noticed, by comparing (5.21) and (5.23), that the passage to first differences has eliminated the constant term β_0 from the model. As a rule this is no great loss, for (as we have argued in section 67) this coefficient is seldom of interest. One exception arises precisely when, in spite of its absence from (5.23), a constant term is nevertheless included in a first difference equation. As inspection will show this term then corresponds to the coefficient β_j of a variable X'_{ji} that among the original observations is identically equal to i. Since i here denotes successive time periods, this is a *trend* variable, and its coefficient should be capable of a reasonable interpretation.

Properties of least-squares estimates

70 We now turn to a very brief review of the estimation of the partial derivatives $\beta_1, \beta_2, \ldots \beta_k$ of (5.10) by the method of least squares. For a given set of observations

$$Y_i, X_{1i}, X_{2i}, \ldots, X_{ki}$$

at our disposal we determine the coefficients $b_0, b_1, \ldots, b_k$ of a linear form

$$Y = b_0 + b_1 X_1 + b_2 X_2 \ldots + b_k X_k$$

by the condition that the sum of squares of the *residuals* E_i, defined by

$$E_i = Y_i - b_0 - b_1 X_{1i} - b_2 X_{2i} \dots - b_k X_{ki} , \qquad (5.24)$$

is minimized, or

$$Q = \sum_1^n E_i^2 \quad \text{a minimum} . \qquad (5.25)$$

Writing

$$\bar{E} = \frac{1}{n} \sum_1^n E_i, \qquad e_i = E_i - \bar{E} \qquad (5.26)$$

we may partition Q as

$$Q = \sum_1^n E_i^2 = \sum_1^n e_i^2 + n\bar{E}^2 .$$

It follows that Q is least if $\bar{E}=0$, and substituting (5.24) into (5.26) we find that this is easily ensured by putting

$$b_0 = \bar{Y} - b_1 \bar{X}_1 - b_2 \bar{X}_2 \dots - b_k \bar{X}_k , \qquad (5.27)$$

where we have extended the notation for sample means of (5.4) to Y as well. Since $\bar{E}$ is now zero the least-squares problem is reduced to determining the remaining coefficients $b_1, b_2, \dots, b_k$ by the condition

$$Q = \sum_1^n e_i^2 \quad \text{a minimum} . \qquad (5.28)$$

As we argued in section 67, the constant term β_0 is rarely of any interest, and we usually wish to estimate the partial derivatives $\beta_1, \beta_2, \dots, \beta_k$ only. We now act on this view and restrict the application of the least-squares principle to the determination of the $b_1, b_2, \dots, b_k$. The preliminaries are therefore concluded by eliminating b_0. To this end we substitute (5.27) and its concomitant $\bar{E}=0$ into (5.24) and obtain

$$e_i = (Y_i - \bar{Y}) - b_1(X_{1i} - \bar{X}_1) - b_2(X_{2i} - \bar{X}_2) \dots - b_k(X_{ki} - \bar{X}_k) .$$

Extending the use of lower case letters for deviations from the sample mean to all variables we write

$$y_i = Y_i - \bar{Y} ,$$
$$x_{ji} = X_{ji} - \bar{X}_j ,$$

and have

$$e_i = y_i - b_1 x_{1i} \dots - b_k x_{ki} . \qquad (5.29)$$

The least-squares problem is now reduced to the determination of the $b_1, b_2, \dots, b_k$ of (5.29) so as to meet the condition (5.28).

71 So far we have proceeded step by step in order to convince the reader that we are at liberty to formulate the least-squares problem entirely in terms of deviations from the sample mean. It is a matter of opinion whether we are right in neglecting the constant term; in respect of $b_1, b_2, ..., b_k$, however, the least-squares problem summarized in (5.29) and (5.28) is fully equivalent to the original statement of (5.24) and (5.25). Having established this much we return to our former practice of drawing freely on the reader's presumed knowledge of least-squares regression, and pass on at once to its matrix representation.

If we were to write (5.29) in full for $i = 1, 2, ..., n$ we would obtain a system of n linear equations which can be written in matrix notation as

$$e = y - Xb .\tag{5.30}$$

Here e and y are column vectors composed of n elements e_i and y_i respectively, X is a $(n \times k)$ matrix of the x_{ji} and b is a column vector consisting of $b_1, b_2, ..., b_k$. The minimum condition (5.28) now refers to

$$Q = e'e ,$$

and upon substitution of (5.30) and differentiation in respect of the elements of b it is found that in order to satisfy

$$\frac{\partial Q}{\partial b_j} = 0 \quad \text{for } j = 1, 2, ..., k$$

b must be a solution of

$$(X'X)b = X'y .\tag{5.31}$$

Provided $(X'X)$ is nonsingular the least-squares estimates b are therefore determined by

$$b = (X'X)^{-1}X'y .\tag{5.32}$$

We recall once more that the elements of X and y here consist of deviations from the sample means and not of the original observed values.

72 In order to establish the probabilistic properties of the estimators (5.32) we must first re-formulate the regression model (5.11) in terms of deviations from sample means. Since by assumption all n observations satisfy

$$\underline{Y}_i = \beta_0 + \beta_1 X_{1i} + \beta_2 X_{2i} ... + \beta_k X_{ki} + \underline{U}_i ,$$

evidently

$$\overline{Y} = \beta_0 + \beta_1 \overline{X}_1 + \beta_2 \overline{X}_2 + \ldots + \beta_k \overline{X}_k + \overline{U}$$

and, upon subtraction,

$$\underline{y}_i = \beta_1 x_{1i} + \beta_2 x_{2i} + \ldots + \beta_k x_{ki} + \underline{u}_i \tag{5.33}$$

with

$$\underline{u}_i = \underline{U}_i - \overline{U}, \qquad \overline{U} = \frac{1}{n} \sum_1^n \underline{U}_i .$$

In the matrix notation introduced above (5.33) can be written as

$$\underline{y} = X\beta + \underline{u} . \tag{5.34}$$

As long as we consider the estimation of β by $\underline{b}$ conditional upon the values taken by $\underline{X}$ we employ this formulation where the X are nonrandom given constants and $\underline{u}$ is the only random term among the determinants of $\underline{y}$. But when we come to the asymptotic properties of $\underline{b}$ we shall acknowledge the random character of the $\underline{X}_{ji}$, and hence of the $\underline{x}_{ji}$ and of $\underline{X}$, already noted in section 66, and we shall then of course write

$$\underline{y} = \underline{X}\beta + \underline{u}$$

instead of (5.34).

The main point to watch is that the elements of $\underline{u}$ are deviations from the sample mean,

$$\underline{u}_i = \underline{U}_i - \overline{U} ,$$

just like the elements of $\underline{y}$ and of X. Since the assumptions made about the disturbances refer to $\underline{U}_i$, not to $\underline{u}_i$, some obvious modifications are in order if we wish to set down the properties of the latter. It is here that assumption 2 (5.13),

$$E(\underline{U}_i) = 0 ,$$

is seen to be unnecessarily restrictive in view of our neglect of β_0 and of the ensuing passage to deviations from the mean: the properties of the $\underline{u}_i$ are not affected if we equate $E(\underline{U}_i)$ to any nonzero constant instead.

73   Substitution of (5.34) in (5.32) yields

$$\underline{b} = \beta + (X'X)^{-1} X' \underline{u}, \tag{5.35}$$

and this is the basic formula for the discussion of the probabilistic properties of $\underline{b}$. Upon taking expectations all elements of $X'\underline{u}$ vanish, so that

$$E(\underline{b}) = \beta ,\tag{5.36}$$

i.e. the elements of $\underline{b}$ are *unbiased* estimators of the corresponding elements of β. We may at once use (5.36) to define the variance-covariance matrix of the elements of $\underline{b}$ as

$$V = E\{(\underline{b}-\beta)(\underline{b}-\beta)'\} ;$$

upon substitution of (5.35), and making use of the properties of $\underline{U}$ this yields the familiar formula[†]

$$V = (X'X)^{-1}\sigma^2 .\tag{5.37}$$

For reasons to be made clear shortly we are often much more interested in the asymptotic properties of b for $n \to \infty$. Evidently these will depend on the behaviour of X for $n \to \infty$, and we must therefore specify some properties of the X_{ji} that are added, as it were, when the sample size increases. By definition a typical element of $(X'X)$ is

$$\sum_{i=1}^{n} x_{hi}x_{ji} ,$$

and such a second moment (around the sample mean) may be written in terms of the sample standard deviations and correlations of the X_j as

$$\sum_{i} x_{hi}x_{ji} = ns_{x_h}s_{x_j}r_{x_hx_j} ,$$

where

$$s_{x_h} = \sqrt{\frac{1}{n}\sum_{i}^{n} x_{hi}^2} , \qquad r_{x_hx_j} = \frac{\sum_{i} x_{hi}x_{ji}}{ns_{x_h}s_{x_j}} .$$

Introducing two $(k \times k)$ matrices S_x and R_x defined as

$$S_x = \begin{bmatrix} s_{x_1} & \cdots & 0 & \cdots & 0 \\ 0 & \cdots & s_{x_2} & \cdots & 0 \\ \vdots & \cdots & \vdots & \cdots & \vdots \\ 0 & \cdots & 0 & \cdots & s_{x_k} \end{bmatrix}\tag{5.38}$$

[†] At first sight the passage to deviations from the mean does not facilitate the derivation of this result. All goes well, however, when we replace $X'u$ in (5.35) by $X'U$, where U is the vector of the original disturbances U_i. We may do so because the difference between $X'u$ and $X'U$ consists element for element of sums of the form $\Sigma_i^n x_{ji}\overline{U}$, or $\overline{U}\Sigma_i^n x_{ji}$; these are identically zero, whatever the value of $\overline{U}$, since $\Sigma_i^n x_{ji}$ is identically zero.

and

$$R_x = \begin{bmatrix} 1 & \cdots & r_{x_1 x_2} & \cdots & r_{x_1 x_k} \\ r_{x_2 x_1} & 1 & & \cdots & r_{x_2 x_k} \\ \vdots & & \vdots & & \vdots \\ r_{x_k x_1} & r_{x_k x_2} & & \cdots & 1 \end{bmatrix} \tag{5.39}$$

we may write

$$(X'X) = n S_x R_x S_x . \tag{5.40}$$

We now assume that the $\underline{X}_j$ have finite variances and correlations

$$\sigma_{x_j}, \ \rho_{x_h x_j},$$

and arrange these like the corresponding sample statistics in two $(k \times k)$ matrices

$$\Sigma_x, \quad P_x$$

respectively. As n increases indefinitely the sample statistics will under quite general conditions tend in probability to the corresponding parameters, so that

$$\underset{n \to \infty}{\text{Plim}} \{ S_x R_x S_x \} = \Sigma_x P_x \Sigma_x . \tag{5.41}$$

At this stage these results merely serve to establish the convergence in probability of $\underline{b}$ itself. Substituting (5.40) into (5.37) we have

$$V = \{ S_x R_x S_x \}^{-1} \frac{\sigma^2}{n} . \tag{5.42}$$

When we consider the probability limit of $\underline{V}$ for $n \to \infty$ we know by (5.41) that the elements of the matrix product in brackets tends to finite limits. Hence

$$\underset{n \to \infty}{\text{Plim}} (\underline{V}) = \{ \Sigma_x P_x \Sigma_x \}^{-1} \underset{n \to \infty}{\text{Plim}} \frac{\sigma^2}{n} = 0 .$$

As the variances (and covariances) of the elements of $\underline{b}$ tend to zero for $n \to \infty$, $\underline{b}$ itself will tend towards its expected value, or – by (5.36) –

$$\underset{n \to \infty}{\text{Plim}} (\underline{b}) = \beta . \tag{5.43}$$

The estimator $\underline{b}$ of (5.32) thus provides *consistent* estimates of β.

74   Besides consistency there are other qualities of estimators that refer to their limiting behaviour as the sample size increases, such as *asymptotic unbiasedness*

$$\lim_{n \to \infty} E(\underline{b}) = \beta \,.$$

In the present case this follows at once from (5.36) which holds regardless of the value of n.

The reason for stressing such asymptotic properties in connection with econometric applications is not, unfortunately, that the observed samples are large or can be increased at will. On the contrary, most econometric studies are based on a limited number of observations, and at first sight it would be more fitting to examine the small sample properties of the estimates rather than their asymptotic behaviour. Often, however, we are forced to estimate certain economic coefficients indirectly, and while asymptotic properties in general carry over to the indirect estimates the latter's other qualities are hard to establish.

In the simple Keynesian model of income formation the *multiplier* γ is related to the marginal propensity to consume β by

$$\gamma = \frac{1}{1-\beta} \,.$$

As we shall show in section 165 we may under certain conditions obtain a least-squares estimate $\underline{c}$ of γ that is both unbiased (by (5.36)) and consistent (by (5.43)) since all assumptions of the regression model apply. If we now wish to determine the marginal propensity to consume it is natural to take, by analogy,

$$\underline{b} = 1 - \frac{1}{\underline{c}}$$

as an estimator of β. What are its qualities? Although $\underline{c}$ is unbiased, $\underline{b}$ need not be so, and indeed in general is not: but for simple linear transformations with fixed coefficients, the expected value of a transformed random variable does not in general coincide with the corresponding transformation of its expectation. The consistency of $\underline{c}$, however, does carry over to $\underline{b}$ in virtue of the general proposition that under quite general conditions the probability limit of a function of random variables is the corresponding function of their probability limits [†].

[†] See CRAMÈR (1945), p. 254–255, and WILKS (1962), p. 102–103.

75   The Keynesian model is not just an isolated instance; we shall frequently come across situations where the economic model specifies a parameter β as a function of one or more others, say

$$\beta = \phi(\alpha, \gamma, \delta, \ldots).$$

When we have consistent estimates $\underline{a}, \underline{c}, \underline{d}, \ldots$ of $\alpha, \gamma, \delta, \ldots$

$$\underline{b} = \phi(\underline{a}, \underline{c}, \underline{d}, \ldots)$$

is a consistent estimate of β. We shall usually leave it at that and not even try to establish the expected value of $\underline{b}$.

If we wish to establish the variance of $\underline{b}$ we are up against the same difficulty as before, and even when the variance and covariances of $\underline{a}, \underline{c}, \underline{d}, \ldots$ are known this will often prove a very intractable problem. We may however in this case employ the approximation

$$\text{var}(\underline{b}) = \left(\frac{\partial \phi}{\partial a}\right)^2 \text{var}(\underline{a}) + \left(\frac{\partial \phi}{\partial c}\right)^2 \text{var}(\underline{c}) + \ldots$$

$$\text{(5.44)}$$

$$+ 2\left(\frac{\partial \phi}{\partial a}\right)\left(\frac{\partial \phi}{\partial c}\right) \text{covar}(\underline{a}, \underline{c}) + 2\left(\frac{\partial \phi}{\partial a}\right)\left(\frac{\partial \phi}{\partial d}\right) \text{covar}(\underline{a}, \underline{d}) \ldots^{\dagger}$$

The structure of the matrix X

76   We now take leave of asymptotic considerations and in the remaining sections of this chapter once more regard $\underline{b}$ as an estimator that is conditional upon the values taken by the X_{ji} in the sample under review. Indeed we shall give substance to this formal point of view by examining how the characteristics of the X_{ji} – i.e. of the matrix X – affect the properties of $\underline{b}$. Insofar as we have some choice in the matter we shall of course in practice modify X so as to increase the precision of the estimates by reducing their variance ††.

Inspection of the arguments invoked in the passage from (5.35) to (5.36) will bring out that $\underline{b}$ is an unbiased estimator of β whatever X, provided only that $(X'X)$ is nonsingular. The latter condition has already been employed in solving the simultaneous equations (5.31); without it $\underline{b}$ is

---

† See KLEIN (1953), p. 258, or, for a proof of the asymptotic validity of this approximation, CRAMÈR (1945), p. 353–4.

†† The quest for minimum variance is discussed in terms of the estimator's *efficiency* when the observed X are taken as given. Since we specifically consider variations in X we are here concerned with a different problem.

undetermined. X does however affect the variance-covariance matrix of $\underline{b}$, V, as is immediately apparent from (5.37),

$$V = (X'X)^{-1}\sigma^2 .$$

We now recall some expressions from section 73, viz. (5.40)

$$(X'X) = nS_x R_x S_x$$

and (5.42)

$$V = \{S_x R_x S_x\}^{-1}\frac{\sigma^2}{n},$$

and rewrite the latter as

$$V = S_x^{-1} R_x^{-1} S_x^{-1}\frac{\sigma^2}{n}. \tag{5.45}$$

Since S_x, as given in (5.38), is a diagonal matrix we have

$$S_x^{-1} = \begin{bmatrix} \dfrac{1}{s_{x_1}} & 0 & \cdots & 0 \\ 0 & \dfrac{1}{s_{x_2}} & \cdots & 0 \\ \vdots & \vdots & & \vdots \\ 0 & 0 & & \dfrac{1}{s_{x_k}} \end{bmatrix} \tag{5.46}$$

where s_{x_j} is the sample standard error of X_j. R_x^{-1} is the inverse of the sample correlation matrix of the X_j; we denote its typical element as

$$r_x^{hj}$$

and recall that

$$r_x^{hj} = (-1)^{h+j}\frac{|R_x^{hj}|}{|R_x|} \tag{5.47}$$

where R_x^{hj} is the cofactor of $r_{x_h x_j}$ in R_x. This concludes the preliminaries.

77 The precision (or lack of it) of any single estimator $\underline{b}_h$ is gauged by its marginal variance in the joint distribution of all k elements of $\underline{b}$, and this marginal variance is the hth diagonal element of V. We use (5.45) and subsequent formulae to write

$$\text{var}(\underline{b}_h) = V_{hh} = \frac{1}{s_{x_h}^2} \, r_x^{hh} \, \frac{\sigma^2}{n}. \tag{5.48}$$

As the last term shows, the variances of all elements of $\underline{b}$ are proportional to σ^2/n. We already knew (from section 73) that precision is improved by increasing n, but this is rarely a practicable proposition. We can however reduce σ^2 by lessening the part of the omitted variables when specifying the regression model (5.11). At that stage we select k variables that are included in the analysis, and the effects of all omitted variables on the sample variation of Y pass into the disturbance term. The larger these effects the larger is σ^2. All unobserved determinants of Y must perforce be omitted; among the observed variables the choice of the retained variables is dictated in the first place by the objective of the analysis. In order to reduce σ^2 we may however add variables of no intrinsic interest that contribute substantially to the variation of Y among the observations in hand. Thus summer temperature has been successfully used in the analysis of beer demand, and rainfall in studies of crop supply. The introduction of such variables eliminates otherwise unexplained shifts of the demand or supply curve, and thereby reduces σ^2. As we shall see, however, we cannot add variables indefinitely: the number of uncorrelated variables available is usually limited, and as we exhaust it the reduction of σ^2 is offset by an increase of r_x^{hh}.

The first term on the righthand side of (5.48) illustrates that the precision of b_h is proportional (since its variance is inversely proportional) to the sample variance $s_{x_h}^2$ of the variable X_h concerned. If we wish to estimate the derivative of Y in respect of one of its determinants at all accurately we must have observations in which this determinant ranges widely: variables must vary or we cannot assess their effect. The limiting case of a variable that is constant for all observations has already been excluded at an earlier stage (see section 63). But if an observed constant is nevertheless retained in the regression analysis, the corresponding row of X will consist of zeros (because it contains deviations from mean), $(X'X)$ will be singular, and $\underline{b}$ undetermined since (5.31) has no determinate solution.

78 The third term of (5.48) is r_x^{hh}. This calls for much more involved arguments than the other two, but since it is directly related to the problem of *multicollinearity* which besets almost all econometric research we cannot avoid it.

Multicollinearity is the technical term for the existence of close but imperfect linear relations among the X_j. Such interrelations seriously impair the precision of the $\underline{b}_j$. This can be illustrated for the simple case where k

equals 2. The observed triplets (Y_i, X_{1i}, X_{2i}) for $i = 1, 2, \ldots, n$ form a scatter in three-dimensional space similar to the two-dimensional example of fig. 24, and by the principle of least-squares estimation b_1 and b_2 are determined by fitting a plane to these points. If the observed points are evenly distributed as in fig. 25a the least-squares criterion will determine this plane, and hence its direction coefficients b_1 and b_2, without ambiguity. But if the observed sample values of X_1 and X_2 are related, the scatter takes the form of a cylinder or cigar as in fig. 25b. We may still fit a plane to these points by the least-squares criterion, and but for pathological cases we will obtain determinate estimates b_1 and b_2. But this is a delicate solution; the position of the plane, and hence the values of b_1 and b_2, are highly sensitive to small shifts among the observed points: while the main axis of the scatter is well determined, the regression plane may turn violently around it upon a slight displacement of any one observation. Hence certain linear combinations of b_1 and b_2 can be established with some precision, but others cannot, and both b_1 and b_2 taken separately have large variances.

79 Technically multicollinearity shows up in the sample correlation matrix R_x, and its ill effects on the variance of b_h in the inverse element r_x^{hh}. By (5.47) we have

$$r_x^{hh} = \frac{|R_x^{hh}|}{|R_x|}.$$

Thus r_x^{hh} is the quotient of determinants of correlation matrices. By the properties of such matrices these determinants are nonnegative and do not exceed unity. They take the latter value if the X_j are completely unrelated in the sense that all their sample correlations are zero; in this case both R_x and R_x^{hh} reduce to unit matrices, and r_x^{hh} equals unity also. This case will of course never arise; some nonzero sample correlations are bound to occur, especially among economic variables. Now any linear interrelation among all or a subset of the X_j will reduce $|R_x|$ quite as much as a close correlation between a pair of them. Such interrelations are more likely to occur among the k variables represented in R_x than among the $(k-1)$ variables that occur in R_x^{hh}. Consequently, we may generally expect $|R_x|$ to be smaller than $|R_x^{hh}|$, so that r_x^{hh} exceeds unity.

A more precise argument is in order. We may without loss of generality alter the order of the k variables X_j, and when we move h to the first position R_x can be represented as a partitioned matrix of the form

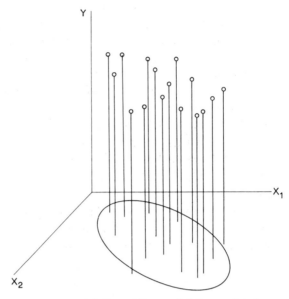

(a) X_1 and X_2 are slightly correlated

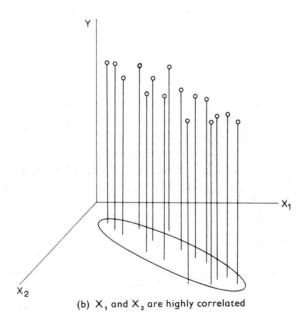

(b) X_1 and X_2 are highly correlated

Fig. 25. Examples of three-dimensional scatter diagrams.

$$
R_x = \begin{bmatrix} 1 & \vdots & r_{x_h x_2} & \cdots & r_{x_h x_k} \\ \hdotsfor{5} \\ r_{x_h x_2} & \vdots & & & \\ \vdots & \vdots & & R_x^{hh} & \\ r_{x_h x_k} & \vdots & & & \end{bmatrix} \tag{5.49}
$$

Now suppose that all k variables that occur in R_x are very nearly linearly dependent, so that $|R_x|$ is small. It is of course conceivable that this condition of strong multicollinearity applies to the $(k-1)$ variables excluding X_h, and that X_h itself is virtually independent of all these other variables. In this case (5.49) reduces to

$$
R_x = \begin{bmatrix} 1 & \vdots & 0 & \dots & 0 \\ \hdotsfor{5} \\ 0 & \vdots & & & \\ \vdots & \vdots & & R_x^{hh} & \\ 0 & \vdots & & & \end{bmatrix},
$$

and we have

$$
r_x^{hh} = \frac{|R_x^{hh}|}{|R_x|} = 1 ,
$$

so that the variance of $\underline{b}_h$ is not unfavourably affected by the multicollinearity among the other variables. As we vary h, however, and consider each coefficient b_j in turn, we must inevitably come across cases in which the condition of near-dependence that obtains among all k variables does not apply to the subset of $(k-1)$ variables that occur in R_x^{hh}. In these cases we have

$$
|R_x^{hh}| > |R_x|
$$

and consequently

$$
r_x^{hh} > 1 ,
$$

and this is where the effect of multicollinearity shows up in the increased variance of the estimate $\underline{b}_h$.

80 The danger of multicollinearity is particularly strong in the analysis of aggregate time series. As we have argued before—in section 69—such macro-economic series tend to move smoothly and in unison, both because there exist very many causal relations among them and because their adjustment to changes in their determinants occurs gradually and may take considerable time. Most analyses of time series are based on a period of some 20 or 30 years, and over such periods most macro-economic variables reflect similar trends and cycles. This leaves little room for independent variation.

By the method of principal components we may decompose the total variation of any number of variables into a smaller number of *independent* components that by linear transformations may account for the whole. STONE (1947) has analysed seventeen macro-economic variables for the United States over the interwar years in this manner; but for some negligible and surely insignificant residual variation three independent factors were sufficient to account for the observed variation. Other analyses of this kind have yielded similar results [†]. Now if there are no more than three independent components among a given set of variables, any subset of four or more of them is bound to be linearly dependent, or almost so since there is inevitably some residual variation present. And this means that some or all of the estimates $\underline{b}_j$ of a regression equation involving four or more variables have large variances.

Thus by the very existence of a large number of intercorrelations among all economic variables we can estimate but a few partial coefficients with tolerable precision. This accounts for the contrast between economic theory and empirical research. The theory is comprehensive: if we list the determinants of, say, consumption or investment that have been discussed by economists we may easily find some ten or twenty distinct effects. But in econometric research we rarely try to estimate more than four or five coefficients for the simple reason that the data do not permit it.

There is no known device to cure multicollinearity. If the data are deficient the proper solution is to add to them, and this has been done by combining cross-section observations with time series data in a single analysis. If this is impossible all we can do is to restrict the number of parameters that are estimated. The simplest way of doing so is to include only a few major determinants in the regression equation, as in the deceptively simple equations of the traditional analysis. Another way of achieving the same end is to allow for a much larger number of variables but to impose so many a priori restrictions on their coefficients that in the end only a few parameters

---

[†] See HOUTHAKKER and TAYLOR (1966), ch. 7.

remain to be estimated. We shall in due course meet several examples of either method which illustrate the importance of multicollinearity in shaping the course of econometric research.

Before we can turn to actual examples, however, we must first discuss another difficulty which has been equally powerful in governing the practice of econometrics. It deserves a chapter of its own.

CHAPTER 6

Simultaneous equations models

Introduction

81 We begin by recalling some characteristics of the fully deterministic relation (5.2) of section 63

$$Y = \phi(X_1, X_2, ..., X_w)$$

that was at the origin of the linear regression model. The first point is that it is meant to be a definitely causal relation, as in (5.1)

$$Y := \phi(X_1, X_2, ..., X_w),$$

the determinants of Y denoted by the X_j being strictly independent variables in the sense that they are *not* in turn determined by Y. If this were not so we could never assume at a later stage that the X_j are nonrandom or, if random, statistically independent of the disturbance term $\underline{U}$. For the disturbances enter into $\underline{Y}$, and if $\underline{Y}$ influences any of the X_j the latter cannot be independent of $\underline{U}$.

The second point is that this basic causal relation which we set out to investigate is assumed to apply directly to the manner in which the actual sample observations arise, or–as in (5.3)–

$$Y_i := \phi(X_{1i}, X_{2i}, ..., X_{wi}), \qquad \text{for } i = 1, 2, ..., n.$$

Hence the regression estimates correspond to the partial derivatives of the deterministic relation that we wish to study.

These specifications are a matter of course whenever the causal character of the observed relation is clear. In the experimental sciences or in the study of heredity (for which regression was originally designed) we can make reasonably sure that the observed data reflect the particular causal relation in which we are interested and no other. But in the case of economic data this is by no means self-evident. The object of econometrics is to obtain empirical evidence of the meaningful causal relations of economics; we select a particular relation, and look for data that may be expected to reflect its operation. But when such data are found it is by no means certain that they arise from the causal relation under review *alone*. The economic process is highly interdependent, and economic variables are often determined by the joint operation of several distinct relations. If this is the case the observed values arise from a system of simultaneous equations, and the assumptions of the regression model no longer apply. Among economic time series in particular interdependence is the rule, and straightforward regression can be used in certain special cases only.

The interdependent character of many economic processes was generally recognized by economists towards 1890, but its statistical implications were not fully realized until much later by HAAVELMO (1944). We shall respect this order and discuss the economic model first before we go on to the problem of estimation. Simultaneous equations after all present a problem of inference that is not particular to *statistical* inference; even if there were no need for disturbance terms because the data reflect fully deterministic relations among observed variables, the problem would remain.

An example: supply and demand

82   The classical example of simultaneous equations is the joint determination of price and quantity by supply and demand, and the classical analysis is that of MARSHALL (1890). We represent the familiar curves or schedules at once by linear functions and write

$$Q_D = \beta_{10} + \beta_{11}P \tag{6.1}$$

for the demand function. This describes the behaviour of buyers in determining the quantity they are willing to buy, Q_D, as a function of price P. Likewise

$$Q_S = \beta_{20} + \beta_{21}P \tag{6.2}$$

is the supply function. Economic theory adduces various reasons why we should expect $\beta_{11} < 0$, $\beta_{21} > 0$ to hold.

A complete model of the market should presumably include an analysis of the process whereby buyers and sellers arrive at the price that equates both quantities. Various imaginative descriptions have been put forward; among these the so-called cobweb theory stands out because of its precise formulation. This theory assumes in substance that either function operates alternatingly as if buyers and sellers announce in turn what prices they set or what quantities they are willing to trade. The result is an iterative process which under certain conditions converges to equilibrium values of P and Q which ensures that the market is cleared. In the present case we assume such convergence, and we also assume that it is rapid; we take our price and quantity variables to refer to a period that is long relatively to the duration of the adjustment process. This permits us to ignore the latter altogether and to adopt as an approximation that buyers and sellers settle instantaneously at the equilibrium values (P^0, Q^0). These values are then determined by the condition that they satisfy both (6.1) and (6.2), or

$$Q_D(P^0) = Q_S(P^0) = Q^0 \; ^\dagger \; . \tag{6.3}$$

Hence (P^0, Q^0) is the point of intersection of the demand and supply functions, and its co-ordinates follow from solving (6.1) and (6.2); we find

$$P^0 = \frac{\beta_{20} - \beta_{10}}{\beta_{11} - \beta_{21}} \; ; \qquad Q^0 = \frac{\beta_{11}\beta_{20} - \beta_{10}\beta_{21}}{\beta_{11} - \beta_{21}} \; ; \tag{6.4}$$

the awkward case $\beta_{11} = \beta_{21}$ is ruled out by the assumption that these coefficients have opposite signs. We see, then, that price and quantity are simultaneously determined by demand and supply, or–as Marshall puts it–that "we might as reasonably dispute whether it is the upper or the lower blade of a pair of scissors that cuts a piece of paper, as whether value is governed by utility or cost of production" ††.

We note two further points about this overfamiliar example. The first is that (6.4) quite properly expresses equilibrium price and quantity as constants. Constants they are when the demand and supply function are fixed as they are here; variations of the equilibrium values can only arise as the result of shifts in either or both functions, and such shifts must in turn be induced by

---

† The real interest of the cobweb theory is of course precisely that it describes the process which we here neglect; see EZEKIEL (1938). The cobweb model would therefore apply in the case under review only if we succeeded in breaking up the observations into much shorter periods. But the reader should note that in that case there would be no longer any question of simultaneous equations.

†† MARSHALL (1890), 8th edition, p. 348.

other variables that determine the level of the demand and supply schedules. If we wish to account for variations in (P^0, Q^0) we must introduce these specific determinants in our model, summarize their effect in random disturbances, or again do both by introducing a few major determinants while all others are relegated to the disturbance term. In either case we shall obtain a model which allows for variations of the observed equilibrium price and quantity data, denoted from now on as (P_i, Q_i) where $i = 1, 2, ..., n$ indicates individual observations.

The second point which should not be overlooked is that it is impossible to deduce any of the four coefficients of (6.1) and (6.2) from a knowledge of the equilibrium values given in (6.4) alone; various solutions are all equally compatible with the observed (P^0, Q^0).

83 Let us first suppose that the observed variations are wholly and exclusively due to demand shifts induced by income (Y) and supply shifts induced by rainfall (Z), and suppose moreover that both these variables have been observed. By the assumption of market equilibrium the (P_i, Q_i) must simultaneously satisfy two equations, viz.

$$\begin{aligned} \text{(demand)} \qquad Q_i &= \beta_{10} + \beta_{11} P_i + \beta_{12} Y_i \,, \\ \text{(supply)} \qquad Q_i &= \beta_{20} + \beta_{21} P_i + \beta_{22} Z_i \,. \end{aligned} \qquad (6.5)$$

Each of these equations represents a distinct economic construction, which here refers to the behaviour of buyers and sellers respectively. Such relations are called *structural relations* and the βs are *structural coefficients*. Solving (6.5) we find that the P_i and Q_i are causally determined by the Z_i and Y_i according to

$$P_i := \frac{1}{\beta_{11} - \beta_{21}} \{\beta_{20} - \beta_{10} + \beta_{22} Z_i - \beta_{12} Y_i\} \,,$$

$$Q_i := \frac{1}{\beta_{11} - \beta_{21}} \{\beta_{11}\beta_{20} - \beta_{21}\beta_{10} + \beta_{11}\beta_{22} Z_i - \beta_{21}\beta_{12} Y_i\} \,. \qquad (6.6)$$

This system is known as the *reduced form* of the structural relations (6.5).

For convenience we may of course take differences from the mean throughout, and employ lower-case letters as before. The structural relations now read as

$$\begin{aligned} \text{(demand)} \qquad q_i &= \beta_{11} p_i + \beta_{12} y_i \,, \\ \text{(supply)} \qquad q_i &= \beta_{21} p_i + \beta_{22} z_i \,, \end{aligned} \qquad (6.7)$$

and the reduced form is

$$p_i : = \pi_{11} z_i + \pi_{12} y_i$$
$$q_i : = \pi_{21} z_i + \pi_{22} y_i$$

(6.8)

with

$$\pi_{11} = \frac{\beta_{22}}{\beta_{11} - \beta_{21}}, \quad \pi_{12} = \frac{-\beta_{12}}{\beta_{11} - \beta_{21}},$$

$$\pi_{21} = \frac{\beta_{11} \beta_{22}}{\beta_{11} - \beta_{21}}, \quad \pi_{22} = \frac{-\beta_{21} \beta_{12}}{\beta_{11} - \beta_{21}}.$$

(6.9)

By assumption the observed values (p_i, q_i, z_i, y_i) satisfy both systems exactly, and provided that the data show sufficient variation there will be no difficulty in determining the direction coefficients of any of the four planes that are each defined in a three-dimensional space of its own by the equations of (6.7) and (6.8). We may therefore determine the structural coefficients directly from the former two equations. But it is also possible (although it would of course be unnecessarily laborious) to determine the reduced-form coefficients of (6.8) first and then to derive the structural coefficients by applying the inverse transformation of (6.9).

The latter possibility is a fortunate property of the particular structural model under review, and it can by no means be taken for granted. The point at issue is whether the transformation (6.9) has an inverse, or more precisely whether there is a one-to-one correspondence between the reduced-form coefficients π and any particular structural coefficient. If this is so the structural coefficient is said to be *identifiable*.

84   A simple example of a model that does not permit identification of the structural coefficients is obtained if we suppose that shifts of both the demand function and the supply function are caused by the *same* variables X. The structural relations now read

(demand) $q_i = \beta_{11} p_i + \beta_{12} x_i ,$

(supply) $q_i = \beta_{21} p_i + \beta_{22} x_i ,$

(6.10)

and the reduced form is

$$p_i : = \pi_{11} x_i ,$$
$$q_i : = \pi_{21} x_i ,$$

(6.11)

with

$$\pi_{11} = \frac{\beta_{22} - \beta_{12}}{\beta_{11} - \beta_{21}},$$

$$\pi_{21} = \frac{\beta_{11}\beta_{22} - \beta_{21}\beta_{12}}{\beta_{11} - \beta_{21}}. \qquad (6.12)$$

We wish to impress on the reader that in this case it is impossible ever to assess the value of any of the structural coefficients. This is not due to any particular coincidence but it holds true regardless of the values of these coefficients (provided they are finite and unknown). Nor is it due to any of the quirks of random variables, for there are no random variables in the model – as before the observations p_i, q_i and x_i satisfy (6.10) and (6.11) exactly by assumption.

Just as in the former example the two equations of (6.10) define two planes in three-dimensional space and the structural coefficients correspond to the direction coefficients of these planes; moreover the observations (p_i, q_i, x_i) once more lie exactly on these planes. But in the present instance the two equations of (6.10) each define a plane in the *same* three-dimensional space with co-ordinates in P, Q and X, and since the observations must satisfy both they must lie on the single line of intersection of these planes. Obviously there is an infinity of pairs of planes that would give rise to the same line of intersection, and we have no means of selecting the true demand and supply planes from among them from a knowledge of the line of intersection alone.

The reduced-form equations of (6.11) are one particular pair of planes from the bundle of planes satisfying the straight line determined by the observations; the first reduced form equation yields a plane perpendicular to the (p_i, x_i) plane, or parallel to the Q-axis, and the second is parallel to the P-axis. We may also determine a third plane parallel to the X-axis, defined by

$$q_i = \frac{\pi_{21}}{\pi_{11}} p_i,$$

$$\frac{\pi_{21}}{\pi_{11}} = \frac{\beta_{11}\beta_{22} - \beta_{21}\beta_{12}}{\beta_{22} - \beta_{12}}. \qquad (6.13)$$

Each of the three equations of (6.11) and (6.13) corresponds to a projection of the line of intersection defined by the observations, and if the reduced form (6.11) is singled out for special treatment this is because it shows how the whole system moves in accordance with the independent variation of X.

Now the coefficients of (6.11) (or of 6.13, for that matter) can easily be determined from the slopes of these projected lines, but this does not solve the problem of determining the structural coefficients; as inspection will show, the transformation (6.12) has no single-valued inverse.

85   In the third and last example of the demand and supply model we return to the first and add a new variable X to the determinants of the demand function but not to the supply function. The structural model reads

$$\text{(demand)} \qquad q_i = \beta_{11}p_i + \beta_{12}y_i + \beta_{13}x_i ,$$
$$\text{(supply)} \qquad q_i = \beta_{21}p_i + \beta_{22}z_i , \qquad (6.14)$$

and the reduced form is

$$p_i = \pi_{11}z_i + \pi_{12}y_i + \pi_{13}x_i ,$$
$$p_i = \pi_{21}z_i + \pi_{22}y_i + \pi_{23}x_i , \qquad (6.15)$$

with

$$\pi_{11} = \frac{\beta_{22}}{\beta_{11}-\beta_{21}} , \quad \pi_{12} = \frac{-\beta_{12}}{\beta_{11}-\beta_{21}} , \quad \pi_{13} = \frac{-\beta_{13}}{\beta_{11}-\beta_{21}} ,$$
$$\pi_{21} = \frac{\beta_{11}\beta_{22}}{\beta_{11}-\beta_{21}} , \quad \pi_{22} = \frac{-\beta_{21}\beta_{12}}{\beta_{11}-\beta_{21}} , \quad \pi_{23} = \frac{-\beta_{21}\beta_{13}}{\beta_{11}-\beta_{21}} . \qquad (6.16)$$

Once more we may determine the structural coefficients directly or deduce them from the reduced-form coefficients; they are identified, as in section 83. The difference, however, is that in the present case the reduced-form coefficients are constrained since by (6.16)

$$\frac{\pi_{22}}{\pi_{12}} = \frac{\pi_{23}}{\pi_{13}} = \beta_{21}$$

so that we need not know all the π in order to determine β_{21}; it may be deduced from either π_{22} and π_{12} or from π_{23} and π_{13}. Since by assumption the observations satisfy the model exactly there can of course be no question as to whether the two procedures will give the same result. All structural coefficients can be determined, or are identified, and β_{21} is said to be *over-identified* because its value can be ascertained independently from the π by two alternative routes.

86   Before we take leave of these examples two remarks are in order. The demand and supply model is simple, and in the examples given we could either determine all structural coefficients or none. As the example of overidentification shows, however, the classification by the identification properties applies to single structural coefficients in a given model, and not to the set of all coefficients as a whole. It is quite possible to devise a more complex model in which the elasticity of demand is overidentified while the elasticity of supply cannot be determined at all.

The second point is much more important. It is that the question of identification refers to a property of the structural model in which the coefficients concerned occurs. The reduced form is merely a particular representation of this model, and if we discuss identification from the point of view of deriving a particular structural coefficient from the reduced form coefficients this is a matter of convenience. Lack of identification is indicated by the fact that a structural coefficient cannot be deduced from the reduced form, but it has the much wider implication that the structural coefficient can in no way be inferred from the observed data. Again there are infinitely many structural coefficients that are observationally equivalent since they can all give rise to the observed values.

The construction of a simultaneous equations model

87 Marshall's model of demand and supply generating market data is about the simplest example of simultaneous equations in economics, and in discussing the simultaneous equations difficulty we usually think of much larger models that run to many more equations. Before considering the identification problem in its general form we shall try to indicate how these larger models arise. We are still concerned with deterministic models, i.e. models without disturbance terms and without statistical estimation problems, and we retain linearity of the equations throughout.

The starting point of an econometric investigation is a particular economic relationship supposedly reflected by a particular set of observed data. The starting point of an economic analysis is a particular phenomenon. In either case we wish to construct a model that "explains" or describes the determination of particular variables within a given framework. In the case of econometrics this framework is set by the conditions of the observed sample, and these correspond to the *ceteris paribus* conditions that can be freely selected in the economic model. Either model consists of a series of *structural relations*.

But for the inevitable simplifications and aggregation that occurs in all model building a structural relation stands for a separate and distinct part of the economic process. Structural relations are *autonomous* in the sense that if any one of them is subject to change this need not affect the operation of the others. By a classification due to Tinbergen we may distinguish three categories of structural relations. The first consists of *behaviour equations* which describe the economic behaviour of particular economic agents in performing a given function. Demand and supply functions are an obvious example, and the consumption function is another. Distinct behaviour relations do not necessarily refer to different groups of individuals; a manufacturer's professional behaviour is subsumed in a supply function, but in his private capacity he participates in the consumption function. Again the same industry may behave differently on the home market than abroad so that there are distinct supply functions for exports and for home supplies. A second group of structural relations describes *technical relations* that govern the production process, and the third consists of *institutional relations* that describe the operation of fiscal regulations and similar arrangements.

A word is in order about the *definitional relations* that occur in almost any of the larger economic models. These relations are variously introduced as *definitions, identities* or *equilibrium conditions*. Thus "current surplus on balance of trade equals exports minus imports" is a definition, "quantity demanded equals quantity supplied" is an equilibrium condition, and "national income equals consumption plus investment" or "savings equals investment" are variously put in any of the three categories. For present purposes we lump all such equations together as definitional relations, regardless of the subtler shades of interpretation. They are distinct from the three classes of structural relations named above in that they are expressions of the model-builder's conventions and are independent of whatever goes on in the real world. Thus the coefficients of definitional relations are known in advance (they are usually plus or minus one) and there is no point in determining them empirically, nor can these coefficients conceivably ever change in the same way as behaviour relations may vary with fashion, or technical relations may change under the effect of new inventions. We shall moreover never have reasons to attach a disturbance term to a definitional relation. By these properties definition equations merely reflect conventional designations of certain economic magnitudes; they may therefore be eliminated from the model at will.

88   In constructing a model, then, we start off from a particular variable and begin listing the structural equations that we believe to be operative in its determination. The first equation expresses the variable under review as dependent upon several others, and each of these determinants may possibly in turn be further described by some other structural relation. At any given stage in the process we therefore have a number of equations, a number of dependent variables that occur on the left-hand sides and a (usually somewhat larger) number of variables that occur exclusively on the right-hand sides. The question is whether we shall continue to add further relations showing what factors influence the latter variables or not.

This decision, and hence the *extent* of the model, depends on several considerations. The first is that we must respect the simultaneous equations character of the economic process under review. If any of the variables that have been introduced as independent variable on the right-hand side of a structural relation is itself in turn influenced by a dependent variable, this further relation must be shown, or we would falsely represent the system as it works. This requirement sets a lower limit to the extent of the model: we cannot stop the process of adding new equations that in turn explain the determinants that already occur, unless these determinants are independent of all the dependent variables present, and hence independent of the outcome of the economic process under consideration. Variables that meet the latter condition are called *predetermined* variables, as opposed to the *jointly dependent* variables that are determined by the process we study.

The predetermined variables correspond to the *data* of the familiar partial economic analysis, and we may again distinguish several classes. The simplest example of a predetermined variable is a *noneconomic variable* or *datum* such as the rainfall variable in the example of section 83. Non-economic data are clearly outside our domain and it would be idle to try to incorporate their determination in our model. Among the predetermined variables of economic character we distinguish between *exogenous variables*, *lagged values of the endogenous variables* and *instruments*. Exogenous economic variables bring out that the distinction between predetermined and jointly dependent variables is related to the model of a particular economic process; they are not affected by the outcome of the process under review (or they would not be predetermined) but depend in turn upon some other economic process. If we consider the national economy of a particular country, the price level of competing products on its export markets is an obvious example of such an exogenous economic variable. The predetermined character of lagged values of the endogenous variables, whose current values constitute the jointly dependent variables, is self-evident; since they precede the operation of the economic process they cannot be affected by its outcome. By *instruments* we finally denote those variables that can be set at will by some policy-making agency in order to achieve given ends. This agency is often personified by a policy-maker who usually closely resembles the model-builder. The policy-maker uses his knowledge of the economic process, that is: of the model, in wielding his instruments; but it is generally assumed that he is not instantaneously affected by the outcome of the economic process since he himself has decided what this outcome should be. Hence the instruments are predetermined variables.

The point of this classification of the predetermined variables is that only in the case of noneconomic data we are barred from extending the model and thus incorporating the predetermined variables in it. Lagged endogenous variables as well as exogenous economic variables are capable of further economic explanation, and both may therefore be turned into endogenous variables by adding further structural relations; some supreme model-builder may conceivably sum up the policy-maker's actions in a behaviour relation, and thus render the instruments endogenous too. If this process were to continue indefinitely, in the end all economic variables would be endogenous variables, linked by a vast system of simultaneous equations to their ultimate noneconomic determinants, the classical *data* like the available productive resources, the state of technology, the preference patterns of the consumers and the behaviour of the economic agents. This is precisely what is intended in the grand design of the general equilibrium models of economists like Walras and Pareto, and it indicates the upper limit to the size of economic models.

These admirable universal models have their place in economic theory, but they do not serve the cause of empirical research. For the latter purpose we wish to restrict the model to an adequate description of the particular variables or phenomena that have attracted our attention. Upon this narrow view there is no point in pursuing the origins of predetermined variables since their determination is immaterial to the problem under review. When predetermined variables thus need no further explanation, the lower limit to the model's size is set by the earlier requirement that we account for all relations that simultaneously enter in a given economic process. As we have already indicated the endogenous quality of variables is contagious, and in constructing a model we add relations and variables like beads on a chain. At each stage in this process we must reflect whether any of the variables in the model is dependent on any endogenous variables already present, and if this is so this dependence must be shown and the variable concerned joins the endogenous variables as a new structural relation is added. The process starts from one endogenous variable which is the dependent variable in the first structural relation which we write down, and it stops when there are no loose ends apart from the predetermined variables. It follows from this prescription that there are exactly as many equations as there are endogenous variables when the model is completed.

The general simultaneous equations model

89   The general model consists of, say, G structural relations which are represented by G linear equations. As we have just shown there occur exactly G endogenous variables in the system, as well as any number K of predetermined variables. We now write all equations in implicit form, and arrange the variables so that the endogenous variables precede the predetermined variables. The system (6.7), for example, would read as

$$
\begin{aligned}
\text{(demand)} \quad & q_i - \beta_{11} p_i - \beta_{12} y_i = 0 \\
\text{(supply)} \quad & q_i - \beta_{21} p_i - \beta_{22} z_i = 0.
\end{aligned}
\tag{6.17}
$$

We now arrange the G endogenous or jointly dependent variables in a column vector y, the K predetermined variables in a column vector x, and the coefficients of the structural equations in a $(G \times G)$ matrix B and a $(G \times K)$ matrix Γ. The structural model then reads

$$
By + \Gamma x = 0.
\tag{6.18}
$$

This system of G simultaneous equations may of course be solved for any G variables we choose. If we select the G jointly dependent variables y we obtain the *reduced form*

$$
y = -B^{-1}\Gamma x
\tag{6.19}
$$

provided of course that B is nonsingular. The reduced form is often written as

$$
y = \Pi x, \qquad \Pi = -B^{-1}\Gamma,
\tag{6.20}
$$

and we shall follow this usage.

The condition that the matrix B is nonsingular is always ensured since it is a basic requirement of economic theory. For if B were singular, the endogenous variables would be indeterminate, and this is generally regarded as an unacceptable conclusion. In the construction of economic theory great care has therefore been taken to rule out this possibility. In the case of supply and demand, for example, B is nonsingular because β_{11} of (6.1) and

β_{21} of (6.2) are taken to have opposite sign; in the last resort it is in order to ensure determinacy that so much trouble has been taken over the law of demand (whereby $\beta_{11} < 0$) and the law of supply ($\beta_{21} > 0$). Another example is the case of constant returns to scale. If the production function is linearly homogeneous, profit maximization is insufficient to fix the level of output of a firm operating under conditions of perfect competition all round. Output would be indeterminate but for an additional assumption, so the additional assumption is made[†].

We note three points in connection with this matrix representation. The first is that the linear structural equations of (6.18) as a rule give a much simplified representation of the economic relations. Even at the present stage where we discuss a fully deterministic model without the benefit of disturbances that take care of all minor determinants, we should think of the structural equations as simple and bare affairs. Only a small number of all the variables of the model will occur in any one equation, and the matrices B and Γ have a considerable number of zero coefficients. This will turn out to have far-reaching implications.

The second point is that in each structural equation one endogenous variable can, by convention, be regarded as the dependent variable. This dependent or "left-hand" variable of the original structural equation will have a coefficient $+1$ in the implicit representation that forms a row of (6.18). There will therefore occur one unit coefficient in each row of B. This is known as the *normalisation rule*. The reader may note that the distribution of these G unit coefficients, one for each row, over the *columns* of B is immaterial and a matter of arbitrary convention.

The third point is that we have suggested, by the example of (6.17), that the variables which occur in y and x are defined as deviations from the mean. In the present discussion this usage was introduced (in section 83) merely for convenience of notation, and once we are using matrices we may abandon it. If we would wish to retain the constant terms of the structural equations (which are, however, seldom of interest), x and y can be taken to refer to the original variables, not deviations from mean, while a *dummy variable* that is identically equal to unity is included among the predetermined variables. It is easily seen that this dummy variable will turn up on the right-hand side of (6.20) as an element of x, and that the reduced form equations will also have constant terms (i.e. a column of Π corresponding to the coefficients of the dummy variable in x) which are otherwise absent.

[†] We return to this subject in ch. 10, section 197.

90   As before, the observed values of x and y by assumption satisfy the structural model (6.18) exactly, and thereby also the reduced form (6.20). Provided there is sufficient independent variation of the elements of x from one observation to another there will therefore be no difficulty in determining the $(G \times K)$ coefficients of Π. The identification problem turns on the question whether or not the coefficients of a particular structural relation – i.e. a row of (6.18) – can be unambiguously inferred from the reduced form coefficients. We shall take considerable trouble over this question, and one may well ask whether it is worth it. After all the reduced form coefficients, which can be known, tell us all we need to know about the economic process under review since they determine the outcome for any given values of the predetermined variables. Surely this is enough for purposes of prediction and policy?

The reasons why it is not, and why we must try to establish the structural coefficients, have been given by MARSCHAK (1953). The fundamental argument is that by its very definition each structural equation describes a specific, distinct, and thereby autonomous link in the economic process. We have already indicated – in section 87 – that this autonomy means that a change in one structural relation does not affect the operation of the others. Thus a change of income tax rates will affect the institutional relation which determines income after tax, but it will not interfere with the marginal propensity to consume; if we know what happens to the tax equation, we may adjust the corresponding row of coefficients of the structural model accordingly while leaving all other coefficients unchanged. But for a full knowledge of all structural coefficients, however, we cannot indicate in what way a tax change will affect the reduced form. Hence reduced-form coefficients can be safely used for prediction only if we are certain that there are no changes in structure, for we have no means of taking such changes into account.

The same autonomous character of structural relations also means that the structural coefficients are more stable, more like physical constants, than are the reduced form composites. Structural coefficients are therefore more easily judged by intuition, and their changes better capable of reasonable discussion and interpretation than is the case with reduced form coefficients. And structural coefficients are certainly more easily compared with the accumulated empirical evidence which invariably refers to economic structure and not to the reduced form.

The identification of a structural equation

91   Now for the algebra. We consider one particular structural equation, which has been moved to occupy the first position in the system (6.18), and wish to know whether the structural coefficients of this equation can be determined from the reduced-form coefficient matrix Π[†]. When we write β_1' and γ_1' respectively for the top row vectors of B and Γ the first structural equation reads

$$\beta_1' y + \gamma_1' x = 0$$

or

$$\beta_1' y = -\gamma_1' x, \tag{6.21}$$

and by assumption all n observed vectors x_i, y_i satisfy these equations exactly. By (6.19), however, they must also satisfy

$$y = \Pi x$$

or again

$$\beta_1' y = \beta_1' \Pi x. \tag{6.22}$$

Since (6.21) and (6.22) hold simultaneously for all observed vectors it follows that ˘

$$-\gamma_1' x_i = \beta_1' \Pi x_i$$

for any x_i, $i = 1, 2, \ldots, n$, whatever. This can only be so if the coefficients on both sides are identical, or, upon returning to column vectors, if

$$-\gamma_1 = \Pi' \beta_1. \tag{6.23}$$

This is a system of K simultaneous linear equations and the question is whether or not it can be solved for the elements of γ_1 and β_1. These elements constitute $(K + G - 1)$ unknowns, viz. K structural coefficients of γ_1, and G coefficients of β_1 of which one is a unitary coefficient fixed by the normalisation rule of section 89. In general it is of course impossible to determine $(K + G - 1)$ unknowns from K equations but for the exceptional case that $G = 1$. In the latter case the model consists of a single structural equation which coincides with the reduced form since there is only one endogenous

---

[†] In what follows we largely repeat the argument of KOOPMANS and HOOD (1953). The discussion is not exhaustive; we deal for instance with the identification of all coefficients in a given structural equation, but not with the identification of a single coefficient.

variable and all variables on the right-hand side are predetermined; the identification problem does not arise. But for this exceptional case, however, we must look for additional restrictions or additional knowledge of the structural coefficients in order to increase the number of equations or to reduce the number of unknowns, if there is to be any hope of a determinate solution.

In the standard case (the only case which we discuss here) we make use of a single type of additional information only, viz. of the *a priori* specification of zero structural coefficients[†]. The vectors x and y contain all variables of the entire structural model, but it stands to reason that they do not all occur in the single equation under review. The absent variables have zero coefficients, and since their absence is laid down in the theoretical specification of the model the position of these zero elements of β_1 and γ_1 is known. We may therefore rearrange the jointly dependent as well as the predetermined variables so that the nonzero coefficients precede the zero elements. Let the relation under review contain G^Δ of the jointly dependent variables, $G^{\Delta\Delta} = G - G^\Delta$ being absent; and let it contain K^* predetermined variables, $K^{**} = K - K^*$ being absent. Upon rearrangement the coefficient vectors take the following form:

$$\beta_1' = [\underbrace{\beta_{11} \; \beta_{12} \cdots \beta_{1G^\Delta}}_{\substack{G^\Delta \text{ nonzero} \\ \text{coefficients}}} \; \underbrace{0 \; 0 \ldots 0}_{G^{\Delta\Delta} \text{ zeros}}],$$

$$\gamma_1' = [\underbrace{\gamma_{11} \; \gamma_{12} \cdots \gamma_{1K^*}}_{\substack{K^* \text{ nonzero} \\ \text{coefficients}}} \; \underbrace{0 \; 0 \ldots 0}_{K^{**} \text{ zeros}}].$$

We now partition these vectors accordingly and write in an obvious notation

$$\beta_1 = \begin{bmatrix} \beta_{1\Delta} \\ 0_{\Delta\Delta} \end{bmatrix}, \qquad \gamma_1 = \begin{bmatrix} \gamma_{1*} \\ 0_{**} \end{bmatrix}.$$

The $(G \times K)$ matrix $\boldsymbol{\Pi}$ is partitioned correspondingly: it need not contain any zeros, but its rows correspond to jointly dependent variables, and its columns to predetermined variables, so that we write

---

[†] For a review of other identifying conditions see FISHER (1966).

$$\Pi = \left.\left[\begin{array}{c:c} \Pi_{\Delta*} & \Pi_{\Delta**} \\ \hdashline \Pi_{\Delta\Delta*} & \Pi_{\Delta\Delta**} \end{array}\right]\begin{array}{l} \} \ G^{\Delta} \\ \\ \} \ G^{\Delta\Delta} \end{array}\right.$$

$$\underbrace{\phantom{\Pi_{\Delta*}}}_{K^*} \quad \underbrace{\phantom{\Pi_{\Delta**}}}_{K^{**}}$$

Substituting the partitioned vectors and matrix into (6.23) we obtain

$$\left[\begin{array}{c} -\gamma_{1*} \\ \hline 0_{**} \end{array}\right] = \left[\begin{array}{c:c} \Pi'_{\Delta*} & \Pi'_{\Delta\Delta*} \\ \hdashline \Pi'_{\Delta**} & \Pi'_{\Delta\Delta**} \end{array}\right]\left[\begin{array}{c} \beta_{1\Delta} \\ \hline 0_{\Delta\Delta} \end{array}\right]$$

Inspection of this expression shows that the system of K simultaneous equations (6.23) falls apart into two separate subsets, viz. a system of K^* equations

$$-\gamma_{1*} = \Pi'_{\Delta*}\beta_{1\Delta}, \tag{6.24}$$

and a system of K^{**} equations

$$0_{**} = \Pi'_{\Delta**}\beta_{1\Delta}. \tag{6.25}$$

The identification problem now turns on the possibility of solving (6.25) for $\beta_{1\Delta}$. If this can be done the result may be substituted into (6.24) to yield γ_{1*}, and all nonzero coefficients of the first structural equation can be determined from the reduced-form coefficients in $\Pi_{\Delta**}$ and $\Pi_{\Delta*}$. In solving (6.25) we need moreover determine the G^{Δ} elements of $\beta_{1\Delta}$ up to a multiplicative constant only, since one of its elements is conventionally equated to unity by virtue of the normalisation rule of section 89.

It is clear that we shall have to examine the matrix $\Pi_{\Delta**}$ in order to decide whether (6.25) can be solved. In practice we take the structural matrices B and Γ and determine Π according to (6.20), writing each of its elements in full as a function of the nonzero elements of B and Γ. The next step is to partition Π and to consider $\Pi_{\Delta**}$. We recall that the discussion of the present section refers to a single structural equation, which has been moved for convenience to the top position of the structural system (6.18). A full investigation of a structural model therefore requires that the rearrangement of variables by zero and nonzero coefficients and the subsequent partitioning of x, y, and Π is carried out anew for each structural equation in turn.

92   Equation (6.25) represents a system of K^{**} linear homogeneous equations. Its solution for $\beta_{1\Delta}$ depends on the *rank* of the $(G^{\Delta} \times K^{**})$ matrix $\Pi_{\Delta**}$.

(1) *The rank of* $\Pi_{\varDelta**}$, $\rho(\Pi_{\varDelta**})$, *cannot exceed* $(G^{\varDelta} - 1)$. Since $\Pi_{\varDelta**}$ has $G^{\varDelta}$ rows its rank cannot exceed $G^{\varDelta}$. But if its rank equals $G^{\varDelta}$, the solution of (6.25) is that $\beta_{1\varDelta}$ is a null vector and this contradicts the requirement that each structural equation must contain at least one of the jointly dependent variables with a nonzero coefficient. Since this requirement is safeguarded by the very construction of the structural model – see section 88 – the case $\rho(\Pi_{\varDelta**}) = G^{\varDelta}$ cannot arise.

If the number of columns of $\Pi_{\varDelta**}$ is small enough, i.e. $K^{**} \leqslant G^{\varDelta} - 1$, this condition is immediately apparent; but we may equally well have $K^{**} > G^{\varDelta}$. In this case the required reduction of $\rho(\Pi_{\varDelta**})$ is brought about by linear dependence of its rows or columns.

(2) *If* $\rho(\Pi_{\varDelta**}) < G^{\varDelta} - 1$ *the structural coefficients cannot be determined.* In this case (6.25) provides no determinate solution for $\beta_{1\varDelta}$ and hence the structural coefficients cannot be established; there is lack of identification or *underidentification.*

This case obviously arises when $K^{**} < G^{\varDelta} - 1$, but it may also happen that the order of the matrix is sufficiently large but that linear dependence of rows or columns reduces its rank below $G^{\varDelta} - 1$.

(3) *If* $\rho(\Pi_{\varDelta**}) = G^{\varDelta} - 1$ *the structural coefficients can be determined.* In this case (6.25) determines the $G^{\varDelta}$ elements of $\beta_{1\varDelta}$ up to a constant and the normalization rule renders the solution unique. The result can then be substituted in (6.24) and yields γ_{1*}.

Once more we distinguish two cases according to the order of $\Pi_{\varDelta**}$. If its rank is set by the number of columns, i.e. if $K^{**} = G^{\varDelta} - 1$ and there is no linear dependence of rows or columns that further reduces its rank, there is *just-identification.* If on the other hand $K^{**} > G^{\varDelta} - 1$, so that the requisite rank must be due to interdependence of rows or columns, there is *overidenti-fication.*

93 The number of rows of $\Pi_{\varDelta**}$ is always equal to $G^{\varDelta}$, the number of jointly dependent variables that have nonzero coefficients in the structural equation under review. The order of $\Pi_{\varDelta**}$ therefore varies exclusively with the number of columns K^{**}, i.e. the number of predetermined variables excluded from this structural equation. We need only count variables to find out whether the *order condition* for identification $K^{**} \geqslant G^{\varDelta} - 1$ is met, and in practice this will rapidly reveal many cases of underidentification. But while this order condition is necessary for identification it is not sufficient, and when it is met we must proceed to examine rank.

Table 11 summarizes the combinations of the order and the rank criteria.

Four out of the nine cases cannot possibly arise. Among the five admissible cases that remain linear dependence of rows or columns of $\Pi_{\Delta**}$ is prevalent: it is certain in three cases, possible in one case and absent in the single case of just-identification alone.

TABLE 11

Rank and order conditions for the identification of a structural equation.

order: \ rank:	$\rho(\Pi_{\Delta**}) < G^{\Delta} - 1$	$\rho(\Pi_{\Delta**}) = G^{\Delta} - 1$	$\rho(\Pi_{\Delta**}) > G^{\Delta} - 1$
$K^{**} < G^{\Delta} - 1$	*underidentification,* regardless of further reduction of rank below K^{**} by interdependence of rows or columns	impossible since rank cannot exceed number of columns	impossible since rank cannot exceed number of columns
$K^{**} = G^{\Delta} - 1$	rank is reduced by interdependence of rows or columns: *underidentification*	*just-identification*	impossible since rank cannot exceed number of columns
$K^{**} > G^{\Delta} - 1$	rank is reduced by interdependence of rows or columns: *underidentification*	rank is reduced by interdependence of rows or columns: *overidentification*	impossible since interdependence of rows or columns will reduce rank to $G^{\Delta} - 1$ at most (see section 93)

It may not be immediately clear how this linear dependence comes about and how its presence can be established. So far we have throughout assumed that the observed vectors x_i, y_i exactly satisfy the structural model. They thereby also satisfy the reduced form and provided there is sufficient obser-vational variation the elements of Π can be determined exactly. In this ideal case linear dependence of rows or columns of $\Pi_{\Delta**}$ would show up in the numerical values of its elements and $\rho(\Pi_{\Delta**})$ could be ascertained directly by numerical inspection. But as the assumed conditions are of course patently unrealistic this is of little avail.

Now identification (like any other property of the model) is determined by the specification of the structural model, and it must therefore be possible to establish it without having recourse to the numerical values of the coeffi-cients. This is indeed the case. We write down the structural model in the form (6.18) and obtain the matrices B and Γ in terms of zero coefficients and unknown nonzero coefficients β_{ij} and γ_{nk}. We then determine Π according to (6.20). When this is done each element of Π, and hence of $\Pi_{\Delta**}$, is given in terms of the unknown but distinct nonzero structural coefficients of B and Γ. And this permits us to detect linear dependence and to evaluate the rank of this matrix[†]. Identification depends on the theoretical specification of zero structural coefficients; it is independent of the numerical values of the non-zero coefficients.

94 In conclusion we return to a few points from the earlier discussion. The first is that underidentification is not just a technical deficiency which prevents the calculation of structural coefficients from the reduced form, but that it is a fundamental obstacle to the evaluation of the structural coefficients by any technique whatsoever. There is no remedy for it but to go beyond the limits of the given model and to use additional information or to impose additional restrictions in order to obtain a determinate solution from the available observations.

Underidentification is not only very troublesome but it is also likely to arise quite frequently, especially among the larger models. By the order condition the identification of a structural equation requires that sufficient predetermined variables are excluded from it relatively to the number of included jointly dependent variables; in short, identification requires many zeros. If this condition is met it is because in empirical models the structural equations traditionally contain but a few variables – rarely more than three or four. But as we have pointed out before – in section 80 – this tradition reflects the dread of multicollinearity rather than a strong conviction as to the bare simplicity of economic relations. It has indeed been argued by LIU (1960) that a proper specification of macro-economic relations in the light of economic theory would lead to the opposite result, each variable being related to almost all others. If this is so, underidentification is the rule rather than the exception, at least in aggregate time-series models, and unless identification can be secured by the use of extraneous information we should perhaps abandon all attempts to advance our empirical knowledge of the economic system by means of aggregate time-series data. Other observational data can be free of this defect. By the argument of section 82 the simultaneous character of an economic process depends in the last resort on the aggregate character of the observed data and on the length of the period to which they refer. A continued subdivision of this period of observation would in principle lead ultimately to the dependent variables being deter-

---

[†] The identification criteria can also be reformulated once and for all in terms of the structural coefficient matrices B and Γ. See JOHNSTON (1963), p. 251.

mined exclusively by lagged endogenous and thereby predetermined variables, so that the identification problem would vanish along with the simultaneous character of the model.

The statistical model

95   We now turn to the statistical problem of estimating the coefficients of one of a set of simultaneous structural equations. We shall adhere to the view expressed in section 90 that there is no point in evaluating the reduced-form coefficients for their own sake; we wish to establish the structural coefficients. Upon this choice all cases of underidentification can be abandoned, and only two out of the nine cases of table 11 remain of interest. These are the cases of just-identification and that of overidentification.

We start with a statistical reformulation of the simultaneous equations model which prepares the way for a discussion of estimation. To begin with we abandon the pretence that the structural equations hold exactly, and add random disturbances which have the same meaning as in ch. 5 (see sections 64 and 65). A disturbance term is in order in all equations that describe causal economic relations – behaviour relations, technical relations and institutional relations – but not in the definitional relations that are supposed to hold identically. As we have already indicated in section 87 the coefficients of the latter equations are set in advance and these identities can therefore be eliminated from the model without loss of generality of the estimation problem. After this has been done there remain G structural equations all of which have a disturbance term; we introduce random disturbances

$$\underline{U}_{ji}, \quad j = 1, 2, ..., G, \ i = 1, 2, ..., n \,,$$

which are attached to the jth structural equation in the ith observed set of values x_i, y_i. The structural model earlier given in (6.18) then reads

$$By + \Gamma x = \underline{u} \,, \tag{6.26}$$

where $\underline{u}$ is a vector of G random variables $\underline{U}_j$, or, as the case may be, of $\underline{u}_j$ whenever we express the model entirely in deviations from the mean.

As before we may solve (6.26) for any G variables. Once more selecting the jointly dependent variables y we obtain the reduced form

$$\underline{y} = -B^{-1}\Gamma x + B^{-1}\underline{u}$$

or

$$\underline{y} = \Pi x + \underline{v} \tag{6.27}$$

with

$$\boldsymbol{\Pi} = -\boldsymbol{B}^{-1}\boldsymbol{\Gamma}, \quad \underline{v} = \boldsymbol{B}^{-1}\underline{u}. \tag{6.28}$$

It is always assumed that $\boldsymbol{B}$ is nonsingular. The interest of this particular solution is again that it shows by what process the observed values of the jointly dependent variables are causally determined, i.e.

$$\underline{y}_i := \boldsymbol{\Pi}\boldsymbol{x}_i + \underline{v}_i \quad \text{for} \quad i = 1, 2, \dots, n. \tag{6.29}$$

96   The introduction of random disturbances does not affect the argument that has been employed in the discussion of identification. The first line of the structural model (6.26) now reads, for any given sample values $\boldsymbol{u}_i$, $i = 1, 2, \dots, n$ of $\boldsymbol{u}$, as

$$\boldsymbol{\beta}_1' \boldsymbol{y}_i + \boldsymbol{\gamma}_1' \boldsymbol{x}_i = U_{1i},$$

or, as in (6.21),

$$\boldsymbol{\beta}_1' \boldsymbol{y}_i = -\boldsymbol{\gamma}_1' \boldsymbol{x}_i + U_{1i}. \tag{6.30}$$

Again, all vectors $\boldsymbol{x}_i$, $\boldsymbol{y}_i$ satisfy the reduced form (6.27)

$$\boldsymbol{y}_i = \boldsymbol{\Pi}\boldsymbol{x}_i + \boldsymbol{v}_i$$

so that

$$\boldsymbol{\beta}_1' \boldsymbol{y}_i = \boldsymbol{\beta}_1' \boldsymbol{\Pi}\boldsymbol{x}_i + \boldsymbol{\beta}_1' \boldsymbol{v}_i. \tag{6.31}$$

By (6.28), however, we have

$$\boldsymbol{v}_i = \boldsymbol{B}^{-1}\boldsymbol{u}_i, \quad \boldsymbol{\beta}_1' \boldsymbol{v}_i = \boldsymbol{\beta}_1' \boldsymbol{B}^{-1}\boldsymbol{u}_i = U_{1i},$$

so that (6.31) reduces to

$$\boldsymbol{\beta}_1' \boldsymbol{y}_i = \boldsymbol{\beta}_1' \boldsymbol{\Pi}\boldsymbol{x}_i + U_{1i}.$$

If we now compare the latter expression with (6.30) the requirement that they both hold simultaneously for all $\boldsymbol{x}_i$ and all values of U_{1i} once more implies that

$$-\boldsymbol{\gamma}_1 = \boldsymbol{\Pi}'\boldsymbol{\beta}_1,$$

and this is the same condition (6.23) that was at the basis of our discussion of the identification problem. Hence the results of that analysis continue to apply after the introduction of random disturbances in the structural model. As a matter of fact additional identifying conditions can be deduced from an analysis of the second moments of these random variables u and their transformation v; since by (6.28)

$$v = B^{-1}u,$$

a careful comparison of the assumed properties of u and the corresponding behaviour of v may throw some light on B itself. But we shall not follow up this train of thought [†].

97   We now attribute much the same basic properties to the random disturbances as in ch. 5. Leaving aside the particular variants that have been discussed there we assume specifically that the U_{ji} have three simple characteristics, viz.

assumption 2 of section 67, (5.13): $E(U_{ji}) = 0$ for all j and i;

assumption 3 of section 68, (5.14): $\mathrm{var}(U_{ji}) = \sigma_j^2$ for all i;

assumption 4 of section 69, (5.19): $\mathrm{covar}(U_{ji}, U_{jk}) = 0$ for all j and all $i \neq k$.

Thus the disturbances of each of the G structural equations share many properties of the disturbances of the single regression equation of ch. 5, except for the first assumption of that chapter, (5.12) of section 66. This is the basic assumption to the effect that the disturbance term is independent of all but one of the variables (and that one the dependent variable) that occur in the equation concerned. We cannot possibly retain this assumption in the simultaneous equations case, for each structural equation is bound to contain more than one of the jointly dependent variables with nonzero coefficients[††], and any jointly dependent variable is by (6.29) and (6.28) related to all the G disturbances that enter into the model.

It is dependence of each of the jointly dependent Y_{ki} upon any disturbance U_{ji} which is the fundamental objection to the use of least-squares estimation of the structural coefficients in a simultaneous equations model. As inspection of the argument of section 73 will show the least-squares estimates are neither unbiased nor consistent when the independence assumption does not hold, and in general there is no point in establishing estimates that are

---

[†] See FISHER (1966).

[††] By the construction of a simultaneous equations model–see section 88–there is no point in adding a structural equation unless it contains at least two jointly dependent variables. If the first equation contains but a single (jointly) dependent variable, and no further interrelations need be taken into account, the whole model consists of that single equation and we have the single regression equation model of ch. 5.

lacking in these attractive properties. But this general argument does not constitute an absolute prescription against the direct least-squares estimation of structural equations. In the simpler models, like the case of demand and supply, the extent of the asymptotic bias of direct least-squares estimates can be indicated and assessed, and in certain particular cases there may be valid reasons to regard it as a negligible effect. We shall come across such cases in ch. 9.

98   While the random disturbances cannot be assumed to be independent of the jointly dependent variables y, the independence condition can apply to the predetermined variables x. By their very definition the values taken by these variables are independent of the outcome of the economic process under review and hence of the disturbances that enter into it. We may therefore write

$$\text{covar}(\underline{X}_{li}, \underline{U}_{ji}) = 0 \quad \text{for } i = 1, 2, ..., n \tag{6.32}$$
$$l = 1, 2, ..., K$$
$$j = 1, 2, ..., G \ .$$

Let us now consider the G reduced-form equations of (6.29). By (6.28) the disturbances $\underline{V}_{ji}$ of these equations are linear combinations of the $\underline{U}_{ji}$ (always provided B is nonsingular), and this implies that they satisfy the same three properties that were ascribed to the latter above; in other words the $\underline{V}_{ji}$ have zero expectation, constant variance for each j, and they are independent of one another for different observations i. Moreover the $\underline{V}_{ij}$ are by (6.32) independent of all the predetermined variables in x_i.

As a result of these properties each of the reduced-form equations exactly meets the requirements of the single equation regression model of ch. 5, and least-squares estimates of the reduced-form coefficients are both unbiased and consistent. It would thus seem that there is no estimation problem at all: estimation makes sense only if the structural coefficients can be established at all, viz. in the cases of just-identification and overidentification, and in those cases the structural coefficients can be derived from the reduced-form coefficients which themselves can be estimated by simple least-squares methods. But this conclusion is too simple: it overlooks the possibility that the structural specification of the model implies certain restrictions of the reduced-form coefficients.

We have earlier discussed – in section 93 – how linear dependence of rows or columns of the submatrix Π_{A**} may arise and how its presence can be established. The same argument applies to the general case of interdependence of elements of the whole reduced-form matrix. Such interrelations follow from the theoretical specification of B and Γ and can be found by inspection of $\Pi = -B^{-1}\Gamma$. Again, the expected values and probability limits of the least-squares estimates of Π correspond to the true parameters, and these will exactly satisfy the implied side relations or the model would not hold. But in contrast to the nonstochastic case this does *not* in general apply to the least-squares estimates: there is no reason why these sample values should meet the same restrictions as their expectations and probability limits do. Hence least-squares estimation of the reduced form must be abandoned whenever restrictions occur because its results are likely to contradict the very model on which the empirical analysis is based.

In discussing estimation we must therefore distinguish two cases according to the presence or absence of restrictions on the reduced-form coefficients. This is related to the distinction between just-identification and overidentification of a particular structural equation, but it is not the same thing. The only link between the two is that the presence of any overidentified equation implies linear dependence of rows or columns of a submatrix of Π and hence restrictions on Π itself; in other words, if there are no restrictions on the reduced-form coefficients no structural equation can be overidentified, and they must all be either just-identified or underidentified. But if there are restrictions the individual structural equations may belong to any of the three identification categories.

The method of indirect least squares

99   If the structural model imposes no restrictions on the reduced form we may use the simple method of *indirect least squares* to estimate the just-identified equations of the model. (There are no overidentified equations or there would be restrictions, and we need not bother about any underidentified equations since they cannot be estimated in any case.) This means that we obtain estimates P of the reduced-form matrix Π by applying the least-squares method of ch. 5 to each of the G equations of (6.27),

$$y = \Pi x + \underline{v},$$

and then deduce estimates c_1, b_1 of the required structural coefficients by solving the equations

$$-c_{1*} = P'_{\Delta*} b_{1\Delta},$$
$$0_{**} = P'_{\Delta**} b_{1\Delta}.$$

(6.33)

The latter equations are of course obtained by substituting the estimates c_1, b_1 and P for the coefficient vectors γ_1, β_1 and for Π in (6.24) and (6.25); since it is assumed that the (top) structural equation of the system with which we are dealing is just-identified there is no difficulty in solving them. If we are interested only in this single structural equation we need not estimate the entire reduced form Π; as (6.33) shows it is sufficient to determine $P_{\Delta*}$ and $P_{\Delta**}$, i.e. the estimates of the first G^Δ reduced-form equations which form the top part of (6.27), or

$$\underline{y}_\Delta = [\Pi_{\Delta*}\Pi_{\Delta**}]x + \underline{v}_\Delta \tag{6.34}$$

where $\underline{y}_\Delta$ and $\underline{v}_\Delta$ have been obtained by partitioning off the first G^Δ elements of y and $\underline{v}$ respectively. Note that x is *not* partitioned. We need only take those reduced-form equations that have as their dependent variables the G^Δ jointly dependent variables occurring in the equation under review; for each of these we must however perform a least-squares regression on *all* the predetermined variables of the entire model.

100   By the argument of section 98 the elements of P are unbiased and consistent estimates of the corresponding elements of Π. Since we have assumed that there are no restrictions among the latter, these estimates cannot contradict the model nor lead to several conflicting values for the same structural coefficient. The structural estimates b_1, c_1 derived by (6.33) are transformations of the unbiased and consistent estimates P. They are therefore not in general unbiased, but they are consistent; as we have earlier indicated – in section 74 – the latter property is preserved under (most) transformations but the former is not. We shall therefore have to be content with estimates with this asymptotic quality alone.

The required absence of restrictions on P limits the application of indirect least squares to small and simple models; in practice any extension beyond a few structural equations usually leads to restrictions. There is therefore a slight chance that the approximation (5.44) of section 75 may be used to evaluate the variances of the structural estimates. This formula does however quickly lose its simplicity when G^Δ increases. For while the elements of u may reasonably be assumed to be independent, the elements of v may not, as can be seen from (6.28). The covariances of the elements of $\underline{v}_\Delta$ of (6.34) must therefore be taken into account and this may soon complicate matters to such an extent that the approximation is of little help.

The estimation of overidentified equations

101   Proceeding in logical order we should now turn to the case of restrictions on the reduced-form coefficients which arises whenever overidentified structural equations occur. It follows from the discussion of identification that estimation is in principle possible; since we are dealing with a system of simultaneous equations least-squares regression is not applicable; it remains to devise another method of estimation. These methods sometimes take the form of a short-cut solution for the particular model under review – we shall come across an example in ch. 10 section 205 – but there are also several general methods. We shall name some of these methods and describe one of them that is used in the sequel; an adequate theoretical discussion is however quite beyond our scope.

102   When one is faced by restrictions on the reduced-form coefficients the obvious theoretical approach is to establish estimators that respect these constraints. This is done in the oldest method, *full information maximum likelihood* estimation[†]. But when we are dealing with a single overidentified equation by itself such perfection is not necessary, and it may suffice only to consider the constraints on the submatrix Π_{A**} in order to reduce its rank as required. This idea has led to the *limited information single equation* method of estimation of Anderson and Rubin which is substantially simpler than the former; but for the equation under review the structural model need not be specified apart from the predetermined variables that occur in it[††]. Both methods are based on the maximization of a likelihood function, which is determined by assuming that the structural disturbances $\underline{u}$ are normally distributed, and they therefore yield consistent estimates.

Like the limited information method, *two-stage least squares* is designed for the estimation of the coefficients of a single overidentified equation and requires no knowledge of the rest of the model other than a complete list of all predetermined variables that occur in it. But this method is not based on the maximum likelihood principle, and hence calls for no further specification of the distribution of the disturbances. As we shall use two-stage least squares a brief description is in order; for the theory of this simple and ingenious method the reader is referred to the original presentation by THEIL (1958), (forthcoming) to whom it is due.

[†] See KOOPMANS et al. (1950).

[††] See ANDERSON and RUBIN (1949), or KOOPMANS and HOOD (1953).

Two-stage least squares

103   We consider a single overidentified equation and once more take it to
be the first equation of the structural model, or

$$\beta_1' y + \gamma_1' x = U_1,$$

so that in terms of the observed variables for $i = 1, 2, ..., n$

$$\beta_1' y_i + \gamma_1' x_i = \underline{U}_{1i},$$

or, upon omitting all variables with zero coefficients,

$$\beta_{1\,A}' \underline{y}_{Ai} + \gamma_{1*}' x_{*i} = \underline{U}_{1i}. \tag{6.35}$$

In the preceding discussion all jointly dependent variables were treated with
impartiality, and the normalisation rule was invoked to equate an arbitrary
element of β_{1A} to unity. We now revert to the earlier view that each structural
equation has one particular dependent variable: among the G^A jointly
dependent variables of y_A *the* dependent variable of (6.35) is that variable to
which the disturbance $\underline{U}_1$ is supposed to refer. Denoting this variable by $\underline{y}_1$
(6.35) is rewritten as

$$\underline{y}_{1i} = -\beta_{1,A-1}' \underline{y}_{A-1,i} - \gamma_{1*}' x_{*i} + \underline{U}_{1i}, \tag{6.36}$$

where $\beta_{1,A-1}$ contains the coefficients that remain after normalisation and
$\underline{y}_{A-1}$ is the vector of the jointly dependent variables other than $\underline{y}_1$, or

$$\underline{y}_{A-1} = \begin{bmatrix} \underline{y}_2 \\ \underline{y}_3 \\ \vdots \\ \underline{y}_{G^A} \end{bmatrix}.$$

104   The problem is how to estimate the elements of $\beta_{1,A-1}$ and γ_1. The
basic objection to the application of least-squares regression to (6.36) is that
the elements of $\underline{y}_{A-1}$ are not independent of the disturbance term $\underline{U}_1$. The
reason why this is so is that by (6.28) and (6.29) we have

$$\underline{y}_i = \Pi x_i + \underline{v}_i, \qquad \underline{v}_i = B^{-1} \underline{u}_i. \tag{6.37}$$

The elements of $\underline{y}_{A-1}$ are therefore determined as functions of x and $\underline{v}$ by
$(G^A - 1)$ rows of the full reduced form which we write as

$$\underline{y}_{A-1,i} = \Pi_{A-1} x_i + \underline{v}_{A-1,i}, \tag{6.38}$$

while by the second part of (6.37) each element of $\underline{v}_{A-1,i}$ is related to $\underline{U}_{1i}$.

The basic idea of two-stage least squares is to remove this interdependence of the elements of $\underline{y}_{A-1,i}$ and $\underline{U}_{1i}$ by replacing the former by their estimates in terms of least-squares regressions on all predetermined variables x. The first stage therefore consists of $G^A - 1$ least-squares regressions, one for each row of (6.38), and the resulting estimates may be arranged in a matrix P_{A-1} that corresponds to Π_{A-1}. No restrictions on the reduced-form coefficients are taken into account, and it is indeed doubtfull whether there are any within Π_{A-1}. As in (6.34) we may consider

$$\underline{y}_A = (\Pi_{A*} \Pi_{A**}) x + \underline{v}_A$$

and since we are dealing with an overidentified equation it is now certain that the rank of Π_{A**} is reduced by linear dependence. But this permits no definite conclusions about Π_{A-1} which is obtained from

$$(\Pi_{A*} \Pi_{A**})$$

by omitting the latter's first row.

The estimates P_{A-1} of Π_{A-1} are now used to compute the values of the $\underline{y}_{A-1,i}$ according to the first stage regression, i.e. the computed values

$$\hat{\underline{y}}_{A-1,i} = P_{A-1} x_i \tag{6.39}$$

and these are substituted for the $\underline{y}_{A-1,i}$ of (6.36). The second stage then consists of a standard least-squares regression of $\underline{y}_t$ on the $G^A - 1$ elements of $\hat{\underline{y}}_{A-1}$ and the K^* elements of x_*, which yields the two-stage least-squares estimates of the structural coefficients under consideration.

105 If we had been able to substitute the true expected values

$$\Pi_{A-1} x$$

for $\underline{y}_{A-1}$ in (6.36), the second stage regression would refer to nonrandom explanatory variables throughout, and the simultaneous equations bias would have disappeared altogether. It is moreover intuitively clear that these regression coefficients would be unbiased estimates of the particular structural coefficients that appear in (6.36) for the simple reason that upon taking expectations throughout the equation must hold identically, all our manipulations of the reduced form and of other transformations notwithstanding.

As a matter of fact we use the estimated $\underline{P}_{A-1}$ instead of the true Π_{A-1}. The elements of $\underline{P}_{A-1}$ have all the qualities of proper least-squares estimates since the application of the first stage regression to (6.38) is perfectly legitimate. Still the approximation is imperfect and the second stage estimates are biased, since the $\hat{y}_{A-1,i}$ defined by (6.39) are not quite independent of $\underline{U}_{1i}$ in (6.36). The chain runs as follows: the $\hat{y}_{A-1,i}$ are random because they depend on the $\underline{P}_{A-1}$, the $\underline{P}_{A-1}$ are related to the $\underline{v}_{A-1,i}$, and the $\underline{v}_{A-1,i}$, are related to $\underline{U}_{1,i}$. Each link represents a linear transformation with fixed, nonrandom coefficients; one of these relations is of particular interest since it vanishes asymptotically. This is the relation of $\underline{P}_{A-1}$ to $\underline{v}_{A-1,i}$. We consider the covariance of one element of the former, say $\underline{P}_{jh}$, with $\underline{v}_{ji}$, i.e. the disturbance of the reduced-form equation concerned, *for the ith observation*; in the absence of serial correlation this is the sole element of $\underline{v}_j$ that is related to $\underline{U}_{1i}$. We now apply some results of section 73 of ch. 5 to the first stage regression under review. By equation (5.35) we have

$$\underline{P}_{jh} = \Pi_{jh} + \sum_{l=1}^{k} (X'X)^{hl} x_l' v_j$$

where X is the $(k \times n)$ matrix of observations of all predetermined variables, x_l is its lth column, and

$$(X'X)^{hl}$$

denotes the indicated element of $(X'X)^{-1}$. Since moreover

$$E(\underline{P}_{jh}) = \Pi_{jh}, \qquad E(\underline{v}_{ji}) = 0$$

we have

$$\text{covar}(\underline{P}_{jh}, \underline{v}_{ji}) = E\left\{ \sum_l (X'X)^{hl} x_l' \underline{v}_j \underline{v}_{ji} \right\}$$

or, by the serial independence of $\underline{v}_{ji}$ and $\underline{v}_{jh}$, $h \neq i$,

$$\text{covar}(\underline{P}_{jh}, \underline{v}_{ji}) = \sum_l (X'X)^{hl} x_{li} E(\underline{v}_{ji}^2) = \sigma^2 \sum_l (X'X)^{hl} x_{li} .$$

Continuing by an analysis of $(X'X)^{hl}$ along the lines of section 73 it is found that this is equivalent to

$$\text{covar}(\underline{P}_{jh}, \underline{v}_{ji}) = C(X) \frac{\sigma_v^2}{n}$$

where $C(X)$ is a transformation of X that tends to a definite limit with increasing n. As a result,

$$\lim_{n \to \infty} \text{covar}(\underline{P}_{jh}, \underline{v}_{ji}) = 0 .$$

Hence the simultaneous equations bias of two-stage least-squares estimates that was pointed out at the beginning of this section is of the order of $1/n$, and vanishes asymptotically.

106 The last point that must be raised is the practical question whether the substitution of $\hat{y}_{A-1}$ for $\underline{y}_{A-1}$ in (6.36) does not introduce perfect multi-collinearity in the second stage regression. After all we introduce G_{A-1} linear combinations of K predetermined variables as explanatory variables in addition to the subset of K^* predetermined variables already present in (6.36), and there is a danger that this results in linear dependence among the explanatory variables. The answer to this question is that the method has specifically been designed for the estimation of an overidentified equation. By table 11 this means that

$$G^A - 1 < K^{**}$$

or, upon adding K^* on both sides,

$$G^A - 1 + K^* < K .$$

Hence the total number of explanatory variables in the second stage regression is less than the number of predetermined variables of which they are linear combinations and there is no reason to fear that they are linearly dependent on this account.

CHAPTER 7

The analysis of family budgets

Consumer surveys

107 Consumer surveys are concerned with the direct observation of the economic behaviour of households or of individuals of varying social and economic conditions. The principal use of these data in econometrics is for the estimation of income elasticities, and we have already used them to this end for certain attributive characteristics of consumer demand in ch. 3. We now turn to the traditional Engel curve, that is the relation of any category of expenditure to income in a cross-section sample of households of varying income levels.

The study of this relation on the basis of family budgets was initiated by Ernst Engel in 1857. One of his major conclusions was that food expenditure increases with income, but at a lesser rate, i.e. that food demand is inelastic with respect to income. This is Engel's (first) law; it is still valid [†]. The collection of household budgets represents an even older tradition which stretches without interruption from the beginning of the nineteenth century to the present day; but with the exception of Engel's work it did not attract much attention among professional economists until interest was revived by ALLEN and BOWLEY (1935). Since then the analysis of family budgets has developed into a firmly established branch of econometric research. Curiously enough it has yielded few further empirical generalizations of the type of Engel's law, and its theoretical content is slight. The wider interest of the

---

[†] See ENGEL (1857) and HOUTHAKKER (1957).

subject lies largely in the specific technical aspects of the micro-economic cross-section sample data which it uses. Almost any analysis of sample survey data can benefit from the experience of Engel curve research.

108 Household surveys vary widely in almost any respect. They may be concerned with the physiological intake of foodstuffs, with purchases of distinct commodities (quantities or expenditure), or again with purely financial matters such as the sources of income or the composition of investment and savings. There is also much variation in the choice of the participants and in the method of data collection. These questions are a matter of specialized technique; we shall but briefly review a few of the main types of survey.

The oldest and best established variety is the *budget survey*, which in principle covers all household expenditure during a given period with a full specification by commodities. The questionnaire may or may not include a few questions about savings and income; since income is generally regarded as a delicate subject, these matters are often treated lightly, e.g. by asking the respondent merely to indicate his position in the broad groups of a given income classification.

Although the choice of participants, the type of questionnaire and the duration of the period may in principle vary independently, we can in practice distinguish two main types of budget survey. The first is the *intensive* survey, which used to be in favour in continental countries. In this case the first concern of survey design is that each individual return shall accurately represent the expenditure pattern of the household concerned. Traditionally these surveys call for highly detailed information which can only be obtained by having the participants keep full account of all purchases; in order to eliminate chance fluctuations in the expenditure on particular items these records must extend over long periods of up to a year's duration. Obviously, these demands on the participants restrict the scope of such surveys to volunteer households or to a small fraction of willing respondents out of a much larger random sample. At the other end of the scale the advocates of the *extensive* method aim primarily at a high response rate in a random sample, and they try to achieve this by a much slighter form of interrogation. The participants may for example merely be asked to recollect their expenditure of the last few days. In the case of infrequent purchases like clothing, however, the individual is notoriously incapable of recalling the exact data of his recent acquisitions, and his recollections may be seriously biased. Moreover even an accurate record of a household's expenditure on say major durables in a single week would be subject to large sampling variation because of the rare incidence of such purchases. Surveys of this type are therefore usually restricted to expenditure on food and simular recurrent items, and even then the individual returns may have a large margin of error.

These two major types of survey illustrate the conflict between the two requirements of a high response rate in a truly random sample on the one hand and of full, precise and detailed individual information on the other. Many ingenious compromise solutions have been put forward, and nowadays surveys often combine an interview, used as a means of obtaining co-operation, with a system of record-keeping over limited periods of different duration for specific expenditure categories. It is amazing what can be done by careful design and the use of trained and skilled interviewers.

109   Outside budget surveys the same techniques of data collection are used extensively in a wide range of special sample surveys. These are concerned with a single commodity, as in market research, or with particular fields of public interest, like housing or saving. Income and savings surveys are the best known example, but there are also many excellent surveys in market research which remain unpublished. The technical problems of using sample survey data for economic analysis are largely the same whatever the subject.

Limitations of budget surveys

110   The income elasticity estimates derived from budget surveys are subject to some reservation because of the possible defects of the data. In principle these data might be made to meet almost any requirement of econometric analysis by the appropriate survey design; because of the large expense involved, however, surveys are rarely undertaken for the specific purpose of econometric research, and the vast majority of the available data have been collected for other ends. The first budget studies, held in the early nineteenth century, were prompted by concern over the living conditions of the poor. Traces of this tradition persist to the present day, and many surveys serve the social scientists' interest in the living conditions of particular classes rather than the statistical determination of economic relations. Since the first world war household budget surveys have moreover acquired official status as a means of measuring the composition of expenditure that provides the weights for a cost of living price index. As a result the emphasis is often on expenditure rather than income, and the sample design aims at proper estimation of the population means of single variables, taken in isolation, rather than at the estimation of relations between variables. While the user is as a rule unable to remedy these imperfections of the data he should be aware that they may affect his conclusions.

111   We leave aside the obvious dangers of observational errors or systematic distortion of the reported expenditure on particular items, and turn to the difficulties connected with the income variable. The respondents frequently conceal or understate their income, and any attempt to inquire further into the matter will reduce the response rate. Some questionnaires therefore leave this point deliberately vague by the use of a broad income classification, and others do not ask for income at all.

The first point we wish to make is that even a purely random error of observation in recorded income will lead to systematic underestimation of the income coefficient by least-squares estimates. Following the familiar regression model of ch. 5 we consider a particular category of expenditure C_j as a linear function of income, X, so that for all $i = 1, 2, ..., n$ households

$$C_{ji} = \beta_{j0} + \beta_{j1} X_i + U_{ji}, \tag{7.1}$$

with U_j a random disturbance term having the standard properties of the regression model as set out in (5.12), (5.14) and (5.19). The complicating factor is now that the variable X in (7.1) is true income whereas our observations refer to recorded income, X', which differs from the former by a random error of observation V, or

$$X_i' = X_i + V_i. \tag{7.2}$$

Denoting deviations from sample means by lower case letters as before the standard least-squares estimate b_{j1} of β_{j1} is given by

$$b_{j1} = \frac{\Sigma c_j x'}{\Sigma x'^2} \dagger.$$

Upon substitution of (7.1) and (7.2) we find

$$b_{j1} = \frac{\beta_{j1} \Sigma x^2 + \beta_{j1} \Sigma xv + \Sigma xu + \Sigma uv}{\Sigma x^2 + 2\Sigma xv + \Sigma v^2}.$$

---

† The summation signs refer to the index i from $i=1$ to $i=n$, i.e. summation takes place over all sample observations. We shall not indicate the extent of summation whenever it is as obvious as it is here.

Since this is a quotient of random variables we consider its probability limit rather than its expectation. Upon the simplest and most favourable assumption that the U_i, V_i and X_i are all pairwise independent all cross-products vanish and we obtain

$$\text{Plim}(b_{j1}) = \frac{\beta_{j1} \, \text{var}(X)}{\text{var}(X) + \text{var}(V)}$$

which demonstrates that the least-squares estimate systematically understates the true income coefficient[†].

errors in variables leads to underreporting of income coefficient

112 This argument is not restricted to straightforward reporting errors but it applies to *any* random difference V between the X that appear in (7.1) on the one hand and the observed X' on the other. According to the permanent income hypothesis put forward by FRIEDMAN (1957) there is such a difference regardless of the common errors of observation. Briefly, this arises because the income concept that actually governs expenditure – i.c. X – does not correspond to any accounting definition of income over a given period, so that the divergence between X and X' would persist even if the latter were a perfectly accurate record of current income. We shall discuss Friedman's theory at greater length in ch. 8 in connection with the consumption function, i.e. the relation of *total* expenditure to income ; in the present context it merely adds strength to the errors-in-income argument given above.

113 If recorded income is highly unreliable, heavily distorted or simply not available, the common device is to use total expenditure in its stead. The ensuing estimates refer of course to total expenditure coefficients, not to income coefficients ; in terms of elasticities the difference between these two is however slight, because the elasticity of total expenditure in respect of income is usually quite close to unity.

While the use of total expenditure avoids the problem of errors in income it may yet lead to inconsistent estimates[††]. We consider an exhaustive set of k expenditure categories and assume that all C_j for $j = 1, 2, ..., k$ satisfy a linear Engel function of the type (7.1),

---

[†] This is of course the classical case of errors in variables ; in view of the errors in X', consistent estimation would require that the regression line takes an intermediate position between the first and second regression. See JOHNSTON (1960), ch. 8.

[††] See LIVIATAN (1961) for a fuller discussion of the problem and for a solution.

$$\underline{C}_{ji} = \beta_{j0} + \beta_{j1} X_i + \underline{U}_{ji} .$$

Total expenditure $\underline{C}_i$ of the ith household is defined as

$$\underline{C}_i = \sum_{j=1}^{k} \underline{C}_{ji} ,$$

or, upon substitution of the former expression,

$$\underline{C}_i = \beta_0 + \beta_1 X_i + \underline{U}_i \qquad (7.3)$$

with

$$\beta_0 = \sum_j \beta_{j0}, \quad \beta_1 = \sum_j \beta_{j1}, \quad \underline{U}_i = \sum_j \underline{U}_{ji} . \qquad (7.4)$$

The least-squares regression estimate for any $\underline{C}_j$ as a function of total expenditure $\underline{C}$ is given by

$$\underline{b}_{j1} = \frac{\Sigma \underline{c}_j \underline{c}}{\Sigma \underline{c}^2} ,$$

and upon substituting (7.1) and (7.4) we find

$$\underline{b}_{j1} = \frac{\beta_{j1}\beta_1 \Sigma x^2 + \beta_{j1}\Sigma x\underline{u} + \beta_1 \Sigma x\underline{u}_j + \Sigma \underline{u}_j\underline{u}}{\beta_1^2 \Sigma x^2 + 2\beta_1 \Sigma x\underline{u} + \Sigma \underline{u}^2} .$$

Once more we take the probability limit of this expression upon the most favourable assumptions, which are here that the disturbances $\underline{U}_{ji}$ for all k expenditure categories are independent of one another and are also independent of the true income determinant of expenditure. As a result of this all cross-products of X_i and $\underline{U}_{ji}$ or X_i and $\underline{U}_i$ vanish, but not so the product of $\underline{U}_{ji}$ and $\underline{U}_i$; by the latter's definition in (7.4) we have

$$\text{Plim}\left(\frac{1}{n} \Sigma \underline{U}_{ji} \underline{U}_i\right) = \text{var}(\underline{U}_j) .$$

Hence we obtain

$$\text{Plim}(\underline{b}_{j1}) = \frac{(\beta_{j1}/\beta_1)\,\text{var}(\underline{X}) + (1/\beta_1^2)\,\text{var}(\underline{U}_j)}{\text{var}(\underline{X}) + (1/\beta_1^2)\,\text{var}(\underline{U})} .$$

We conclude that $\underline{b}_{j1}$ is not necessarily a consistent estimate of even the total expenditure coefficient β_{j1}/β_1, and that the sign and extent of its systematic deviation from this value depend on a comparison of

$$\frac{\beta_{j1}}{\beta_1} \quad \text{and} \quad \frac{\text{var}(\underline{U}_j)}{\text{var}(\underline{U})} .$$

Both expressions are proper fractions, provided we rule out the case $\beta_j < 0$ for any j; the quotients β_{j1}/β_1 sum to unity by the definition of β_j of (7.4), and the variance quotients do so by the definition of $\underline{U}$ coupled with the assumption that all $\underline{U}_j$ are independent of one another.

114 In the preceding sections we have demonstrated the two major imperfections of least-squares estimates for the simple case of linear Engel functions and of disturbance terms and errors of observation with highly convenient properties. In either case the basic argument continues to hold good under more conditions. As inspection will show the actual *extent* of the effects that have been indicated may vary considerably; much depends on the nature of the income data and on the definition of the expenditure categories respectively. Either defect of least-squares estimates can in principle be avoided by the use of more sophisticated methods of estimation; in practice it is however common usage to retain the least-squares method and to take its known imperfections into account in assessing the ensuing estimates. We shall take the same view. Two possible shortcomings of least-squares estimates have been pointed out; their importance in any particular analysis of budget survey data is a matter of judgment.

115 Leaving aside questions of bias we turn to the *efficiency* of the income coefficients estimates from budget survey data. By (5.37) the variance of the least-squares estimate of β_{j1} of (7.1) is given by

$$\frac{\sigma^2}{\Sigma x^2},$$

and this expression serves for a brief comparison of the merits of family budgets and aggregate data. On the one hand the disturbance variance σ^2 is larger for individual, micro-economic observations than for aggregate data [†]; on the other hand, the much larger number of observations and the much wider range of observed income variation both contribute to Σx^2 and thus improve the precision of regression estimates based on survey data. On balance the latter factor outweighs the former.

In principle the efficiency of the estimates might be considerably advanced by increasing Σx^2 through the appropriate sample design, i.e. by extending the range of observation to the extremes of high and low incomes. The

[†] But not so much as one might think. See section 145, where we examine the disturbance term of aggregate relations.

efficiency would be particularly improved by increasing the number of observations among the higher income groups, because many Engel curves are definitely heteroskedastic with σ^2 increasing along with the income level. Unfortunately most sample surveys are designed for other ends; as we have pointed out earlier (in section 110) their main purpose is usually to obtain estimates of population means rather than of regression coefficients, and the two considerations do not lead to the same sample design.

116   This distinction is of practical interest for the *weighting* of the sample observations. As we have indicated in section 68 the available survey data should be weighted in the regression analysis in order to account for the heteroskedasticity of the Engel curve. These weights serve the efficiency of the regression estimates; they should not be confounded with an altogether different set of weights that is often attached to sample data in the interest of unbiased estimation of population means.

The need for the latter weights arises whenever the data do not constitute a fair sample, i.e. a random sample with equal effective sampling rates in all sections of the population concerned. This may be the result of differential response rates or of conscious sample design by stratification; efficiency of the population mean estimate requires that the sampling rate is increased in strata suspected of having a relatively large dispersion. As a result the number of sample observations in the hth stratum, n_h, is not proportional to the corresponding stratum population N_h. If the true stratum means are μ_h, the overall population mean over all strata is

$$\mu = \frac{1}{N} \sum_h N_h \mu_h, \qquad N = \sum_h N_h,$$

and it is the estimation of this overall mean μ that is at issue. Now, provided the sample is random within each stratum, the sample stratum means $\bar{X}_h$ are unbiased estimators of the μ_h,

$$E(\bar{X}_h) = \mu_h,$$

and it follows that the unbiased estimator $\bar{X}'$ of μ is

$$\bar{X}' = \frac{1}{N} \sum_h N_h \bar{X}_h.$$

This differs from the unweighted sample mean

$$\bar{X} = \frac{1}{n} \sum_h n_h \bar{X}_h, \qquad n = \sum_h n_h,$$

since the n_h are not proportional to the N_h. Hence the use of weights designed to reconstitute the sample in accordance with the composition of the population.

These considerations do not apply to regression estimates. By section 73, a sufficient condition for least-squares estimates to be unbiased is that

$$\text{covar}(X_{ji} U_i) = 0 \quad \text{for } i = 1, 2, ..., n \text{ and all } j$$

where U is the disturbance term and the X_j are the independent variables of the regression equation. Thus no amount of weighting will affect bias or its absence, and efficiency considerations for the case of heteroskedasticity alone dictate the use of weights.

The two motives that we have distinguished may lead to quite different weighting systems. If the higher income groups are underrepresented because of their poor response rate, unbiased estimation of the population mean requires that large weights are attached to these observations; but by the heteroskedasticity argument they should be weighted lightly.

We conclude that the weights attached to sample data in order to make them conform to the composition of the population are irrelevant to the estimation of regression coefficients and should as a rule be disregarded in the interest of efficiency. Unfortunately these weights are often introduced implicitly at an early stage of processing the survey data, and it is then impossible to remove their effect from the published tabulations.

The use of group means

117 The number of individual households in a survey may run from a hundred or so to well over a thousand. It is standard practice to reduce this mass of data to manageable proportions by taking group means over a much smaller number of distinct classes; published survey results almost invariably take the form of cell means for a given classification of the sample households, and the individual household records are seldom accessible. As a result most Engel curves are fitted to group means, even though by the advance of electronic equipment the analysis of large numbers of individual data is nowadays perfectly possible.

The use of group means in regression raises no major problems; the case of a single explanatory variable is particularly simple. We consider the same relation as in (7.1), viz. a linear Engel function for expenditure on a particular category j, but we omit the latter index in order to make room for an additional index h which denotes the cells of a given classification of the sample households. Within each cell the individual households are denoted by $i = 1, 2, ..., n_h$. By assumption all individual data satisfy the same linear relation under review, or

$$C_{hi} = \beta_0 + \beta_1 X_{hi} + U_{hi} \quad \text{for all } h \text{ and } i.$$

Taking the X_{hi} to be nonrandom variables we attribute the usual properties to the U_{hi}, i.e. they have zero mean and they are independent of one another; for the sake of the argument we moreover assume homoskedasticity, or

$$\text{var}(U_{hi}) = \sigma^2 \quad \text{for all } h \text{ and } i.$$

It follows at once by summation over i that the cell means, defined as

$$\bar{C}_h = \frac{1}{n_h} \sum_i C_{hi}, \quad \bar{X}_h = \frac{1}{n_h} \sum_i X_{hi}, \quad \bar{U}_h = \frac{1}{n_h} \sum_i U_{hi},$$

satisfy

$$\bar{C}_h = \beta_0 + \beta_1 \bar{X}_h + \bar{U}_h \text{ for all } h. \tag{7.5}$$

Like the U_{hi}, the disturbances $\bar{U}_h$ of this equation have zero mean and are mutually independent, but (7.5) is no longer homoskedastic; $\bar{U}_h$ is the mean of n_h independent variates with a common variance σ^2, so that

$$\text{var}(\bar{U}_h) = \frac{\sigma^2}{n_h}. \tag{7.6}$$

Hence (7.5) is heteroskedastic, and efficient estimation of β_0 and β_1 requires that the group means are weighted in all regression formulae with weights inversely proportional to the disturbance variance. By (7.6) this means that the group means must be weighted by the n_h, i.e. by the number of individual observations that they each represent.

118 Thus in the case of grouped data, weighted least-squares regression on the basis of the cell means is an appropriate procedure, and it will yield unbiased and efficient estimates. This holds for any given classification of the individual observations whatever. Some classifications are however better than others. In the case of weighted regression, the variance of the estimate b_1 is

$$\frac{\sigma^2}{\sum_h n_h \bar{X}_h^2}, \tag{7.7}$$

where the lower case $\bar{x}_h$ stands for the deviation of $\bar{X}_h$ from the overall sample mean,

$$\bar{X} = \frac{\sum_h n_h \bar{X}_h}{\sum_h n_h}, \qquad \bar{x}_h = \bar{X}_h - \bar{X}.$$

In the classical partition of the total sample sum of squares,

$$\sum_{h,i}(X_{hi} - \bar{X})^2 = \sum_h n_h \bar{x}_h^2 + \sum_{h,i}(X_{hi} - \bar{X}_h)^2, \qquad (7.8)$$

$\sum_h n_h \bar{x}_h^2$ appears as the between-classes component. By (7.7) the precision of the estimate $\underline{b}_1$ will be improved by increasing this quantity; since the left-hand term of (7.8) is constant for any given sample of individual observations, the between-cell component can only be increased by selecting a classification which reduces within-cell variation. This is of course best achieved by classifying the individual observations according to the value of X itself. Hence the prevalence of classifications by income groups, and hence the ready use of income group means in Engel curve estimation[†].

Even with this classification by income groups the use of group means does of course somewhat reduce the precision of the estimates below what is attained with the full use of the individual observations. When the variance of the estimate for the latter case is compared with (7.7), it is seen that grouping increases the variance of the regression coefficient by a factor

$$\frac{\sum_{h,i}(X_{hi} - \bar{X})^2}{\sum_h n_h \bar{x}_h^2},$$

which by (7.8) is always > 1. In the common type of classification by income groups this factor equals about 1.1[††].

119 The discussion of grouping has been restricted to the two-variable case; insofar as we are concerned with Engel curves there is no need to extend the argument to multiple regression. In the latter case the least-squares

---

[†] When respondents have been asked merely to indicate in what income class they belong, the mean incomes within income classes are unknown and the mid-points of the intervals are used instead, completed by ad hoc evaluations for the two extreme classes. The mean income of the open-ended top income class can be evaluated by the Pareto formula (4.6) of section 44 for some reasonable value of α.

[††] See CRAMER (1964).

estimates based on group means are again unbiased, and efficient estimation for a given classification requires as before that all group means are weighted by the number of observations concerned. The choice of an optimal classification is however complicated by the fact that grouping may well affect the correlation among the explanatory variables and hence lead to serious multicollinearity, even when this does not occur in the individual observations. So far this problem has received little attention[†].

The Engel curve

120 We now turn to the substance of Engel curves which is the effect of income on consumer behaviour in respect of distinct commodities or expenditure categories. Several aspects of this behaviour may be singled out for investigation; the decision-making process of the individual consumer defies complete description. As a convenient artifice we may however think of the consumer's behaviour in respect of any commodity as the outcome of three distinct and consecutive decisions. The first decision is whether or not to consume a given commodity at all. If the consumer decides to do so, the second question is how much he will consume. And thirdly he must decide on the quality that he will buy.

Each of these three decisions is reflected in a separate variable that can be related to income. The presence of a particular commodity in a household's budget, or the ownership of a particular durable good, is an attribute of the household concerned; this calls for a probability model of its incidence as a function of income. We have discussed one such model in ch. 3. The other two variables, quantity and quality consumed, can be treated as continuous variables; no particular probabilistic model is required, and their relation to income can be studied by regression methods. Even so we need some theoretical considerations, however slight, that specify the regression model. To this problem we now turn.

121 As we have seen in section 65 the general justification of the linearity of the regression model is that it is a first order approximation to some other function which is left undefined. This is acceptable when the observations are confined to a relatively narrow interval where curvature matters little

---

[†] An investigation of optimal grouping in multiple regression should start from the general statement of grouping in terms of matrix algebra of PRAIS and AITCHISON (1954).

or nothing. As we have already noted in section 115, however, it is a major attraction of survey data that they may cover a considerable income range. Hence curvature of the Engel curve cannot be neglected, and we must discuss the shape of this curve and the mathematical function by which it can be represented.

Three considerations govern the choice of an Engel curve. The first is that it should broadly fit the data and reproduce any marked curvature the observations may possess. In the second place it will be convenient to select a function that can be put in linear form by a simple transformation of the data, so that linear regression can be applied to the correspondingly transformed observations. Finally we may adduce some plausible inductive requirements. These are of little importance when we merely wish to describe general tendencies over the observed range of variation, but they come into their own when the result is to be used in projection or extrapolation beyond the observed interval.

122   There are few such inductive or theoretical considerations and their content is slight; economic theory, and the pure theory of consumer behaviour in particular, have little to offer in this respect. The latter theory provides an analysis of how an individual with given preferences allocates a given income over various commodities with given prices; even within these severe limitations there result no useful conclusions about the shape of the Engel curve or the properties of income elasticities of demand. Virtually the only element that is taken over in empirical analysis is the view that expenditures on all commodities sum to income. This is the *budget restriction*

$$\sum_j C_j = X ,$$
(7.9)

which implies

$$\sum_j \frac{dC_j}{dX} = 1 .$$
(7.10)

The latter constraint may of course be expressed in terms of income elasticities. As in section 30, the elasticity of expenditure on the jth commodity in respect of income is defined as

$$\eta_j = \frac{d \log C_j}{d \log X} = \frac{X}{C_j} \frac{dC_j}{dX} ,$$

so that

$$\sum_j \frac{C_j}{X} \eta_j = 1 ;$$
(7.11)

in words, the income elasticities weighted by the budget shares C_j/X sum to unity.

In what follows we shall repeatedly refer to these simple constraints. The budget restriction may be read as an identity or a definitional relation, and as a matter of fact the household budget data are generally made to satisfy it identically either by equating X to total expenditure (see section 113), or by a suitable definition of the expenditure categories. In the latter case there appears a residual category, often labelled "savings", which is exceptional in that it may be negative.

With such pains being taken over the data, logic demands that the Engel functions, too, are made to satisfy the budget restriction identically, i.e. at all values of X. Several *expenditure systems* that meet this requirement have been put forward, but they all suffer from the defect of uniformity: in order to keep the system at all manageable, their authors impose the additional condition that the expenditure functions for all k commodities have the same mathematical form[†]. This is an understandable simplification, but it may lead to rather artificial results. In our view it is preferable to allow for the particular characteristics of each single commodity, and to select suitable Engel functions regardless of the overall restraint of (7.9), especially when the observations range widely over the income scale. As long as the analysis does not cover all k commodities exhaustively, the problem is evaded since there remains a residual category, presumably with a residual Engel function. In the other case – of a complete analysis – the mathematical form of the Engel functions will often be equally incompatible with (7.9); among the simpler formulae, linear Engel functions alone will strictly satisfy (7.9) for all X, but these are ruled out because of their poor fit. The more complex nonlinear systems that meet (7.9) give rise to estimation problems; the parameters of the k expenditure functions are obviously restrained, and as a rule it is not possible to take the functions one at a time in estimating them. But even when unrestrained nonlinear functions are fitted to data that satisfy (7.9) identically, the ensuing estimates will still approximately satisfy (7.10) or (7.11), at least within the observed income range[††].

[†] Most of these systems include prices besides income among the determinants of demand, and we therefore discuss them in ch. 9, sections 181 and ff. For examples of actual equation systems that meet the budget restriction the reader will have to follow up the references given there, since we do not deal with such details, or he may turn at once to LESER (1965).

[††] For a discussion of this and related questions, see CHAMPERNOWNE and WORSWICK (1954) and NICHOLSON (1957).

123   In the absence of any substantial contribution from economic theory we construct a rough scheme of the Engel curve on the arbitrary but simple basis of intuitive considerations[†]. We do so by examining an individual consumer's behaviour in respect of a particular commodity as he moves through the income scale. The variety of goods that is available is very large, but for most of them the individual will have a positive threshold income at which he first adds the commodity concerned to this budget. At very low incomes consumption is restricted to a small number of goods; as income increases new commodities enter one by one into the expenditure pattern. At and near the threshold income the commodity in question is a luxury which is just coming within the consumer's reach; when income continues to rise, expenditure will at first increase steeply. By (7.10), however, the slopes of the Engel curves of the commodities already present must inevitably decline to make room, as it were, for the new entrant. But expenditure on this good will in turn be affected in the same way as it is succeeded by other newly introduced goods, and the slope of the Engel curve will decline with increasing income until it becomes zero at the stage of saturation.

At this stage we must distinguish between demand in physical quantities and expenditure. After physical demand for a given commodity has reached saturation, expenditure may continue to rise as highly priced varieties are substituted for the cheaper kind. It depends on the commodity classification how this affects the Engel curve. In the case of restrictive commodity definitions there is a separate Engel curve for the cheaper good, i.e. expenditure on this particular item declines as it is replaced by superior varieties. But when a group of similar products is lumped together in a single expenditure category the Engel curve continues to rise[††].

124   By this description the individual Engel curve for expenditure on a given commodity will typically look like fig. 26a; when we consider a group of consumers with different preference patterns and different threshold incomes, the average Engel curve will have the shape of fig. 26b. In either case the ultimate decline is problematical and largely a matter of commodity classification; with the fairly broad commodity groups that are generally employed it will rarely occur. Most Engel curves are therefore probably

---

[†] The following description of the Engel curve has been largely inspired by HOUTHAKKER (1953). But Houthakker derives his conclusions much more rigorously from the maximization of a suitable individual preference function under linear restraints.

[††] We discuss this point more fully in sections 129 and 130.

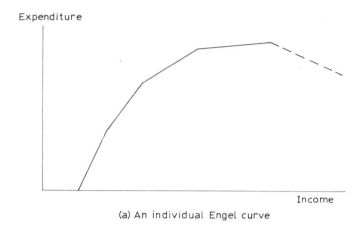

(a) An individual Engel curve

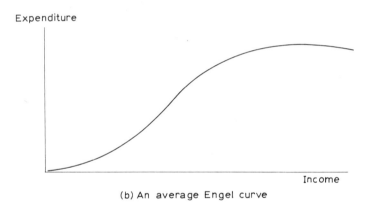

(b) An average Engel curve

Fig. 26. The shape of an Engel curve.

sigmoid in shape; but they may require a very wide income range indeed to reveal this in full. It depends therefore on the commodity concerned and on the observed income range whether all or part of fig. 26b is appropriate.

These arguments are sufficiently vague to apply to other characteristics of the demand for a given commodity as well as to expenditure. Attributes like durable ownership reach saturation quickly, and in the case of common durables like shoes or a radio there is virtually 100% ownership at all observed income levels. But durables that have more recently been introduced and are more expensive, like motorcars, may still constitute a luxury for many households, so that the ownership rate ranges over the whole sigmoid curve at the observed income levels. Quantity demand is already much slower to approach saturation, and although sigmoid functions have been fitted to this variable we usually observe either the lower part of the curve where the commodity is a luxury and the increase is rapid, or the upper branch where saturation makes itself felt. As for quality, i.e. the unit price of a given commodity group, we may confidently expect this variable to reach saturation very slowly indeed if at all.

125   In the last section we have in fact been discussing the requirement of an acceptable fit to the observed curvature. A great many Engel functions have been put forward to allow for a variety of assumptions about the variation of income elasticities and derivatives with income, about saturation, and so on, and it is tempting to select for each application in turn the particular function that best fits observed behaviour. The trouble is however that when we consider individual observations, as in fig. 27a, the dispersion is so large that almost any Engel function will give an equally poor fit. It is only when the individual observations are grouped together in income class means, as in fig. 27b, that systematic curvature appears. Since group means cannot possibly provide more information than the individual data on which they are based, it would seem that this phenomenon is an optical illusion which is moreover dependent on the particular income class limits adopted.

This argument is illustrated in table 12. Three types of Engel curve – the linear function and the double-logarithmic and semi-logarithmic forms to be discussed below – have been fitted to individual data of expenditure on several foodstuffs, and the exercise has been repeated for group means of two sets of income classes. The table shows the resulting estimates of the income elasticity at the mean and the values of R^2, the coefficient of determination, which provide a measure of the goodness of fit. Here as in all subsequent tables the standard errors of the regression estimates are given in brackets. Inspection shows that the elasticity estimates are on the whole little affected by the grouping of the data, but that R^2 increases systematically and quite considerably as the data are grouped together. The former result confirms the argument of sections 117 and 118 to the effect that the use of income group means leaves the properties of the regression estimates largely intact; as for the increase of R^2, this can be shown to be a natural concomitant of grouping[†]. When we return to the present issue and compare the

---

[†] See CRAMER (1964).

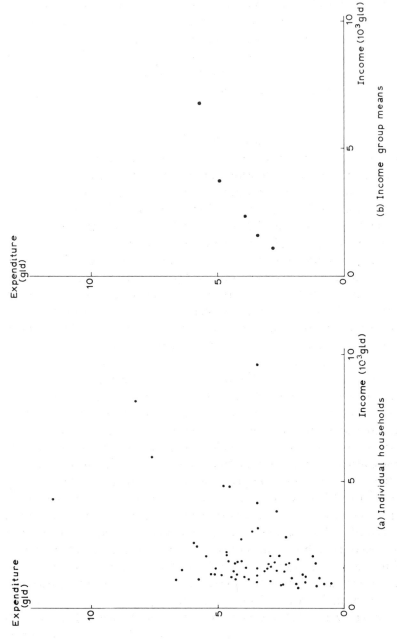

Fig. 27. Income and expenditure on beef of 65 households; effect of grouping (Holland, 1935–1936). For notes see appendix B.

TABLE 12

Income elasticity estimates and goodness of fit of different Engel functions at various degrees of grouping (Germany, 1962).

commodity and degree of grouping*		$\bar{E}$, income elasticity estimate at mean			R^2, coeff. of determination		
		linear	iso-elastic	semi-log	linear	iso-elastic	semi-log
meat	a	.04 (.06)	.09 (.07)	.18 (.09)	.003	.010	.026
	b	.04 (.06)	.13 (.09)	.18 (.09)	.016	.078	.132
	c	.09 (.12)	.20 (.12)	.21 (.15)	.104	.346	.337
eggs	a	.13 (.05)	.30 (.10)	.25 (.08)	.036	.051	.058
	b	.13 (.06)	.25 (.08)	.26 (.08)	,182	.266	.290
	c	.18 (.10)	.25 (.08)	.26 (.10)	.440	.490	.522
milk	a	.15 (.05)	.25 (.08)	.26 (.08)	.046	.051	.062
	b	.15 (.05)	.28 (.08)	.26 (.08)	.229	.281	.309
	c	.17 (.06)	.27 (.07)	.26 (.06)	.672	.746	.850
cheese	a	.21 (.07)	.52 (.12)	.46 (.10)	.051	.105	.107
	b	.21 (.09)	.43 (.11)	.47 (.13)	.178	.379	.376
	c	.33 (.16)	.48 (.09)	.51 (.16)	.645	.854	.822
butter, fats	a	.10 (.04)	.20 (.06)	.22 (.06)	.029	.055	.066
	b	.09 (.05)	.20 (.07)	.22 (.07)	.108	.233	.251
	c	.14 (.06)	.24 (.05)	.24 (.05)	.550	.795	.824
vegetables	a	.33 (.12)	.64 (.14)	.62 (.19)	.041	.110	.064
	b	.33 (.13)	.67 (.15)	.62 (.19)	.231	.414	.365
	c	.31 (.27)	.64 (.21)	.58 (.32)	.325	.648	.640
fruit	a	.47 (.14)	.70 (.15)	.92 (.22)	.065	.111	.109
	b	.49 (.26)	.74 (.17)	.94 (.40)	.185	.418	.294
	c	.70 (.24)	.91 (.10)	.99 (.16)	.900	.947	.979

* a: 173 individual households

  b: same data, group means of 29 income classes

  c: same data, group means of 7 income classes

For notes see appendix A.

results of fitting different Engel curves to the same data we find that the two logarithmic functions have much in common while the linear function differs; this holds for the elasticity estimates as well as for the goodness of fit. Indeed, for all commodities and for all degrees of grouping shown, the fit of the linear function is uniformly worse than that of the two other Engel curves. The choice between the latter is difficult, since their relative merits in respect of fit in several cases vary with the degree of grouping adopted; fortunately the choice is of little importance since the elasticity estimates are hardly affected.

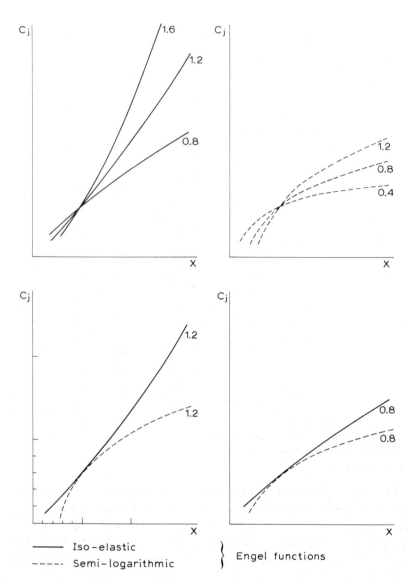

the values given denote elasticities at the common point

Fig. 28. Iso-elastic and semi-logarithmic Engel functions. For notes see appendix B.

In view of these results it would seem that considerations of fit are sufficiently served by the distinction of a few main types of Engel curve, and that
in selecting these we may rate analytical convenience higher than the pursuit
of subtler shades of curvature. We here restrict the discussion to the two
simple standard functions that are commonly employed[†].

126   The first of these is the *iso-elastic* or *double-logarithmic* function

$$C_j = A_j X^{\beta_j} \tag{7.12}$$

with constant income elasticity β_j. This curve, shown in fig. 28, is in order
when we observe the lower part of the sigmoid curve where the commodity
is a luxury, or at any rate the income elasticity shows no tendency to decline.

The simplest way of estimating the parameters is of course to take
logarithms of the observed values and to apply least-squares regression to
the linear relation between the transformed variables. When the data refer to
individual households the incidence of zero values usually precludes a
logarithmic transformation, but with the use of group means this difficulty
hardly arises. We may then write

$$\log \bar{C}_{jh} = \alpha_j + \beta_j \log \bar{X}_h + \bar{U}_{jh} ,$$

$$\alpha_j = \log A_j ,$$

where $\bar{C}_{jh}, \bar{X}_h$ denote the mean values of expenditure on the jth commodity
and of income respectively in the hth income group[††]. The parameters α_j
and β_j can now be estimated by least-squares regression, the group means
being weighted by the number of households they represent according to
the argument of section 117. Over and above this weighting procedure the
logarithmic transformation of the dependent variable C_j will take care of
heteroskedasticity of the underlying micro-economic relation among the
individual data, as has been indicated in section 68.

127   The second standard Engel curve applies to necessities which do
already exhibit a marked decline of the income elasticity indicating the
onset of saturation. This is the *semi-logarithmic* Engel function

$$C_{ji} = \alpha_j + \beta_j \log X_i + U_{ji} ; \tag{7.13}$$

[†] For other Engel curves see LESER (1965), PRAIS and HOUTHAKKER (1955), AITCHISON and
BROWN (1957) and WOLD and JUREEN (1953).

[††] For the argument of section 117 to apply we should have taken group means of logarithms,
i.e. $\bar{C}_{jh}$ and $\bar{X}_h$ should be geometric averages; in practice they invariably are arithmetic means.
The difference is however slight unless the income class is very wide; see also sections 146–7.

which is also shown (for $U_{ji}=0$) in figure 28. Along this curve the income elasticity varies inversely with the level of consumption attained since

$$\eta_j = \frac{\partial \log C_j}{\partial \log X} = \frac{1}{C_j}\frac{\partial C_j}{\partial \log X} = \frac{\beta_j}{C_j}.$$

This function can be fitted by least-squares regression to individual data as well as to group means upon taking logarithms of observed income. With the use of group means the standard weighting procedure of section 117 is in order; if it is believed that the underlying relation among individual data is strongly heteroskedastic, additional weights should presumably be superimposed on the former.

While the estimates a_j and b_j of α_j and β_j of (7.13) are thus readily obtained, a minor technical problem arises when we wish to give an estimate of the income elasticity. Substitution of the estimates for the unknown parameters yields

$$\underline{E}_j(X_0) = \frac{\underline{b}_j}{\underline{a}_j + \underline{b}_j \log X_0}$$

as an estimate of the income elasticity at some given income level X_0; when the elasticity is meant as an estimate of the characteristic Engel curve slope for the sample under review, it should be evaluated at the mean sample income $\bar{X}$, and this leads to

$$\bar{E}_j = \frac{\underline{b}_j}{\bar{C}_j}$$

where $\bar{C}_j$ is the sample mean of $C_j{}^\dagger$. Either elasticity estimate is a quotient of random variables so that its variance can be established approximately only by the method of section 75. Upon applying (5.44) to the elasticity at the sample mean we find that its relative standard error, i.e.

$$\frac{\sigma(\bar{E}_j)}{\bar{E}_j} = \sigma\sqrt{\left\{\frac{1}{\underline{b}_j^2\Sigma x^2} + \frac{1}{n\bar{C}_j^2}\right\}},$$

is only slightly larger than the relative standard error of $\underline{b}_j$, that is

$$\frac{\sigma(\underline{b}_j)}{\underline{b}_j} = \sigma\sqrt{\frac{1}{\underline{b}_j^2\Sigma x^2}},$$

where the x in Σx^2 stand for deviations from the mean of logarithms of income.

$\dagger$ We assume all logarithms to have base e. If the observed incomes have however been transformed into decimal logarithms, the ensuing regression coefficient b_j must be multiplied by $^{10}\log e = .4343$ before being substituted in the income elasticity formulae given above.

128 So far, the argument of the present chapter may be briefly summarized as follows. In principle Engel curve analysis is concerned with scatter diagrams of the sort shown in fig. 27a; in practice matters are simplified by the use of grouped data and complicated by the introduction of nonlinear Engel curves. We have suggested that the closeness of fit to individual data is about the same for various nonlinear Engel functions, and that grouping by income does not materially affect the estimates of a given Engel function. In short, the estimate of a typical sample slope coefficient like the income elasticity at the mean is about the same, whatever way the data are handled.

TABLE 13

Engel curve estimates of income elasticities of expenditure on selected commodities.

commodity	Germany 1950–51	United States 1955	France 1956	Great Britain 1958
bread	.02	.12	−.12	−.05
milk	.11	−.18	.00	.27
butter	.76	.37	.31	.30
cheese	.73	.30	.59	.24
meat	.50	.30	.64	.25
fish	.43	.06	.70	.41
vegetables	.56	.66	.83	.42
fruit	1.02	.14	1.10	.70
sugar	.12	−.04	−.09	.07
eggs	.66	.16	.43	.37
all food	.47	.21	.57	.28
clothing	1.55		1.35	
rent	.61		1.35	

For notes see appendix A.

In table 13 we bring together a number of income elasticity estimates from different studies. The methods of analysis employed vary, and for a full account of the technical details the reader is referred to the original studies cited. Yet there is some similarity in the results; notwithstanding national differences, for example, food commodities rank nearly uniformly as necessities, although the precise order of their income elasticities shows how table habits vary from one country to another.

Quality variation

129 So far we have glossed over the distinction between quantity and expenditure of a particular commodity and ignored the consumer's decision as to what quality he will buy. A moment's consideration of a commodity like meat will show that these matters are closely related. Meat is sufficiently homogeneous for a single quantity measure to apply – we may add pounds of beef to pounds of mutton and obtain pounds of meat – yet it is at the same time a composite commodity group which covers a variety of cuts from all sorts of stock. When we narrow down the definition of a separate commodity within such a group, we end up with a large number of distinct goods that are strictly homogeneous in the sense that each is sold at a single price of its own. These prices are of course the same for all customers, and we take it that they do not vary in the course of the budget survey that provides the Engel curve data.

We now consider C, expenditure on meat, as the sum total of expenditures C_k on the kth homogeneous kind of meat available. Each expenditure variable C_k can be written as the product of quantity Q_k and price P_k. By the definition of what constitutes a single homogeneous good, P_k is a constant that does not vary between individual customers and that is independent of income; the quantity bought Q_k, on the other hand, does vary with income X, and we may write

$$C_k(X) = Q_k(X)P_k .$$
(7.14)

By definition, expenditure and quantity for the commodity group as a whole are given by

$$C(X) = \sum_k C_k(X), \qquad Q(X) = \sum_k Q_k(X) .$$
(7.15)

We now consider the *unit price* of the composite commodity group as a whole,

$$P(X) = \frac{C(X)}{Q(X)},$$
(7.16)

and take this as a measure of quality. $P(X)$ is of course a weighted average of the prices P_k, the weights being the quantity shares of the homogeneous goods, or, by (7.14) and (7.15),

$$P(X) = \sum_k \frac{Q_k(X)}{Q(X)} P_k .$$

Since the prices P_k are constants, the variation of $P(X)$ with income X comes about through systematic shifts of the quantity shares which move in favour of the higher-priced varieties as income increases[†].

Having distinguished between expenditure and quantity we correspondingly define two separate income elasticities. For a single homogeneous good the two coincide since by (7.14)

$$\log C_k(X) = \log Q_k(X) + \log P_k ,$$

where P_k is a constant, irrespective of income X; we may therefore introduce a single income elasticity

$$\eta_k = \frac{d \log C_k(X)}{d \log X} = \frac{d \log Q_k(X)}{d \log X} ,$$

which can of course also be written as

$$\eta_k = \frac{X}{C_k(X)} \frac{dC_k(X)}{dX} = \frac{X}{Q_k(X)} \frac{dQ_k(X)}{dX} . \tag{7.17}$$

For the commodity group as a whole the income elasticities of expenditure and quantity generally differ, and we write

$$\eta_C = \frac{d \log C(X)}{d \log X} , \qquad \eta_Q = \frac{d \log Q(X)}{d \log X} .$$

By alternate substitution of derivatives and elasticities as in (7.17) both these overall elasticities can be written as a weighted average of the η_k, viz.

$$\eta_C = \sum_k \frac{C_k}{C} \eta_k , \qquad \eta_Q = \sum_k \frac{Q_k}{Q} \eta_k . \tag{7.18}$$

The point is of course that these two elasticities differ because the weights differ. By (7.16) we have

$$\log P(X) = \log C(X) - \log Q(X)$$

so that

$$\eta_P = \eta_C - \eta_Q \tag{7.19}$$

with

$$\eta_P = \frac{d \log P(X)}{d \log X} .$$

[†] The description of this phenomenon as quality variation measured by unit prices is due to PRAIS and HOUTHAKKER (1955).

This is the elasticity of the unit price in respect of income, or *quality elasticity* for short–any reference to price might cause confusion with elasticities in respect of price. By a final substitution of (7.18) into (7.19) we find

$$\eta_P = \sum_k \left\{ \frac{C_k(X)}{C(X)} - \frac{Q_k(X)}{Q(X)} \right\} \eta_k. \tag{7.20}$$

130 As an empirical generalisation we may say that the quality elasticity is nonnegative and takes higher values the more heterogeneous is the commodity group concerned. By (7.20) it is a product sum of the η_k with factors

$$\left\{ \frac{C_k}{C} - \frac{Q_k}{Q} \right\} = \frac{Q_k}{Q} \left\{ \frac{P_k}{P} - 1 \right\},$$

where we have omitted the income level X involved. The first term on the right-hand side is a weight, but the price term which follows can be of either sign: by (7.15) the weighted sum over k is zero. The quality is thus formally equivalent to a (weighted) *covariance* of income elasticities and prices within a commodity group, and if it is positive this brings out that these two vary together: the more expensive varieties are more of a luxury. Hence the quality elasticity describes the substitution of dearer goods for the cheaper

TABLE 14

Quality elasticities of a commodity group and of its constituent parts (Germany 1950).

	expenditure		quantity		quality	
	mean value C_k	elasticity η_C	mean quantity, Q_k	elasticity η_Q	unit price P_k	elasticity η_P
butter	95	.76	17	.74	5.6	.02
margarine	77	.01	33	.01	2.3	.00
shortening etc.	73	.18	24	.16	3.1	.02
all fatstuffs	245	.35	74	.24	3.3	.12

For notes see appendix A.

items within the commodity group under consideration, and a positive quality elasticity may arise for a group of homogeneous goods, each of which by definition has a zero quality elasticity. It follows that quite high quality elasticities can be obtained by adding together composite commodities that already show a moderate variation. Table 14 illustrates how the quality elasticity of the group comes about by the disparity between quantity and expenditure weights in (7.18) and in (7.20), and it also demonstrates how the value of η_p depends on the heterogeneity of the group, or, more precisely, on the spread of prices and of income elasticities of the constituent commodities.

Household composition

131   Apart from income many other factors affect household consumption, and insofar as they have been observed we may chose between three possible courses of action: we can altogether ignore these other variables, thus including their effect in the disturbance term of the Engel curve; we can introduce them as a separate independent variable in the regression model; or we may eliminate their effects by analysing selected samples in each of which they are constant.

Of all the factors other than income, *household composition* has been studied most intensively. Although there is no empirical evidence to this effect it is generally held to be the second most important determinant of household consumption, following immediately after income; its effect on the expenditure pattern is moreover of considerable interest in itself. As we indicated before the early budget surveys were often motivated by concern over the living conditions of the working classes, and it is clear that any discussion of the adequacy or otherwise of income levels must take family size into account. More recently interest in the relation of expenditure to household composition has revived in connection with the introduction of family allowances and tax relief for the larger families. The persistent and plausible idea underlying the discussion is that larger households have in some sense greater needs than small families; the difficulty is that these needs must be inferred from expenditure patterns that have been constrained by the budget restriction. Several quite sophisticated methods have been put forward to solve this problem.

132   Households consist of individuals of different sex, age and family status, and since their needs (however defined) may be expected to vary with these characteristics there is no single natural measure of family size. We shall shortly return to the problem of measurement of family size; the mere fact that this does present a problem would recommend the fitting of separate Engel curves to distinct subsamples, each consisting of households of strictly the same composition. Although this course is rarely feasible without a severe reduction of the number of observations, it is undoubtedly the best procedure for the estimation of income elasticities, for the *ceteris paribus* condition is very nearly attained. But this approach will not answer the demand for better insight into the needs of families of different composition, unless we proceed to compare the estimates of the distinct subsamples; and in order to do so we shall need some kind of model of household composition after all. Therefore we may as well introduce family size explicitly into our model at the very outset.

133   Apart from the difficulty of measuring family size we must reckon with the presence of a strong positive correlation between income on the one hand and family size, measured on any sensible scale, on the other. Large families tend to have high incomes, and conversely. This is not due to a direct causal link between the two variables but to fortuitous characteristics of our social structure, as may be illustrated by the two extreme instances which largely determine the observed correlation. At one end of the scale we have households of one or two persons, which usually represent the very young –bachelors and young couples–or the old; both categories tend to have substantially lower incomes than the active adult population. At the other end of the scale very large families of say eight or more persons often include more than one wage-earner, either because they are in fact composite households or because of the natural age-structure of families with six or more children.

   Whatever the reason for the positive correlation of income and family size, the statistical consequences are the same. The first is that even if we are prepared to ignore the family size effects altogether we cannot simply relegate them to the disturbance term of the Engel curve. For if we do so the disturbance will not be independent of the remaining explanatory variable, income, the assumption of section 66 will no longer be valid and simple least-squares estimates of the income elasticities will be biased. An illustration is in order. We introduce a variable F for family size, measured on some reasonable scale, e.g. by counting the number of individuals in the household, and we suppose that logarithmic transformation of the variables is appropriate throughout. The correct Engel curve model then reads as

$$\log \underline{C}_{jh} = \alpha_j + \beta_j \log X_h + \gamma_j \log F_h + \underline{U}_{jh}$$

where the index j identifies a commodity and h serves to distinguish the observations. By assumption the disturbances $\underline{U}$ are uncorrelated with the income and the family size variable. Passing on to deviations from the sample means we have equivalently

$$c_{jh} = \beta_j x_h + \gamma_j f_h + u_{jh} \tag{7.21}$$

where the lower-case roman letters stand for deviations from the sample mean of the (logarithmically) *transformed* variables.

If we omit the family size variable F, the income elasticity β_j is estimated by a simple regression of c on x, i.e. by

$$b_j = \frac{\sum\limits_h c_{jh} x_h}{\sum\limits_h x_h^2}.$$

Upon substitution of (7.21) and taking expectations, using the independence of u from both X and F, we find

$$E(b_j) = \beta_j + \gamma_j \frac{\sum\limits_h x_h f_h}{\sum\limits_h x_h^2}.$$

Clearly b_j is a biased estimator of β_j insofar as (i) $\gamma_j \neq 0$, i.e. family size affects consumption, and (ii) $\sum_h x_h f_h \neq 0$, i.e. x and f are correlated in the observed sample at hand.

134   The third alternative is to estimate both β_j and γ_j by applying multiple regression to (7.21). But in this case the correlation between X and F turns up as multicollinearity among the explanatory variables with the unfortunate result, set out in section 78, that the estimates will have large variances. The only way of improving the precision of the estimates is to impose an additional *a priori* condition which restricts the joint variation of the estimates; and this is in fact the course that is generally adopted in the present case.

The simplest and most commonly adopted way of restricting the estimates is to assume that

$$\beta_j + \gamma_j = 1 \quad \text{for all } j, \tag{7.22}$$

and to impose the same condition on the estimates of these elasticities. Since we are dealing with elasticities this implies that consumption of any commodity is a linearly homogeneous function of income and family size, or again that budget shares are constant, irrespective of family size, provided income keeps in step with the latter variable: households have no economies or diseconomies of scale.

By (7.22) the original model can be rewritten as

$$\log \underline{C}_{hj} - \log F_h = \alpha_j + \beta_j (\log X_h - \log F_h) + \underline{U}_{jh}$$

or

$$\log (\underline{C}_{hj}/F_h) = \alpha_j + \beta_j \log(X_h/F_h) + \underline{U}_{jh} .$$

This is equivalent to a simple constant-elasticity Engel curve for per capita consumption as a function of per capita income. The estimation of β_j presents no problems, and the estimate of γ_j, the family size elasticity, follows from (7.22).

135   The reduction of both income and consumption to a per capita basis implies that for each commodity the Engel curves of distinct household types can be made to coincide by a single scale transformation of all the variables involved; alternatively, the procedure may be regarded as an attempt to bring households of varying composition into a position where they have in some sense equal needs. Since it will depend on the definition of the family size variable F whether the assumption (7.22) is an acceptable approximation or not, a discussion of the scale of measurement of family size is in order.

   To define F as the number of individuals in the household is widely felt to be a very crude procedure, and many attempts have been made to improve on it by attaching different weights to individuals of different sex and age groups. If there are K_{lh} individuals of the lth type in a household h, its family size F_h is defined as

$$F_h = \sum_l \lambda_l K_{lh} .$$

Since it is standard practice to normalize the λ_l by attaching unit weight to the adult male, such sets of weights are known as *equivalent adult scales*. Table 15 gives a few examples of such scales, which have flourished until the 1940's; since then their usage is generally restricted to food consumption if they are not altogether abandoned in favour of a tabulation of the survey results by a highly detailed household composition classification[†]. As a matter of fact these scales are rarely based on any coherent argument, and the general impression is that they represent a very crude idea of an individual's needs, largely determined by reference to his bare physiological need for food. This is of course irrelevant; the only sound argument in favour of a particular

---

[†] See note to table 15, appendix A, page 258.

TABLE 15

Some equivalent adult scales.

source	coefficients of children	coefficients of adults
League of Nations	rising with age from .20 to .80 at the age of 14.	1.00 for a man, .80 for a woman, .80 for anyone over 60.
Amsterdam scale	rising with age from .15 to .90 at the age of 14.	1.00 for a man, .90 for a woman.
C.R.E.D.O.C. – I.N.S.E.E.	.50 up to the age of 15	first adult 1.00, all others in the household .70.

For notes see appendix A.

scale of measurement of F would be to the effect that it is appropriate to (7.22), i.e. that its use for the reduction to per capita values makes the Engel curves of households of varying composition coincide.

136 While it is possible that equivalent adult scales may be devised which bring about the desired result for a set of Engel curves for a particular commodity, it is unlikely that a single transformation will do so for all commodities. If we intuitively consider individual needs it is manifest that no single scale will at the same time cover, say, milk as well as cigars. It is therefore natural to extend the notion of an equivalent adult scale to a whole set of such scales, one for each commodity and one for income[†]. In this approach the Engel curves are cast in the general form

$$Cj/Fj = f_j(X/F) \quad \text{for all } j , \tag{7.23}$$

where f_j is the specific Engel function for commodity j,

$$F_j = \sum_l \lambda_{l_j} K_l \quad \text{for all } j , \tag{7.24}$$

$$F = \sum_l \Lambda_l K_l ;$$

at this stage we omit the index h which should denote the household or observation concerned. The equivalent adult weights λ_{l_j} are known as the

---

[†] The idea was first put forward by SYDENSTRICKER and KING (1921) and later rediscovered by PRAIS and HOUTHAKKER (1955).

specific coefficients for the *j*th commodity, and the Λ_l as the *income coefficients*, of the *l*th type of individual.

The intuitive appeal of this approach is strengthened by the fact that the income coefficient of any given type of individual can be expressed as a weighted sum of the specific commodity coefficients of that individual. This is so because an exhaustive set of Engel curves of the type (7.23) must satisfy the budget restriction of section 122. If income varies while family composition is constant we must therefore have, as in (7.10),

$$\sum_j \frac{\partial C_j}{\partial X} = 1 .$$ (7.25)

Likewise the budget restriction must continue to hold good when household composition varies while income is kept constant, so that

$$\sum_j \frac{\partial C_j}{\partial K_l} = 0 \quad \text{for all } l .$$ (7.26)

Writing (7.23) as

$$C_j = F_j \cdot f_j(X/F)$$ (7.27)

we have

$$\frac{\partial C_j}{\partial X} = \frac{F_j}{F} f'_j$$

or, by (7.25),

$$F = \sum_j F_j f'_j .$$ (7.28)

Differentiating (7.27) in respect of K_l and using (7.24) we find

$$\frac{\partial C_j}{\partial K_l} = \lambda_{l_j} f_j - \Lambda_l \frac{X}{F^2} F_j f'_j$$

or, by (7.26),

$$\Lambda_l \frac{X}{F^2} \sum_j F_j f'_j = \sum_j \lambda_{l_j} f_j ,$$

and substitution of (7.28) and (7.23) leads to

$$\Lambda_l = \frac{F}{X} \sum_j \lambda_{l_j} f_j = \sum_j \frac{(C_j/F_j)}{(X/F)} \lambda_{l_j} .$$ (7.29)

This shows the income coefficient as a weighted average of the corresponding specific coefficients, the weights being the budget shares of the commodity concerned corrected by the appropriate equivalent adult scales.

137   The result (7.29) is intuitively satisfactory, and it would moreover seem to simplify the problem of estimation of equivalent adult coefficients: since the income coefficients can be expressed in terms of the specific coefficients, we need only estimate the latter. Unfortunately, however, it appears that even with this help the estimation of a complete set of coefficients of this type is impossible. Prais and Houthakker proposed an iterative procedure, but they did not put it into practice; it was left to FORSYTH (1960), who set out to complete the work, to discover that the specific coefficients cannot be identified, i.e. that no amount of information about observed Engel curves will render these coefficients determinate. A strict demonstration of this fact would call for protracted algebraical exercises on the basis of a particular mathematical specification of the Engel functions f_j of (7.23); we shall try to summarize the main argument by means of a simplified example.

Suppose that Engel functions for a complete set of s distinct commodities have been fitted separately, without any regard for household composition, to two subsamples of observations. The first subsample refers to standard households to which we attribute unit coefficients on all scales, i.e. for these households all s specific coefficients as well as the income coefficient are unity by normalization. The second subsample refers to households which contain exactly one additional person of type l. The problem is to estimate the equivalent scale coefficients of this type of individual, and it would seem that we have assumed a situation which is well adapted to this end. We dispose of two sets of fitted Engel curves; the estimated functions for the standard subsample are denoted by

$$C_j = f_j(X) \quad \text{for } j = 1, 2, ..., s,$$ (7.30)

and those for the second subsample by

$$C_j = g_j(X) \quad \text{for } j = 1, 2, ..., s.$$ (7.31)

All we have to do is to determine $(s+1)$ coefficients

$$\lambda_{l_j} \text{ for } j = 1, 2, ..., s, \quad \Lambda_l,$$

subject to (7.29), such that the scale transformations

$$C_j^* = \frac{C_j}{1 + \lambda_{l_j}}, \qquad X^* = \frac{X}{1 + \Lambda_l},$$

will make the functions fitted to the second sample coincide with the standard set, or

$$g_j(X) = (1 + \lambda_{l_j}) f_j(X^*) \quad \text{for all } j. \tag{7.32}$$

Since both sets (7.30) and (7.31) represent estimated functions we must presumably allow for sampling variation in determining the coefficients that will bring about the best possible correspondence between the Engel curves from either sample; moreover the derivation of such optimal coefficients will obviously vary with the specific Engel functions f_j, g_j adopted. But it stands to reason that when these technical problems have been solved the required coefficients λ_{l_j}, Λ_l will finally emerge as functions of the estimated parameters of the s pairs of Engel curves fitted. Since Λ_l is by (7.29) a function of the λ_{l_j}, there are altogether s coefficients that must be determined, and there are s paired comparisons of parameter estimates available. On the face of it this seems a simple problem, but in fact it does not allow for a determinate solution. This is so because the budget restriction (7.9) must obtain in either subsample and must be met by either set of fitted Engel curves. Thus neither set of s estimated functions f_j and g_j for each of the two subsamples is independent: in either set one function refers to a residual commodity, and its parameters can be derived from the $(s-1)$ others. As a result, there are only $(s-1)$ independent pairs of parameter estimates that allow for a comparison, and this is insufficient to determine the s specific coefficients λ_{l_j}.

138   The only way to remedy this situation is to impose yet another restriction on some or all of the coefficients in order to ensure that the set of equivalent adult scales is determinate. Thus Prais and Houthakker succeed in estimating the specific coefficients because they assume at the very outset that the income coefficients Λ_l are unity for all l.[†] Since this is an arbitrary assumption it would seem preferable to revive a method due to NICHOLSON (1949). If we translate this method in the terms of the present discussion, it consists of estimating the income coefficients of children by considering commodities for which the child's specific coefficients may be reasonably fixed at zero. In Nicholson's analysis these commodities are men's and women's clothing, tobacco and drink; since his Engel curves are not based on logarithmic transformations, his estimates refer to income differentials (or the "cost of a child") rather than to income scales. Un-

---

[†] See PRAIS and HOUTHAKKER (1955), ch. 9. The authors treat this as a mere computational simplification and do not seem aware that they would be unable to estimate the λ_{l_j} without it.

fortunately the empirical results are disappointing, largely because the commodities concerned are liable to larger disturbances as well as observational errors than others. But the principle of Nicholson's approach is sound, and it is the only justifiable solution to the problem of indeterminacy that we have indicated above.

We end up with an example which shows the simplicity of Nicholson's method as well as its empirical defects. We borrow the results of FORSYTH (1960) for double logarithmic Engel curves of equal slope but varying intercept, fitted to four family types consisting of a couple with 0, 1, 2 and 3 children respectively. We consider expenditure on alcoholic drink, tobacco and entertainment, and take it that children have zero specific coefficients for these commodities. For these goods the Engel functions (7.30) and (7.31) can therefore, by the double-log specification, be written as

$$\log C_{jk} = \alpha_j + \beta_j \log \left\{ \frac{X}{1 + k\Lambda_l} \right\},$$

where l refers to a child and k indicates the number of children in the household; the Λ_l are normalized by attributing unit value to a couple rather than to an adult male. Since this can also be written as

$$\log C_{jk} = \beta_j \log X + (\alpha_j - \beta_j \log(1 + k\Lambda_l))$$

the term $(1 + k\Lambda_l)$, and hence Λ_l itself, is easily evaluated by a comparison of the intercepts of the fitted curves for different k.

TABLE 16

Values of the income coefficient Λ of a child obtained by Nicholson's method (England 1953).

commodity used in the analysis	value of Λ of a child in households consisting of a couple and k children		
	$k=1$	$k=2$	$k=3$
	income coefficient of a couple $= 1$		
alcoholic drink	.09	.15	.12
tobacco	−.05	.01	−.05
entertainment	−.01	.06	.08

For notes see appendix A.

The results obtained in this manner are shown in table 16, and they are rather disappointing. There may of course be some doubts about the uniformity of the type of individual denoted as a child (this covers all ages up to 15), but this would affect all three commodity analyses equally while in fact the main trouble is that they do not yield coherent results. The values for alcoholic drink are very roughly in line and suggest that on the overall income scale a child is equivalent to about .12 of an adult couple, or to about a quarter of an adult; this is just about acceptable. For tobacco and entertainment, however, we obtain negative values which make no sense. Upon inspection of Forsyth's original analysis the odd results for tobacco can be attributed to the fact that the Engel curves for this commodity show a poor fit, so that it is presumably ill suited as an indicator of the standard of living. In the case of entertainment, however, this excuse is not open to us, and we must conclude that the specific coefficient of a child for this commodity is nonzero. In short, while we have set out to illustrate Nicholson's method because it is the only valid solution to the problem of constructing equivalence scales, the illustration mainly brings out that its actual application is rarely practicable. It is dependent on the presence of expenditure categories that are closely related to income while we can at the same time be sure that children have zero specific coefficients. These two conditions go seldom together.

CHAPTER 8

The consumption function

The consumption function

139 In the traditional view of consumer behaviour the typical decisions of the consumer bear on the allocation of a given income to various ends. The Engel curves of the preceding chapter describe the allocation of income to a large number of specific expenditure categories, provided they meet the budget restriction of section 122. We now turn to a simple dichotomy whereby income is exhaustively divided between consumption on the one hand and saving on the other. The proportions may vary with the income level, and the *consumption function* describes the relation of consumption to income; since savings are the complement of consumption, it is equivalent to a *savings function*.

The terms of this dichotomy are defined by their role in the Keynesian model of aggregate income determination: consumption represents those allocations of income that contribute directly to effective demand, and savings is the remainder. Adopting the standard notation of this model we denote consumption by C and income by Y, and write the consumption function as

$$C_t = C(Y_t) . \tag{8.1}$$

In the simplest representation of the Keynesian model this is the only behaviour relation involved. It is supplemented by the identity

$$Y_t = C_t + I_t \tag{8.2}$$

which indicates that apart from consumption there is only one other component of effective demand which is called investment, I. We note for the
record that

$$I_t \text{ is autonomous} \tag{8.3}$$

which simply means that I_t is *not* related to C_t or Y_t; by the classification of
section 88 it is a predetermined (exogenous) variable. In this simple presentation of the model all variables refer to the same time period denoted by t.

140   We have put the consumption function immediately in the context of
the macro-economic model of income determination because this is where
it belongs. Any realistic version of this model will of course be much more
elaborate and allow for taxes, government expenditure and foreign trade.
But even then private consumption is invariably by far the largest single
component of effective demand, and it is of obvious interest to know what
relation determines this formidable aggregate.

This question has been tackled by the study of aggregate time-series as well
as by micro-economic analyses of savings behaviour, based on special
surveys of the financial operations of consumer households[†]. Since the
major part of savings is due to the higher income classes, such surveys
require another sample design than do household expenditure surveys. In
principle the savings function that appears among such data is of course
very much like an Engel function, but in practice the analysis is beset by
several complicating factors. Individual savings show far more variation
than, say, food expenditure, and these variations are moreover to a much
larger extent related to systematic factors other than income, such as age,
professional and occupational status, and wealth; indeed among many
survey data these factors may well predominate to such an extent that
it becomes difficult to isolate the effect of income variation in which we are
primarily interested. Another difficulty of the micro-economic analyses is
that the distinction between savings and current expenditure that is relevant
to individual decisions may well differ from the macro-economic definitions
intended. Expenditure on durable goods, for example, may for the individual
at least in part represent investment, i.e. a form of saving, while in the macro-

---

[†] The first of these were the Surveys of consumer finances of the Survey Research Center,
Michigan, which began in 1948. Some years later the Oxford University Institute of Statistics
ran a series of Savings Surveys. Similar surveys have since been held in France, in Holland
and in other countries.

economic model it must of course be counted as consumption since it contributes immediately to effective demand. For these reasons micro-economic analyses, however fruitful and rewarding they may ultimately be, seldom bear directly on the consumption function with which we are here concerned.

141   A number of specific hypotheses concerning the consumption function have been put forward. We shall first review these theories and then illustrate them by applications to Dutch annual time-series data for the period 1949–1964. Inevitably, we shall have to deal at some length with technical questions that arise in any analysis of aggregate data.

A simple formulation; Keynes' own

142   In Keynes' view the consumption function is a relation between current consumption and current income, or, as in (8.1),

$$C_t = C(Y_t).$$

This function is not further specified, but Keynes does argue that the marginal propensity to consume is positive but less than one, i.e.

$$0 < \frac{dC}{dY} < 1. \tag{8.4}$$

He also suggests, but with less conviction, that the income elasticity of consumption will be less than one, or

$$0 < \frac{d \log C}{d \log Y} = \frac{Y}{C} \cdot \frac{dC}{dY} < 1^{\dagger}. \tag{8.5}$$

These additional hypotheses have important consequences for the economic analysis, but they do not add to the specification of the consumption function (8.1). We are free to write this as a linear function in C and Y or in their logarithms, either specification being meant as an approximate description of the observed variation that is dictated by convenience and justified by the argument of sections 62 to 65 of ch. 5. The assumptions (8.4) and (8.5) are then equivalent to certain restrictions on the parameters of such equations, and these may or may not be borne out by the subsequent

---

† See KEYNES (1936), p. 96–98.

estimates[†]. But they do not contribute to the prior specification of the consumption function.

While the consumption function is postulated as a relation between aggregates it is quite clearly meant to reflect individual behaviour. Assumption (8.4), for example, is presented by Keynes as a fundamental psychological law. Adopting a linear representation and adding a disturbance term we may write the consumption function of the ith household as

$$\underline{C}_{it} = \beta_{0i} + \beta_{1i} Y_{it} + \underline{U}_{it} \quad [††}. \tag{8.6}$$

Several observations are in order. The first is that (8.6) is meant to represent individual behaviour and that hence the variable Y must be defined as that income which the household is in fact free to allocate at will to savings or to consumption. Thus Y must be defined as *disposable income*, i.e. the part of income that remains after deduction of income tax, social security contributions and any other statutory obligations that the household may incur[†††].

Secondly, since the consumption function is concerned with variations in real income, care must be taken to measure income correspondingly and not to confound nominal and real income variations. In practice this is done by expressing both C_t and Y_t in constant prices, i.e. by reducing the nominal variables expressed in current prices to a common denominator by dividing them by an appropriate price index. This use of real magnitudes does of course reflect a material hypothesis about behaviour to the effect that the consumer is impervious to the money illusion and that his allocation of income to saving and consumption is invariant to changes in the overall price level. We might of course approach this question with an open mind and introduce both nominal income Y^* and the price level P as separate variables in an analysis of nominal consumption, deciding by the ensuing

---

[†] This is one of the rare instances of an economic hypothesis that is at least in principle amenable to a statistical test (see section 3); but in fact (8.4) is so innocuous that it is almost certain not to be rejected.

[††] By (8.4) we should have $0 < \beta_{1i} < 1$, and if we accept (8.5) as well $\beta_{0i} > 0$.

[†††] While the idea is clear, the implementation of this definition may raise difficult technical questions. Some theorists further restrict the consumer's freedom by assuming that part of income is *committed* to necessary or routine expenditure, and is hence excepted from the free choice between saving and spending. This affects the specification of the behaviour relation rather than the definition of income; the level of committed income is not imposed beforehand but established by estimation. See STONE (1954) for an example, which is however concerned with expenditure functions for various commodity groups rather than with the consumption function.

estimates whether consumers have a money illusion or not. But these estimates must be derived from aggregate data (we shall shortly discuss the passage involved) and as we have argued before, in section 80, aggregate time series tend to be highly correlated because of their common cyclical movements. This certainly holds for Y^* and P. Thus multicollinearity would effectively prevent a clear conclusion on the money illusion issue, and it would also adversely affect the precision of the estimated income coefficient. For this reason we prefer to impose the absence of a money illusion by assumption, and to define consumption and income as constant price magnitudes.

Aggregation

143   So far we have merely discussed what definitions of consumption and income are appropriate to the individual consumption function (8.6), and we must now pass on from this micro-economic relation to a macro-economic formulation that is amenable to estimation from aggregate data. This is the problem of aggregation, and it is fair to say that it is usually handled by analogy. The consumption function theories that we shall discuss below, for example, are as a rule conceived in micro-economic terms and subsequently applied to macro-economic variables without much regard for the aggregation involved. As a matter of fact there is little to be said about this subject; while we may set out quite plausible conditions that justify the aggregate relation, it is just as easy to think of conditions that would lead to an altogether different specification[†]. But since we have no independent evidence about the issues involved there is not much point in repeated and prolonged speculation about these matters.

144   The simplest form of aggregation is summation, and the linear micro-economic relation (8.6) lends itself quite easily to this operation. For the ith household we have

$$C_{it} = \beta_{0i} + \beta_{1i} Y_{it} + U_{it}$$

with the usual properties of zero expectation, constant variance and independence of the disturbance term U_{it}. Adding this relation over all N_t households in the economy we obtain

---

[†] For a systematic treatment see THEIL (1954).

$$\sum_i^{N_t} \underline{C}_{it} = \sum_i^{N_t} \beta_{0i} + \sum_i^{N_t} \beta_{1i} Y_{it} + \sum_i^{N_t} \underline{U}_{it} .$$

Now although $\Sigma_i^{N_t} \underline{C}_{it}$ equals total consumption this equation does not amount to a simple relation between aggregate variables of the type readily amenable to standard statistical analysis. For one thing we cannot separate total income, $\Sigma_i^{N_t} Y_{it}$, from the composite term $\Sigma_i^{N_t} \beta_{1i} Y_{it}$; moreover, unless we pretend that N_t is constant and that the summation extends for all t over exactly the same households, there is no reason why the aggregate parameters should be at all stable.

Some of these problems are solved if we make the stringent assumption that all micro-parameters are equal, i.e.

$$\beta_{0i} = \beta_0' , \qquad \beta_{1i} = \beta_1 \quad \text{for all } i ; \tag{8.7}$$

this leads to

$$\sum_i^{N_t} \underline{C}_{it} = \beta_0' N_t + \beta_1 \sum_i^{N_t} Y_{it} + \sum_i^{N_t} \underline{U}_{it} .$$

Unless N_t is constant for all t the right-hand side of this equation contains two variables but no constant term. The absence of a constant raises the minor technical problem of adapting the standard regression theory to meet this case; it is more important that N_t and $\Sigma_i^{N_t} Y_{it}$ are likely to move together, so that multicollinearity will lessen the precision of the estimates. Both difficulties are turned if we divide all variables by N_t and consider

$$\frac{1}{N_t} \sum_i^{N_t} \underline{C}_{it} = \beta_0' + \beta_1 \frac{1}{N_t} \sum_i^{N_t} Y_{it} + \frac{1}{N_t} \sum_i^{N_t} \underline{U}_{it} . \tag{8.8}$$

We may equally well divide the aggregates by a series that is proportional to N_t, say λN_t, and then obtain

$$\frac{1}{\lambda N_t} \sum_i^{N_t} \underline{C}_{it} = \beta_0'/\lambda + \beta_1 \frac{1}{\lambda N_t} \sum_i^{N_t} Y_{it} + \frac{1}{\lambda N_t} \sum_i^{N_t} \underline{U}_{it} .$$

The point of using λN_t instead of N_t is that we seldom have reliable data about the number of households and therefore take total population instead as a proxy variable that can reasonably be assumed to be proportional to the number of households; λ then stands for the average household size which is supposed to be constant. Upon this interpretation the last equation is equivalent to

$$\underline{C}_t = \beta_0 + \beta_1 Y_t + \underline{U}_t \tag{8.9}$$

where $\underline{C}_t$ and Y_t are the familiar *per capita* aggregate consumption and income variables, and where moreover

$$\beta_0 = \beta'_0/\lambda\,, \qquad \underline{U}_t = \frac{1}{\lambda N_t}\sum_i^{N_t} \underline{U}_{it}\,.$$

Thus the constant term is affected by the factor λ, but as we have argued repeatedly we are anyhow little concerned with this parameter. The properties of the disturbance term $\underline{U}_t$ will have to be derived with some care from assumptions about the micro-economic disturbances $\underline{U}_{it}$; we return to this question below.

145 The above argument rests heavily on the primitive assumption (8.7) to the effect that the individual relations of all households have the same micro-parameters. This is patently unrealistic, and we may give a somewhat more acceptable justification of (8.9) by considering the micro-parameters as random variables with expected values

$$E(\underline{\beta}_{0i}) = \beta'_0\,, \qquad E(\underline{\beta}_{1i}) = \beta_1 \tag{8.10}$$

and with finite variances. Upon summation of the micro-relations and division by N_t, as before, we obtain

$$\frac{1}{N_t}\sum_i^{N_t} \underline{C}_{it} = \frac{1}{N_t}\sum_i^{N_t} \underline{\beta}_{0i} + \frac{1}{N_t}\sum_i^{N_t} \underline{\beta}_{1i}\,Y_{it} + \frac{1}{N_t}\sum_i^{N_t} \underline{U}_{it}\,. \tag{8.11}$$

The first term on the right-hand side,

$$\frac{1}{N_t}\sum_i^{N_t} \underline{\beta}_{0i}$$

is a simple sample mean; the second term can be rearranged as

$$\left\{\sum_i^{N_t} \underline{\beta}_{1i} \cdot Y_{it}\Big/\sum_i^{N_t} Y_{it}\right\} \frac{1}{N_t}\sum_i^{N_t} Y_{it}$$

and the term between brackets is a weighted sample mean. The sample size involved is of course enormous – in the case of the Dutch data N_t is about 3.5 million – and if the variates $\underline{\beta}_{0i}$ and $\underline{\beta}_{1i}$ are independent as from one i to another, the variance of these sample means will be negligibly small, however large the original variances of the micro-parameters can reasonably be. Upon adopting the independence of the individual micro-parameters – and this is the crucial assumption – we therefore have little qualms in replacing both sample means that occur in (8.11) by their expected values according to (8.10). This leads to

$$\frac{1}{N_t}\sum_i^{N_t} C_{it} = \beta'_0 + \beta_1 \frac{1}{N_t}\sum_i^{N_t} Y_{it} + \frac{1}{N_t}\sum_i^{N_t} U_{it}$$

which is identical to (8.8). The passage to (8.9) upon the introduction of λ follows the same lines as before.

We now turn to the properties of the aggregate disturbance

$$\underline{U}_t = \frac{1}{\lambda N_t}\sum_i^{N_t} U_{it}$$

of (8.9). Apart from the constant λ, which raises no major problems, it might seem that we can employ the same argument as in the case of β_{0i} and β_{1i}; but if this were so $\underline{U}_t$ would virtually vanish since it is the sample mean of a very large number of variates with zero expectation. In fact this is not so, and the reason is that the assumption of independence may well hold for the micro-parameters but certainly does not apply to the micro-disturbances. These disturbances represent the effect of all neglected factors, and these include certain systematic factors that affect all households in the same sense. The choice between saving and consumption is certainly influenced by economic conditions and expectations about future conditions that are largely shared by all households; hence the individual disturbances $\underline{U}_{it}$ are not independent, and even with sample sizes of several millions the variance of their mean value is not nearly so much reduced as in the case of independence. By this argument the aggregate disturbance term does not represent individual vagaries nor sampling variation, but reflects the operation of quite general systematic factors that have nevertheless been neglected in the specification of the regression equation.

To show this in more detail we suppose that the $\underline{U}_{it}$ have the standard properties of disturbances, viz. for all i and t

$$E(\underline{U}_{it}) = 0, \quad \text{var}(\underline{U}_{it}) = \sigma^2, \quad \text{covar}(\underline{U}_{i,t}, \underline{U}_{i,t+1}) = 0 \,{}^{\dagger}.$$

For any pair of individual disturbances the correlation is ρ if they refer to the same date and zero otherwise, i.e.

$$\text{covar}(\underline{U}_{it}, \underline{U}_{jt}) = \rho\sigma^2, \quad \text{covar}(\underline{U}_{i,t}, \underline{U}_{j,t+1}) = 0 \quad \text{for } i \neq j.$$

[†] In fact the individual disturbances will show a positive serial correlation, and so will the aggregate disturbances; we here ignore this complication and act as if such autocorrelation has already been removed by suitable transformation of the micro-variables.

The properties of

$$\underline{U}_t = \frac{1}{\lambda N_t} \sum_i^{N_t} \underline{U}_{it}$$

can now be derived. It is easily seen that

$$E(\underline{U}_t) = 0, \qquad \text{covar}(\underline{U}_t, \underline{U}_{t+1}) = 0 \ ;$$

for the variance we find

$$\text{var}(\underline{U}_t) = \frac{1}{\lambda^2} \frac{1}{N_t^2} E \left\{ \sum_i^{N_t} \underline{U}_{it} \right\}^2 = \frac{1}{\lambda^2} \frac{1}{N_t^2} \{ N_t \sigma^2 + N_t(N_t - 1)\rho\sigma^2 \} \ ,$$

which simplifies to

$$\text{var}(\underline{U}_t) = \frac{1}{\lambda^2} \sigma^2 \left\{ \frac{1}{N_t} + \left(1 - \frac{1}{N_t}\right)\rho \right\} \ .$$

For the very large values of N_t which we have in mind we may neglect the terms $1/N_t$ and write

$$\text{var}(\underline{U}_t) = \frac{1}{\lambda^2} \rho\sigma^2 \ .$$

But for the constant $1/\lambda^2$, which is merely the result of changing from a per household to a per capita basis, the variance is therefore reduced through aggregation by a factor ρ, $0 < \rho < 1$, which corresponds to the positive correlation between any pair of micro-economic disturbance terms. Otherwise the disturbances of the aggregate relation have the same properties as those of the micro-economic relations, and if the latter permit least-squares estimation so do the former.

146 At times (but not in the present chapter) we shall feel free to write the macro-economic equation in terms of the logarithms of aggregate observations. Such an equation can be derived from a micro-economic relation that equally runs in terms of logarithms by the same arguments as we have applied to a linear function. The only difficulty is that by this argument the observed series $\underline{C}_t$, Y_t in

$$\log \underline{C}_t = \eta_0 + \eta_1 \log Y_t + \underline{U}_t \tag{8.12}$$

should represent per capita aggregate consumption and income by geometric mean values, whereas in fact the observed series invariably refer to common arithmetic averages. We have already come across this problem in section 126, where it was argued that the two means would very nearly coincide because of the limited variation of the individual observations concerned; after all if the individual values are identical the two means will be identical too. But in the present case this clearly will not do, and we must examine the matter in more detail.

147   We consider N values Z_i of a micro-economic variable that is always positive (as prices, incomes and consumption are) so that

$$V_i = \log Z_i$$

exists for all i. The arithmetic average is

$$\bar{Z}_a = \frac{1}{N} \sum_i Z_i \tag{8.13}$$

and the geometric average is

$$\bar{Z}_g = \sqrt[N]{\prod_i Z_i} \; ; \tag{8.14}$$

we also write

$$\bar{V} = \log \bar{Z}_g = \frac{1}{N} \sum_i V_i . \tag{8.15}$$

We shall express $\bar{Z}_a$ in terms of $\bar{Z}_g$ and the V_i. To begin with Z_i is written as an exponential and then expanded in a power series:

$$Z_i = \exp(V_i) = \exp(\bar{V}) \exp(V_i - \bar{V})$$

$$= \exp(\bar{V})\left(1 + (V_i - \bar{V}) + \frac{1}{2!}(V_i - \bar{V})^2 + \frac{1}{3!}(V_i - \bar{V})^3 \ldots\right);$$

Substitution in (8.13) yields

$$\bar{Z}_a = \exp(\bar{V})\left(1 + \frac{1}{N}\sum_i (V_i - \bar{V}) + \frac{1}{2!}\frac{1}{N}\sum_i (V_i - \bar{V})^2 + \ldots\right),$$

and since by (8.15) $\exp(\bar{V})$ equals $\bar{Z}_g$ and $\sum_i(V_i - \bar{V})$ vanishes identically the final result is

$$\bar{Z}_a = \bar{Z}_g \left(1 + \frac{1}{2!}\frac{1}{N}\sum_i (V_i - \bar{V})^2 + \frac{1}{3!}\frac{1}{N}\sum_i (V_i - \bar{V})^3 \ldots\right) . \tag{8.16}$$

The ratio of the arithmetic average to the geometric average is thus expressed in the higher order sample moments of the V_i, i.e. of the logarithms of the original observed values Z_i. If the latter have the positively skew distribution that is characteristic of so many economic variables, the distribution of their logarithms will be approximately symmetrical, and we may often assume that all odd central moments of V_i will disappear; if the distribution of the Z_i is approximately lognormal we can even go further and apply the formula for the expected value of a lognormal variate, writing

$$\bar{Z}_a \simeq \bar{Z}_g \exp\left(\tfrac{1}{2}\frac{1}{N}\sum_i (V_i - \bar{V})^2\right).$$

Regardless of such further refinements we may in the case of aggregate time-series assume that the distribution of the individual values concerned is very much the same from one year to another so that the higher order moments of their distribution are constant. The two means will then be proportional for all time periods, and their logarithms will differ by a constant. The use of arithmetic averages for C_t and Y_t in (8.12) instead of the geometric means that would be appropriate thus merely results in the addition of unknown positive constants to both log C_t and log Y_t. As far as the elasticity η_1 is concerned the specification of the consumption function remains the same; only the constant term η_0 is affected, but we persist in our disregard of this parameter.

148   In the preceding pages we have tried to show that the Keynesian consumption function may reasonably be specified as

$$\underline{C}_t = \beta_0 + \beta_1 Y_t + \underline{U}_t$$

or, alternatively, as

$$\log \underline{C}_t = \eta_0 + \eta_1 \log Y_t + \underline{U}_t$$

where C is aggregate real per capita consumption and Y aggregate real per capita disposable income. Some of the arguments put forward are highly speculative, in particular in the justification of the aggregation of micro-economic relations. There is therefore little point in repeating the exercise anew for each new aggregate behaviour relation that is introduced. As a rule we shall feel free to extend micro-economic considerations without further ado to aggregate variables.

Friedman's theory: permanent income

149   An alternative specification of the consumption function of a much more technical and detailed character than Keynes' seemingly nonchalant presentation has been put forward by FRIEDMAN (1957)[†]. This is a strictly micro-economic theory of individual behaviour which is based on at least four distinct and quite strong assumptions. Friedman's thesis has given rise to much lively controversy, partly because of the interdependence of its component parts; a seemingly straightforward test of one of his hypotheses may turn out to be debatable and open to alternative interpretations when the other elements of his theory are taken into account.

We give a brief and perhaps inadequate summary of Friedman's theory in four points. The first is that, as far as the individual is concerned, consumer durables should be treated as capital goods: their services (or depreciation) should be counted as consumption, and expenditure at the time of purchase represents at least in part investment of accumulated savings. Consumption in Friedman's theory thus differs from the macro-economic definition of section 140. This is a minor point[††], but it may render many debates inconclusive since by strict standards measured consumption never conforms to this definition.

Friedman's second point is that both income and consumption can be divided in a permanent and a transitory component. We denote these by subscripts P and T and write

$$Y_i = Y_{P_i} + Y_{T_i},$$
$$C_i = C_{P_i} + C_{T_i},$$

where the index i serves as a reminder that these variables refer to the individual consumer; they also refer to the same time period t but we shall omit this index in order to simplify the formulae. If we may take the variables C and Y to be sufficiently defined, we need only define one of their components and the other will follow from these identities. It is however hard to define either permanent or transitory components, and even harder to measure them. The underlying idea is that the individual consumer largely disregards fortuitous variations of current income, and that his decisions are based on his view of his normal or expected income over a longer period which may even extend to his lifetime. This constitutes permanent income, and transitory income is its difference from current income.

[†] Friedman's theory in some respects represents the ultimate stage in a process of refinement of the consumption function which began soon after Keynes' introduction of the concept. We shall review some of the earlier ideas below; here we only mention as a direct precursor of Friedman's theory the paper of MODIGLIANI and BRUMBERG (1951).

[††] We shall not even trouble to introduce a separate symbol for consumption in Friedman's sense.

Once the distinction between permanent and transitory income is accepted the corresponding division of consumption follows from a third assumption to the effect that permanent consumption is a function of permanent income,

$$C_{P_i} = f(Y_{P_i}),$$
(8.17)

and that there are no other relations between the four variables that have been introduced; but for (8.17) they are all independent of one another.

The fourth and final element is the specification of the consumption function (8.17) as

$$C_{P_i} = kY_{P_i}, \qquad 0 < k < 1,$$
(8.18)

which is based entirely on theoretical considerations about individual behaviour. Apart from the passage to permanent income and consumption in lieu of current variables this specification accords with Keynes' "fundamental psychological law" (8.4) but not with (8.5): in Friedman's theory the elasticity of (permanent) consumption in respect of (permanent) income is unity.

Friedman's theory is often loosely referred to as the *permanent income hypothesis*, but in practice this term may cover any selection of the separate elements involved with various shifts of emphasis. For our part we shall ignore the redefinition of consumption, which is very hard to respect in empirical applications, and concentrate on the last three assumptions.

150 Friedman's theory explains many empirical results and notably accounts for the disturbing inconsistency that the income elasticities of consumption obtained from cross-section data are generally much lower than the long-term aggregate elasticity estimated from time series.

To show this we restate the theory in statistical terms. Permanent and transitory income are regarded as independent random variables, the latter having zero expectation; we note

$$E(\underline{Y}_{P_i}) = \mu_y, \qquad E(\underline{Y}_{T_i}) = 0,$$

$$\text{var}(\underline{Y}_{P_i}) = \sigma_P^2, \qquad \text{var}(\underline{Y}_{T_i}) = \sigma_{YT}^2,$$
(8.19)

$$\text{covar}(\underline{Y}_{P_i}, \underline{Y}_{T_i}) = 0.$$

The consumption function (8.18) which does not include a disturbance term now reads as the transformation of a random variable, i.e.

$$\underline{C}_{P_i} = k\underline{Y}_{P_i},$$
(8.20)

so that by the properties of $\underline{Y}_{P_i}$ we have

$$E(\underline{C}_{P_i}) = k\mu_y, \qquad \text{var}(\underline{C}_{P_i}) = k^2\sigma_p^2 ,$$
$$\text{covar}(\underline{C}_{P_i}, \underline{Y}_{P_i}) = k\sigma_p^2 . \qquad (8.21)$$

Transitory consumption is again a random variable that is independent of all others and has zero expectation, so that

$$E(\underline{C}_{T_i}) = 0, \qquad\qquad \text{var}(\underline{C}_{T_i}) = \sigma_{CT}^2 ,$$
$$\text{covar}(\underline{C}_{T_i}, \underline{Y}_{T_i}) = 0, \qquad \text{covar}(\underline{C}_{T_i}, \underline{Y}_{P_i}) = 0 . \qquad (8.22)$$

Observed income and consumption are now defined as

$$\underline{Y}_i = \underline{Y}_{P_i} + \underline{Y}_{T_i} ,$$
$$\underline{C}_i = \underline{C}_{P_i} + \underline{C}_{T_i} ;$$

and their expectations, variances and covariance follow from the earlier assumptions. Thus by (8.19), (8.20), (8.21) and (8.22) we find

$$E(\underline{Y}_i) = \mu_y, \qquad E(\underline{C}_i) = k\mu_y ,$$
$$\text{var}(\underline{Y}_i) = \sigma_P^2 + \sigma_{YT}^2 , \qquad \text{var}(\underline{C}_i) = k^2\sigma_P^2 + \sigma_{CT}^2 , \qquad (8.23)$$
$$\text{covar}(\underline{C}_i, \underline{Y}_i) = k\sigma_p^2 .$$

By the stochastic properties of the transitory elements this system very closely resembles the regression model in which errors of observation are taken into account. Transitory consumption corresponds to the sum of the disturbance term of the consumption function and errors of measurement in consumption, and transitory income plays exactly the same part as an error of observation in the explanatory variable[†]. The only difference is that by the particular interpretation of transitory income we may discuss its behaviour in any specific application somewhat more easily.

151   If we have survey data and plot individual values or income class means of observed income and consumption against each other the elasticity of the regression line is invariably less than one[††]. An example is given in fig. 29. According to Friedman the true permanent elasticity of unity is still there, but it is hidden by the transitory elements.

The argument is best demonstrated for the case that a linear regression

---

[†] See sections 111 and 112.
[††] See sections 117–119 about the use of income class means.

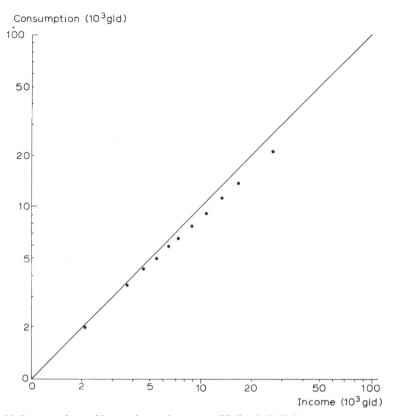

Fig. 29. Consumption and income in a savings survey (Holland, 1960). For notes see appendix B.

line is fitted to the observed C_i, Y_i, the elasticity being evaluated at the sample mean just as in section 127. Since we have

$$\eta = \frac{d \log C}{d \log Y} = \frac{Y}{C} \frac{dC}{dY}$$

for the elasticity η, we take

$$\underline{E} = \frac{\overline{Y}}{\overline{C}} \frac{\Sigma \underline{c} \, y}{\Sigma \underline{y}^2}$$

as its estimate; as before $\overline{Y}$, $\overline{C}$ denote sample mean values and the lower-case letters indicate deviations from these means, the summations extending over all n sample values. We now consider

$$\mathrm{Plim}(\underline{E}) = \mathrm{Plim}(\overline{Y}/\overline{C}) \, \mathrm{Plim}(\Sigma \underline{c} \, y / \Sigma \, y^2)$$

and upon assuming convergence substitute expected values throughout. By (8.23) this leads to

$$\text{Plim}(\overline{Y})/\text{Plim}(\overline{C}) = \mu_y/k\mu_y = 1/k$$

and

$$\text{Plim}(\Sigma \underline{cy}/\Sigma \underline{y}^2) = \text{Plim}\left(\frac{1}{n}\Sigma \underline{cy}\right)/\text{Plim}\left(\frac{1}{n}\Sigma \underline{y}^2\right) = k\sigma_P^2/(\sigma_P^2 + \sigma_{YT}^2).$$

Upon substitution this yields

$$\text{Plim}(\underline{E}) = \frac{1}{k}\frac{k\sigma_P^2}{\sigma_P^2 + \sigma_{YT}^2} = \frac{\sigma_P^2}{\sigma_P^2 + \sigma_{YT}^2}. \tag{8.24}$$

By this result $\text{Plim}(\underline{E})$ is less than unity, and in Friedman's view $\underline{E}$ cannot therefore be a consistent estimate of the permanent income elasticity of consumption. This under-estimation is entirely due to the underestimation of k by the estimated slope coefficient; in this respect transitory income has exactly the same effect as errors of observation in income. There is a difference, however, in that in Friedman's theory the true value of the elasticity is known to be unity. Consequently $\underline{E}$ is not merely known to be an underestimate of an otherwise unknown parameter but by (8.24) is seen to reflect the relative parts of permanent and transitory income in the total income variation. We recall that by (8.23) the latter can be partitioned into these two components.

On this view $\underline{E}$ should thus vary inversely with the relative importance of transitory elements in the total observed income variation, and this in turn depends on the composition of the sample, on the method of data collection, the definition of income employed and the like. Friedman analyses the evidence of a large number of household surveys in this manner, and by way of an example we quote some of his comparisons in table 17[†]. In the first example the value of E for 1944 is clearly out of line, and this is attributed to the larger part of transitory income in the unsettled conditions of wartime. The second suggests that transitory income variation is relatively larger in the United States than in Great Britain, and in the third example the differences of E between occupational groups are similarly attributed to the larger part of transitory income that goes together with income variability. All three examples lend themselves quite easily to Friedman's interpretation.

[†] We restrict the discussion to values of E alone and much simplify the subtle arguments put forward by Friedman in his detailed discussion of these and other statistics.

TABLE 17

Estimates of the apparent income elasticity of consumption from survey data, as compared by Friedman.

surveys compared	E
1. United States surveys of urban or nonfarm families in different years:	
— 1941	.87
— 1944	.70
— 1947	.85
— 1950	.80
2. United States, survey of urban and rural spending units, 1950	.82
Great Britain, survey of urban and rural income units, 1950–51	.87
3. United States surveys of various years by occupational groups:	
— 1935–36, families, nonfarm	.82
families, farm	.63
— 1941, families, nonfarm	.87
families, farm	.64
— 1948–50, spending units, independent business	.70
spending units, farm	.69
spending units, other	.86

For notes see appendix A.

152 So much for the underestimation of the income elasticity in cross-section data. We must now demonstrate that the same argument is capable of explaining the apparent discrepancy between the cross-section estimate $\underline{E}$ and the elasticity estimate from aggregate time-series data $\underline{E}^*$. We shall do this by showing that $\underline{E}^*$ is generally less than unity and therefore under-estimates the permanent income elasticity too, but less so than $\underline{E}$.

As a matter of fact the aggregate estimate $\underline{E}^*$ can be derived in exactly the same manner as the cross-section elasticity $\underline{E}$. Applying the aggregation methods of sections 143 to 145 we may introduce permanent and transitory varieties of aggregate per capita income and consumption which have much the same stochastic properties as their micro-economic counterparts; the variances are of course reduced, but expected values and correlations remain unchanged. The result is consequently exactly the same as before, viz. from (8.24)

$$\mathrm{Plim}(\underline{E}^*) = \frac{\sigma_P^{*2}}{\sigma_P^{*2} + \sigma_{YT}^{*2}},$$

where the asterisks indicate that all magnitudes refer to aggregate data. It follows immediately that $\mathrm{Plim}(\underline{E}^*)$ is less than one and that its exact value depends on the relative importance of transitory elements in the variation of aggregate per capita income over the period concerned. The reason why $\underline{E}^*$ is generally closer to unity than $\underline{E}$ is precisely that the part of transitory elements in the variation of aggregate income is smaller than in the income variation between individuals that occurs in cross-section data. In the aggregate average individual windfall gains and losses cancel to a much larger extent than they do in the construction of income class means from survey data, and the only transitory elements that persist in time series data are the unexpected income variations that affect a majority of the individual consumers. The aggregation of transitory income which is a random variable with zero expectation is indeed very similar to the aggregation of the disturbance term of a micro-economic relation; we refer the reader to section 145.

153   By now it will be appreciated that Friedman's theory can account for a variety of empirical results; it is indeed hard to think of any evidence that cannot be interpreted in its terms. As a rare exception we quote a study by BODKIN (1959). By good fortune it was possible to select from a large American survey some 1400 households of veterans who received a back payment in connection with a wartime insurance scheme. Since this bonus was entirely unexpected it would seem to qualify as transitory income. Its effect on consumption could moreover be estimated with some precision since the size of individual payments varied considerably.

Bodkin uses these data to test one specific element of Friedman's theory, viz. the assumption that transitory income affects neither permanent nor transitory consumption. To this end he fits a multiple regression for consumption as a function of observed income (exclusive of the bonus payment) Y and of the bonus itself B, i.e.

$$\underline{C}_i = \beta_0 + \beta_1 Y_i + \beta_2 B_i + \underline{U}_i.$$

Now Y still contains some transitory elements other than B, and B may for a very small part contribute to permanent income insofar as a very large windfall gain may raise expected lifetime income. But even if we grant this much Friedman's theory would seem clearly to imply that β_1 should be much larger than β_2 even if the latter is significantly greater than zero.

A proper test requires that consumption is defined to include the services of durables but not expenditure on durables. Since this cannot be measured Bodkin employs two alternative definitions. The first is C_1 which excludes durable expenditure without any provision for their services and thus understates Friedman's concept. The second, C_2, includes current expenditure on durables and presumably overstates Friedman's concept for many households. Bodkin's estimates are:

for C_1: $b_1 = .56$ (.01), $b_2 = .72$ (.11)
for C_2: $b_1 = .75$ (.02), $b_2 = .97$ (.01).

By these results the marginal propensity to consume out of transitory income is if anything larger than that out of other income which contains both permanent and transitory elements; it certainly is not zero. This contradicts the major assumption of permanent income theory at issue.

154   We return to the macro-economic consumption function which was our point of departure. Having seen how the common estimates of the income elasticity are interpreted as underestimates of its assumed unitary value we may ask what the correct specification would be. It turns out that when aggregates are concerned transitory consumption is indistinguishable from the disturbance term. Translating (8.18) in aggregate terms we may thus write

$$\underline{C}_t = k Y_{Pt} + \underline{U}_t , \qquad (8.25)$$

where C stands for observed aggregate per capita consumption. Note that this equation contains no constant term. The major problem is of course how Y_P, aggregate permanent income, is to be measured.

Friedman courageously tackles this question. He takes the line that permanent income, being essentially a subjective concept, can be identified with the income level which consumers expect to hold. The consumers will of course continuously revise their expectations in the light of current development, and it is assumed that they do so by a gradual and incomplete adjustment of expected income to the income level that actually materializes. Since we are dealing with annual data this process is described by a year-to-year revision of expected income that is proportional to the difference between current income and the expectations previously held. This leads to

$$Y_{P,t} - Y_{P,t-1} = \gamma (Y_t - Y_{P,t-1}) \qquad (8.26)$$

with $0 < \gamma < 1$ since the adjustment is supposed to be incomplete. It will be appreciated that if current income is constant expected income will gradually converge to it. Successive substitution of Y for Y_p when it appears with a lag in (8.26) yields

$$Y_{P,t} = \gamma \{ Y_t + (1 - \gamma) Y_{t-1} + (1 - \gamma)^2 Y_{t-2} \dots \}, \tag{8.27}$$

so that permanent income can be expressed as a weighted average of past income levels with weights that decline geometrically and sum to one.

Friedman actually constructs a series of Y_p from the first seventeen terms of the infinite series on the right-hand side of (8.27) and subsequently fits equation (8.25) to American data for the years 1905–1951[†]. The adjustment coefficient γ is estimated from the data by an iterative procedure and evaluated at .66; the corresponding estimate of k is .88.

While equation (8.26) pertains to aggregate variables, the argument leading up to it draws its intuitive plausibility from considerations about the individual adjustment of private expectations. In the absence of any further discussion aggregation is apparently accomplished without effort by mere analogy. It can reasonably be objected that this practice turns aggregation into a metaphysical process of doubtful validity. We shall have to get used to this, however, as the discussion of other models will presently show.

Other models; the treatment of lags

155 There is a wide variety of alternative specifications of the consumption function. Some models add other variables like liquid assets to income as a determinant of consumption; others distinguish separate components of aggregate income like wages and profits, and thus allow for variations in the income distribution[††]. We disregard these obvious developments as well as variations in the form of the function and continue to consider the role of income in a linear consumption function. Even within this limited field there are several alternative views, which are both by chronological order and by the degree of elaboration intermediate between Keynes' simple relation among current variables and Friedman's sophisticated theoretical innovations.

[†] For details see FRIEDMAN (1957), p. 147. The method of estimation disregards the simultaneous equations problem discussed below in sections 163 and ff.

[††] See for example GRILICHES et al. (1962), ZELLNER (1957) and ZELLNER et al. (1965) and the literature there cited.

156   An obvious improvement of the simple function (8.9),

$$C_t = \beta_0 + \beta_1 Y_t + U_t,$$

is to introduce last year's income as a determinant of current consumption along with current income. For many consumers, especially among the self-employed, current income is not actually known until after the year's close, and several income components like profit and interest, while established on an annual basis, are paid with considerable delay. This makes for an institutional time-lag between income generation as recorded in the national income accounts and the actual receipt and spending of the earnings concerned. We may represent this by considering total consumption as the sum of two distinct parts which are linearly related to last year's income and current income respectively; alternatively, we may define the relevant determinant of current consumption as a weighted average of current and lagged values and substitute

$$Y_t^* = w_1 Y_t + w_2 Y_{t-1}$$

with

$$w_1, w_2 > 0; \quad w_1 + w_2 = 1$$

for current income in the simple function given above[†]. In either case the result is an aggregate behaviour relation of the form

$$C_t = \beta_0 + \beta_1 Y_t + \beta_2 Y_{t-1} + U_t; \tag{8.28}$$

on any reasonable assessment of the importance of the institutional lag or of the relative weights w_1 and w_2 we may expect that

$$\beta_1, \beta_2 > 0; \quad \beta_1 > \beta_2. \tag{8.29}$$

Psychological considerations, by their nature again of an individual character, can lead to much the same model. It may for instance be argued that the consumer views an increment in income with more diffidence than this established income level so that the propensity to consume out of these two elements of current income differs[††]. Denoting these coefficients by α_1 and α_2 we have

---

[†] When all lags within the calender year are ignored, current income has a zero lag and last year's income a lag of one year; in a sense the average lag of the income variable Y_t^* equals w_2 years. Some authors refer loosely to Y_t^* as 'income lagged w_2 years' and denote it as Y_{t-w_2} or Y_{-w_2}. Note that w_2 is a proper fraction. See e.g. TINBERGEN (1939), p. 46.

[††] See MACK (1955).

$$C_t = \alpha_0 + \alpha_1 Y_{t-1} + \alpha_2 (Y_t - Y_{t-1}) + U_t$$

and this is of course equivalent to (8.28) with $\beta_1 = \alpha_2$ and $\beta_2 = (\alpha_1 - \alpha_2)$. Since the argument implies $\alpha_1 > \alpha_2 > 0$ both β_1 and β_2 should be positive, but there are no grounds for the inequality of (8.29) to hold.

157 It has been argued in much the same vein that consumers attach different weights to the highest income level they have ever previously experienced and the deviation from it that currently obtains[†].
   We define

$$Y_t^0 = \text{maximum of } Y_j \text{ for } j < t$$

and translate the theory under review into the linear relation

$$C_t = \alpha_0 + \alpha_1 Y_t^0 + \alpha_2 (Y_t - Y_t^0) + U_t .$$

As before this is of course equivalent to

$$C_t = \beta_0 + \beta_1 Y_t + \beta_2 Y_t^0 + U_t, \qquad (8.30)$$

again with $\beta_1, \beta_2 > 0$.

158 The effect of consumers' inertia and nostalgia can of course equally well be taken into account by introducing lagged values of consumption rather than of income. We need merely assume that some consumption is habitual and that the habits concerned persist from one year to another in order to write

$$C_t = \beta_0 + \beta_1 Y_t + \beta_2 C_{t-1} + U_t . \qquad (8.31)$$

Once more assuming a potent and unending nostalgia for previous highs rather than for last year's condition we define

$$C_t^0 = \text{maximum of } C_j \text{ for } j < t$$

and write

$$C_t = \beta_0 + \beta_1 Y_t + \beta_2 C_t^0 + U_t . \qquad (8.32)$$

Although we may reasonably expect both β_1 and β_2 to be nonnegative in (8.31) as well as in (8.32) there are no grounds for further specifications about the values of these coefficients[††].

[†] See MODIGLIANI (1949) and DUESENBERRY (1952).
[††] The model (8.31) has been used by BROWN (1952), and (8.32) by DAVIES (1952).

159   We return to the simple case (8.28) where a single lagged value of the independent variable has been added, viz.

$$C_t = \beta_0 + \beta_1 Y_t + \beta_2 Y_{t-1} + U_t .$$

Once the existence of institutional and psychological lags has been admitted there is no reason why we should not extend the argument and write quite generally

$$C_t = \beta_0 + \beta_1 Y_t + \beta_2 Y_{t-1} + \beta_3 Y_{t-3} + \dots + U_t , \tag{8.33}$$

treating the termination of this series as a matter of estimation, the only reasonable requirements being that the coefficients are all nonnegative and that they successively decline as the lag lengthens[†]. In practice, however, this is impossible because of the serial correlation of aggregate time series to which we have alluded in section 69: in (8.33) the correlation between successive values of Y leads to multicollinearity which effectively prevents the estimation of the coefficients and thereby makes it impossible to determine the number of terms that can usefully be retained. When the data fall short of what is required, the standard remedy is to strengthen the model by further restrictions, and in the present case this is easily accomplished by imposing a definite pattern on the successive coefficients. It is common practice to assume that they decline according to a geometric series, so that (8.33) is turned into

$$C_t = \beta_0 + \beta_1 Y_t + \beta_1 \lambda Y_{t-1} + \beta_1 \lambda^2 Y_{t-2} + \dots + U_t , \ 0 < \lambda < 1 . \tag{8.34}$$

The reader should note that but for the constant term β_0 this expression is equivalent to (8.25) and (8.27) which yield

$$C_t = k\gamma \{ Y_t + (1-\gamma) Y_{t-1} + (1-\gamma)^2 Y_{t-2} \dots \} + U_t . \tag{8.35}$$

The argument behind these two equations is however quite different: (8.34) is obtained by a technical simplification of the general distributed lag scheme (8.33), whereas Friedman's specification follows from the assumption that consumer behaviour is at least in certain respects characterized by incomplete adjustment[††].

By the additional assumption involved in the passage from (8.33) to (8.34) the number of parameters has been reduced to three, and their estimation is facilitated by the procedure put forward by KOYCK (1954). The prescrip-

---

[†]   See ALT (1942).

[††] For a further discussion of various schemes that by assuming inertia or incomplete adjustment lead up to distributed lags see NERLOVE (1958).

tion is to write $\lambda\underline{C}_{t-1}$ in full according to (8.34), and to substract the resulting expression from (8.34) itself. This yields

$$\underline{C}_t - \lambda\underline{C}_{t-1} = \beta_0(1-\lambda) + \beta_1 Y_t + \underline{U}_t - \lambda\underline{U}_{t-1}$$

or

$$\underline{C}_t = \beta_0(1-\lambda) + \beta_1 Y_t + \lambda\underline{C}_{t-1} + (\underline{U}_t - \lambda\underline{U}_{t-1}). \tag{8.36}$$

But for the composite disturbance term this is again fully equivalent to the earlier specification (8.31) involving last year's consumption as a reflection of habit formation. It goes without saying that the same simplification of a distributed lag scheme can be applied to Friedman's expected income specification (8.35), leading to

$$\underline{C}_t = k\gamma Y_t + (1-\gamma)\underline{C}_{t-1} + (\underline{U}_t - (1-\gamma)\underline{U}_{t-1}). \tag{8.37}$$

This is again indistinguishable from (8.36) but for the absence of a constant term.

Short-term and long-term effects

160 We have seen that the same intuitive argument may at times lead to alternative consumption functions while conversely different approaches can result in equivalent specifications. The reader may well feel bewildered and ask what effective difference the choice of a particular consumption function makes. One answer is to review the economic implications and the interpretation of the parameters by examining the short-term effect and the long-term effect of a given change in income. For this purpose we disregard the disturbance terms by equating them to their expected value which invariably is zero. Most consumption functions can then be solved for current consumption as a function of current and past incomes alone, say

$$C_t = C(Y_t, Y_{t-1}, Y_{t-2}, \ldots). \tag{8.38}$$

We now define the stationary consumption level for a given income Y as

$$\tilde{C}(Y) = C(Y, Y, Y, \ldots). \tag{8.39}$$

This is the level of consumption that would ultimately hold if by some curious process income were indefinitely held constant*.

---

* In these expressions we consider the consumption function in isolation although it is of course one of a set of simultaneous equations. While the attendant interrelations are here ignored in fact quite particular conditions would be required to hold income constant.

By the short-term effect of a change in income we mean its immediate impact on consumption, and this is measured by the derivative of current consumption in respect of current income, or, from (8.38),

$$\frac{\partial C_t}{\partial Y_t}.$$

The long-term effect is the ultimate change in consumption from a once-for-all change in the income level, and it is measured by the derivative of (8.39) [†]

$$\frac{d\tilde{C}(Y)}{dY}.$$

It must be admitted that this method of evaluating the long-term effect runs into difficulties when the consumption function involves the highest previous level of income or consumption, as in (8.30) and in (8.32). In both cases the actual time-path of consumption following a once-for-all income change will vary according to the initial situation; it depends on the question of whether the new development at some stage supersedes the earlier maximum or not. In the case of (8.30), which includes the highest previous *income*, the present definition of the long-term propensity to consume can be used, but the asymmetry to which we have just alluded is lost; (8.39) does not allow for different historical situations, and we must equate Y^0 along with any other previous income level to the same Y. In the case of (8.32), which involves previous highest *consumption*, our definitions break down because it cannot be written in the form (8.38). We shall therefore use a particular definition of the stationary consumption level corresponding to a constant income Y which we obtain by putting $\tilde{C} = C_t = C_t^0$, so that

$$\tilde{C} = \frac{\beta_0}{1-\beta_2} + \frac{\beta_1}{1-\beta_2}\, Y.$$

The long-term effect then follows as before.

In table 18 the various consumption functions reviewed above are brought together and the implied short-term and long-term effects shown. It will be appreciated that in the end there are basically five different functions; Friedman's model is treated as a variant of the other specification from which it can be obtained by suppressing the constant term. In some cases the interpretation of the parameters will of course vary according to the underlying argument.

[†] Since we have chosen to write all consumption functions in linear form we consider derivatives rather than short-term and long-term elasticities which can be defined analogously.

TABLE 18

Alternative specifications of the consumption function.

model	consumption function	effect of income change	
		short-term	long-term
1 simple keynesian; section 144, eqn. (8.9)	$C_t = \beta_0 + \beta_1 Y_t$	β_1	β_1
2 simple lag (income); section 156, eqn. (8.28)	$C_t = \beta_0 + \beta_1 Y_t + \beta_2 Y_{t-1}$	β_1	$\beta_1 + \beta_2$
3 previous high (income); section 157, eqn. (8.30)	$C_t = \beta_0 + \beta_1 Y_t + \beta_2 Y_t^0$	β_1	$\beta_1 + \beta_2$
4 previous high (consumption); section 158, eqn. (8.32)	$C_t = \beta_0 + \beta_1 Y_t + \beta_2 C_t^0$	β_1	$\beta_1/(1-\beta_2)$
5 simple lag (consumption); section 158, eqn. (8.31)	$C_t = \beta_0 + \beta_1 Y_t + \beta_2 C_{t-1}$	β_1	$\beta_1/(1-\beta_2)$
distributed lag (income); section 159, eqn. (8.36)	$C_t = \beta_0(1-\lambda) + \beta_1 Y_t + \lambda C_{t-1}$	β_1	$\beta_1/(1-\lambda)$
5′ permanent or expected income; section 154 and 159, eqn. (8.37)	$C_t = k\gamma Y_t + (1-\gamma)C_{t-1}$	$k\,\gamma$	k

A final word concerns restrictions on the parameters. Nearly all the β_1, β_2, λ, k and γ that appear in table 18 are marginal propensities to consume, incomplete adjustment coefficients or distributed lag series ratios. It can be argued for each of these parameters that they must be nonnegative and not larger than one. To this we can now add the further requirement that the derivatives reflecting the short-term and long-term effects, being themselves propensities to consume, must lie within this range.

An empirical comparison of the alternative specifications

161 We conclude by an empirical comparison of the alternative consumption functions of table 18 on the basis of Dutch aggregate time-series data for the years 1949–1964. This is a period of modest length which is moreover characterized by predominant post-war growth trends in virtually all aggregate economic variables; the ensuing multicollinearity makes for poor quality of the estimates. But these difficulties beset most time-series analyses, and the present application is a fair example of such a study.

In the context of aggregate data the consumption function is of course part of a set of simultaneous equations, and in estimating its parameters we must therefore call on the theory of ch. 6. We shall employ two alternative methods of estimation, viz. indirect least squares and two-stage least squares.

162 The simplest way to set up a complete model is to follow the original Keynesian theory of section 139. But as we shall see the application of this highly abstract model to empirical data is subject to some reservations.

Upon retrieving the disturbance term temporarily suppressed in table 18 the simplest consumption function reads as

$$\underline{C}_t = \beta_0 + \beta_1 Y_t + \underline{U}_t, \tag{8.40}$$

and this looks very much like a specification of (8.1). The difference is however that we have redefined C as real per capita consumption and Y as real per capita disposable income (see sections 142–144). We must moreover abandon the pretence that apart from consumption investment is the only other component of effective demand; instead of (8.2) we write

$$Y_t = C_t + R_t, \tag{8.41}$$

whereby the variable R is defined as a remainder. Apart from investment proper this term reflects the net contribution to effective demand of imports, exports, government expenditure and variations in stocks as well as the effects of taxes and of other categories involved in the passage from gross income to disposable private income. It is therefore highly hazardous (if not downright wrong) to complete the analogy with the Keynesian model by writing, as in (8.3),

$$R_t \text{ is autonomous}.$$

163 If we nevertheless take this step and regard R as a predetermined variable the estimation problem is easily solved by the use of indirect least squares of section 99. The complete system consists of two equations and contains two jointly dependent variables, C and Y, and one predetermined variable, R. Upon eliminating the identity (8.41) and either C or Y the reduced form is found to consist of a single equation with the remaining dependent variable and the sole predetermined variable, viz.

$$\underline{Y}_t = \pi_0 + \pi_1 R_t + \underline{V}_t \tag{8.42}$$

or alternatively

$$\underline{C}_t = \pi_0 + \pi_2 R_t + \underline{V}_t \tag{8.43}$$

with

$$\pi_0 = \frac{\beta_0}{1-\beta_1}, \quad \pi_1 = \frac{1}{1-\beta_1}, \quad \pi_2 = \frac{\beta_1}{1-\beta_1},$$

and

$$\underline{V}_t = \frac{1}{1-\beta_1} \underline{U}_t .$$

If the $\underline{U}_t$ satisfy the standard assumptions of least-squares regression theory the $\underline{V}_t$ will do so too, and least-squares estimates of π_1 or π_2 can validly be derived from (8.42) or (8.43); since R is defined as a remainder in (8.41), observed values are easily obtained by taking the difference of Y and C. In this simple case we need no matrix algebra to see that the parameters of (8.40) are just identified and can be derived from the estimates of π_0 and π_1 of (8.42) or from the estimates of π_0 and π_2 of (8.43)[†].

164   The same argument applies to the other consumption functions of table 18. They all include a lagged variable which we denote by Z_t and treat as if it were predetermined. The system therefore consists of two equations, the consumption function

$$\underline{C}_t = \beta_0 + \beta_1 Y_t + \beta_2 Z_t + \underline{U}_t \tag{8.44}$$

and the same identity (8.41) as before. Solving for C we obtain the reduced-form equation

$$\underline{C}_t = \pi_0 + \pi_1 R_t + \pi_2 Z_t + \underline{V}_t \tag{8.45}$$

with

$$\pi_0 = \frac{\beta_0}{1-\beta_1}, \quad \pi_1 = \frac{\beta_1}{1-\beta_1}, \quad \pi_2 = \frac{\beta_2}{1-\beta_1}$$

and

$$\underline{V}_t = \frac{1}{1-\beta_1} \underline{U}_t$$

As before, indirect least-squares estimation is readily seen to be feasible. We omit the alternative but completely equivalent procedure of solving for Y.

[†]   The reduced form parameter π_1 is of course known in economics as the multiplier. Inspection will show that the indirect estimation of β_1 leads to identically the same estimate whether we use (8.42) or (8.43), provided the data employed satisfy (8.41) (as they must do by our definition of R_t).

165 The least-squares estimation of the reduced form is based on certain assumptions in respect of the structural equation (8.44) to the effect (i) that its disturbance term has the requisite properties and (ii) that the variable Z_t is not correlated with this disturbance and hence predetermined. But in the present case (8.44) does not always represent consumer behaviour directly, as a structural equation should do; the consumption functions of table 18 are indeed at times more like reduced-form equations since they are derived by algebraical manipulation from different underlying behaviour relations. In such cases the disturbance is of course transformed along with the other variables and this can have awkward consequences. We refer to the incomplete adjustment process of section 154 and to Koyck's device for dealing with distributed lags of section 159. These models lead to equations (8.36) and (8.37). Now the composite disturbances of these expressions contain $\underline{U}_{t-1}$ (where $\underline{U}_t$ refers to the underlying behaviour relation) and hence cannot be independent of $\underline{C}_{t-1}$. This lagged variable is therefore not predetermined. In the second place, the disturbances of (8.36) and (8.37) are not serially independent unless the original disturbances follow a particular autocorrelation scheme. Since the $\underline{V}_t$ take their properties from the $\underline{U}_t$ of (8.44) these complications extend immediately to the reduced form[†].

In the present case we disregard both theoretical considerations and treat autocorrelation of the disturbances empirically. The reduced-form equation (8.45) has been fitted by least-squares regression for the six alternative specifications of table 18, i.e. with the variable Z suppressed in specification 1, various variables substituted for Z in numbers 1–5', and no constant term in specification 5'. We have next computed the residuals and constructed the Durbin-Watson statistic mentioned in section 69 to test for serial independence of the disturbances. The resulting values are shown in table 19; although the test statistic by a narrow margin fails to register significance in one instance, they all point to positive autocorrelation. We have therefore adopted the device of section 69 and recast all equations in terms of first differences.

In the absence of a trend variable the passage to year-to-year differences suppresses the constant terms. This holds for π_0 of the reduced-form equation (8.45) and for β_0 of the consumption function (8.44) alike, and it has the unexpected consequence of removing the distinction between the specifications 5 and 5' of table 18. As we turn to empirical application the numerous

---

[†] See Koyck (1954), Klein (1960) and Griliches (1967). Conceivably a theoretical analysis along these lines may serve to distinguish between alternative theories that are represented by the same specification in table 18.

TABLE 19

Indirect least-squares estimates of propensities to consume (Holland, 1948–1964).

model (as in table 18)		Durbin-Watson $\underline{d}^1$)	estimates of propensity to consume[2]) short-term	long-term
1	simple keynesian	.45 (14) **	.19 (.20)	
2	simple lag (income)	.92 (13) **	.10 (.12)	.63 (.12)
3	previous high (income)	.90 (13) **	.10 (.16)	.64 (.13)
4	previous high (consumption)	1.10 (13) **	.15 (.16)	.43 (.14)
5	simple lag (consumption), distributed lag (income)	1.38 (13) *	.07 (.19)	.25 (.50)
5′	permanent or expected income	· 1.41 (14) n.s.		

[1]) Test statistic for autocorrelation of disturbances of the reduced-form equation for consumption; significant positive autocorrelation * at 5 % level, ** at 1 % level. Degrees of freedom in brackets

[2]) Based on first-difference regression equations.

theoretical ideas discussed earlier can be summarized in five distinct consumption functions only.

166   An empirical comparison of these five functions must ultimately turn on the values of the short-term and long-term marginal propensities to consume to which they lead. We present these estimates, together with their standard errors, in table 19, omitting the intermediate results of the tedious calculations by which they have been derived. These involve two successive transformations of the regression estimates p_1 and p_2 of the first-difference equivalent of (8.45), the constant term π_0 being suppressed: at first we obtain the estimates $\underline{b}_1$ and $\underline{b}_2$ of β_1 and β_2 of (8.44) from the reduced-form estimates, and next we translate $\underline{b}_1$ and $\underline{b}_2$ into short-term and long-term effects according to the formulae given in table 18. The standard errors follow from repeated application of the approximation formula of section 75.

The results are very disappointing. To begin with the estimates have very large standard errors. This is understandable since they are based on a series of first differences from a period characterized by a strong and persistent trend; such observations cannot be expected to show much independent variation. The lack of precision is therefore largely due to the nature of the data, and not so much to the method employed. What is worse, however, is that both short-term and long-term estimates are consistently much too low to be acceptable. This is probably due to the error that we have committed in treating the residual expenditure variable R as if it were predetermined like the autonomous investment I of Keynes' theory. By its definition R is a composite of many macro-economic aggregates; by the construction of its "observed" values, which were obtained by subtracting C from Y, it may however be expected to vary inversely with the disturbance $\underline{U}$ rather than to be independent of the unaccountable elements of consumption which this term represents. As inspection of the simple case of section 163 will show such a negative covariance of R and $\underline{U}$ will explain the low values of $\underline{b}_1$ and $\underline{b}_2$, and therefore of the short-term and long-term effects, that we have obtained.

In short, this exercise casts reflections on the data and on the method, but it certainly does not contribute to a proper appreciation of the alternative consumption models.

167 Faced with the failure of the indirect least-squares approach we turn to the alternative method of two-stage least-squares estimation described in section 103. Instead of closing the consumption function model by the familiar national income identity (or a variant thereof) we regard the consumption functions of table 18 each in turn as part of a much larger model of the Dutch economy. This model can be left unspecified but for the predetermined variables that enter into it – i.e. the ultimate autonomous determinants of the economic process under consideration. As such we have selected three expenditure categories, viz. (i) exports, (ii) government consumption and (iii) net government investment. The reduced-form equation relating the variable Y to these three variables is estimated by least-squares regression, and the estimated values, say Y^*, according to the regression coefficients obtained are substituted for Y in the second stage least-squares regression analysis of equation (8.45). This procedure has again been carried out in terms of first differences of all variables, so that the analysis is in this respect comparable to the indirect least-squares estimation; the reason for this was that the first stage regression, i.e. the reduced-form equation for Y, already showed significant positive autocorrelation. Once more, the change to first differences suppresses all constant terms and removes the distinction between the models 5 and 5' of table 18.

The results, again presented by the estimated short-term and long-term effects, are shown in table 20. As before, the estimates have large standard errors, especially in the case of models 4 and 5 where previous consumption levels enter into the equation; the general lack of variation of the data that we have already mentioned in connection with the preceding analysis is here worsened by strong multicollinearity. But while we cannot hope to improve

TABLE 20

Two-stage least-squares estimates of propensities to consume (Holland, 1946–1964).

model	estimates of propensity to consume	
(as in table 18)	short-term	long-term
1 simple keynesian	.65 (.20)	
2 simple lag (income)	.33 (.18)	.79 (.15)
3 previous high (income)	.31 (.18)	.79 (.15)
4 previous high (consumption)	.39 (.23)	.77 (.37)
5 simple lag (consumption), distributed lag (income) 5′ permanent or expected income	.35 (.20)	.77 (.39)

on the quality of the data it is gratifying to find that the strong downward bias of the former estimates has disappeared now we are using a better method of estimation. The propensities to consume are still somewhat lower than one would expect, but they are not unacceptable; in assessing the short-term effects it must be borne in mind that the mere distinction between short-term and long-term effects will in general depress the former below the value that holds in the simple Keynesian model.

The similarity between the estimates for the various alternative consumption function theories is very striking indeed. If we had hoped to judge them by the plausibility of their empirical results we would be severely disappointed, for their performances in this respect differ hardly at all. This does not mean that the theories are indistinguishable, but it does mean that they are indistinguishable on the basis of the poor aggregate data that are generally available. We can conclude that in this field at least the further refinement of economic theory is of little help unless it is matched by a marked improvement in the available empirical evidence.

CHAPTER 9

Demand analysis

The origins of demand analysis

168 Demand analysis offers the earliest example of the application of linear regression to aggregate economic data. This example was set by MOORE (1914) in the early years of this century, and Moore's work established a tradition of which some traces persist to the present day. We shall see that this is not a matter of sentiment alone.

The starting point of demand analysis is the wish to give empirical substance to the classical model of price determination. The neat Marshallian analysis of the operation of a market in terms of a demand schedule and a supply schedule naturally invites attempts to establish the slopes of these curves. The very minimum required for such a study is however that price and quantity data are available, and this has tended to restrict the field very largely to agricultural commodities. Since these commodities are often traded in bulk on well organised markets, statistics of quoted prices are easily available; in many instances quantity data can be obtained from authoritative estimates of home supply, if necessary supplemented by foreign trade returns of imports and exports. Historically, at least, the collection of price and quantity data for staple agricultural products was very much easier than for manufactured products. Quantity data of the latter are often simply nonexistent; competitive considerations may hinder the collection and publication of trade figures about individual commodities like shoes or stockings, and when we turn to larger categories like footwear or clothing, output is so heterogeneous that a measure of quantity is hard to find. In respect of prices there is so much heterogeneity even within a single product that no uniform quoted price exists. For most manufactured goods we must therefore have recourse to price indices and total expenditure series for vast commodity groups such as clothing, household goods, electrical appliances and the like. Data of this type are not spontaneously observed (as the price and quantity on agricultural markets were) and their construction is a comparatively recent innovation[†].

169   In the past, therefore, the availability of price and quantity data has oriented the study of the classical market mechanism towards agricultural produce; and this in turn is the reason why there is a substantial body of demand analysis but little analysis of supply. Demand and supply are of course the classical example of simultaneous equations – we have used them as such in ch. 6 – and the question of identification therefore arises. It so happens that in the case of agricultural products the demand elasticity can be identified and estimated by simple methods while the supply curve is much more elusive. Rather rashly we may even say that the availability of similar data about manufactured goods would have led to the widespread estimation of supply elasticities.

The basic model; Schultz's method

170   We return to the basic model of price and quantity determination of section 82 and make two minor technical modifications. First we adopt the almost universal usage of taking logarithms of price and quantity, or indeed of all variables, so that the linear slope coefficients are elasticities. We also suppress the constant terms in all relations by taking deviations from the sample mean for all observed variables. We use lower-case roman letters to denote such deviations from the mean of logarithms, i.e.

$$z_i = \left\{ \log Z_i - \frac{1}{n} \sum_i \log Z_i \right\}.$$

The structural relations now read as

(demand) $\underline{q}_i = \beta p_i + \underline{u}_i \,, \qquad \beta < 0 \,,$ (9.1)

(supply) $\underline{q}_i = \gamma p_i + \underline{v}_i, \qquad \gamma > 0 \,,$ (9.2)

and β and γ are elasticities of demand and supply respectively. We can reasonably assume that the disturbances $\underline{U}$ and $\underline{V}$, which are here represented by the deviations from the mean

$$\underline{u}_i = \underline{U}_i - \frac{1}{n} \Sigma \underline{U}_i \,, \quad \underline{v}_i = \underline{V}_i - \frac{1}{n} \Sigma \underline{V}_i \,,$$

each meet the standard assumptions of the regression model and that they moreover are independent of one another. If we solve the model for p and q we obtain the reduced form

$$\underline{p}_i = \frac{\underline{u}_i - \underline{v}_i}{\gamma - \beta} \,,$$

$$\underline{q}_i = \frac{\gamma \underline{u}_i - \beta \underline{v}_i}{\gamma - \beta} \,. \tag{9.3}$$

The structural relations (9.1) and (9.2) can, if this is desired, be derived from individual demand and supply schedules by aggregation along the lines of section 143 and following. But since their specification has been dictated by convenience and involves no considerations of individual behaviour we may equally well postulate these equations at once as descriptions of aggregate market phenomena.

171   In section 97 we have argued in quite general terms that the structural equations of a simultaneous equations model do not in general admit of estimation by direct regression because the right-hand variables may not be independent of the disturbance term. In the present instance $\underline{p}_i$ is seen by (9.3) to be dependent upon both $\underline{u}_i$ and $\underline{v}_i$, and consequently neither (9.1) nor (9.2) satisfy the basic requirement of the regression model. In fact the erroneous application of least-squares regression yields the statistic

$$\underline{\delta} = \frac{\Sigma \underline{pq}}{\Sigma \underline{p}^2} \tag{9.4}$$

which is a consistent estimate of neither β nor γ. Upon substitution of (9.3) we find

$$\underline{\delta} = \frac{\gamma \Sigma \underline{u}^2 - (\gamma + \beta) \Sigma \underline{uv} + \beta \Sigma \underline{v}^2}{\Sigma \underline{u}^2 - 2 \Sigma \underline{uv} + \Sigma \underline{v}^2} \,,$$

and when we recall the assumed independence of $\underline{U}_i$ and $\underline{V}_i$ and introduce a self-evident notation for their variances we obtain

$$\text{Plim}(\underline{\delta}) = \frac{\gamma\sigma_u^2 + \beta\sigma_v^2}{\sigma_u^2 + \sigma_v^2}.$$ (9.5)

This confirms that in general $\underline{\delta}$ is a mongrel estimate involving both β and γ which will serve for neither elasticity.

172   There are, however, certain particular conditions in which $\underline{\delta}$ may still provide an acceptable estimate of the demand elasticity β, and these conditions are in large part present in the demand studies of Moore's disciple SCHULTZ (1938). In order to appreciate this point we must briefly review the method adopted in these painstaking investigations of the demand for staple agricultural commodities. Schultz uses simple least-squares regression estimates of quantity on price, but he does so only after having taken a number of preliminary precautions. The first is that the price P is defined as a relative price, i.e. quoted prices are deflated by the general price index. In the second place the quantity data are expressed on a per capita basis. Thirdly, a trend line is fitted to either variable separately and the variables that enter into the regression equations are defined as deviations from the fitted trend. Finally, Schultz distinguishes three historical periods–1875–1895, 1895–1914 and 1915–1929–each of which corresponds to a definite phase in the business cycles of these years, and separate analyses are made for each period in turn.

The result of all these preliminary operations is that the main factors making for shifts of the demand schedule are eliminated. The first two corrections of the data take care of variations in the general price level and of population movements; the effect of changes in income is taken up by the trend factor. Schultz's method of removing trends from variables is equivalent to the introduction of a suitably defined trend factor into a (multiple) regression equation for the original variables, as has been shown by FRISCH and WAUGH (1933); by the restriction of the analysis to separate periods that each correspond to an upswing or a downswing of the larger cyclical movements, this trend factor will fairly represent the variations of the income level. In short, the extensive preparations made by Schultz permit the observation of the demand curve under very nearly *ceteris paribus* conditions: the factors that may cause demand shifts are not neglected but effectively eliminated from the data under review. As we have explained earlier in section 77 this will naturally reduce the variance of the disturbance concerned, i.e. of $\underline{U}$, but not of $\underline{V}$. The point is that Schultz's efforts are uniquely aimed at the demand curve and that he does not take the least trouble to eliminate shifts of the supply curve. We may therefore confidently expect that

$$\sigma_u^2 \ll \sigma_v^2 \, ^\dagger \; . \tag{9.6}$$

The second point which saves Schultz's estimates from serious error is the fact that during the periods under review the supply of agricultural crops was virtually perfectly inelastic; in the absence of any regulation of the commodity markets the quantity supplied was a matter of acreage and harvests alone, and neither was dependent upon the current price. This means that in the present formulation we may put

$$\gamma = 0$$

so that (9.5) is reduced to

$$\text{Plim}(\underline{\delta}) = \frac{\beta \sigma_v^2}{\sigma_u^2 + \sigma_v^2} \; . \tag{9.7}$$

When we now take (9.6) into consideration we find

$$\text{Plim}(\underline{\delta}) \sim \beta$$

so that the least-squares regression coefficient $\underline{\delta}$ of (9.4) is at least approximately an acceptable estimate of the elasticity of demand.

Leaving aside further refinements of Schultz's analyses (such as the introduction of the price of substitutes and the estimation of cross price elasticities) we present some of his estimates of the price elasticity of demand in table 21. The main empirical result is that demand for agricultural products is price inelastic; the major methodological finding is that the demand elasticity is by and large stable, and that its empirical determination is feasible.

173 The fact that only special circumstances permit the estimation of demand elasticities in this manner has not always been recognized. A notorious example is the attempt by MOORE (1914) to estimate the demand elasticity of pig iron by the least-squares regression coefficient $\underline{\delta}$ of (9.4). In this case shifts in the demand curve, induced by the cyclical behaviour

---

† The question of the units of measurement of these variances does not arise; by (9.1) and (9.2) $\underline{U}$ and $\underline{V}$ both refer to the same variable (i.e. $\underline{q}$), and their variances are therefore necessarily expressed in the same unit.

TABLE 21

Schultz's estimates of price elasticities of demand (United States, 1875–1929).

commodity	period		
	1875–1895	1896–1914	1915–1929 (excl. 1917–1921)
wheat	−.03 (.26)	−.15 (.16)	−.08 (.04)
barley	−.13 (.11)	−.22 (.12)	−.42 (.20)
sugar	−.40 (.12)	−.26 (.08)	−.28 (.09)
cotton	−.37 (.17)	−.32 (.11)	[1])
rye	−.36 (.17)	−.43 (.14)	−2.40 (.45)
potatoes	−.66 (.04)	−.59 (.07)	−.31 (0.3)
oats	−.62 (.14)	−.73 (.13)	−.54 (.42)
corn	−.76 (.11)	−.68 (.07)	−.48 (.15)
hay	−.78[2])	−.66 (.15)	−.62 (.28)
buckwheat	−1.32 (.25)	−.60 (.35)	−1.20 (.43)

[1]) estimated price elasticity positive

[2]) arbitrary adjustment of dependent variable precludes the calculation of standard error.
For further notes see appendix A.

of investement, are quite likely, while the supply schedule may be expected to be reasonably stable; moreover there are reasons to believe that the elasticity of demand is small. Hence we have

$$\sigma_u^2 \gg \sigma_v^2, \qquad |\beta| \text{ is small},$$

and upon substitution into (9.5) we find

$$\text{Plim}(\underline{\delta}) \sim \gamma.$$

Under these conditions $\underline{\delta}$ is therefore an approximate estimate of the elasticity of supply rather than of the demand elasticity, and this explains why a positive estimate was found. Moore however took this as evidence of a peculiar demand curve with a positive slope. The misunderstanding was cleared up in a neat diagrammatical demonstration by WORKING (1927), long before simultaneous equations were discovered in the late 1940's.

The estimation of price flexibilities

174   The observation that the supply of agricultural products is for practical purposes perfectly inelastic has led to an alternative method of estimating demand elasticities which has superseded Schultz's approach. The basis of these analyses is that the quantity supplied, being independent of current price, is a predetermined variable–either exogenous or of the lagged endogenous type by being related to last year's price. The appropriate method of estimation follows immediately.

As an example we take the demand studies of Fox (1958). Instead of eliminating demand shifts from the data (as Schultz did) Fox includes the shift factors in the demand equation. On the face of it his structural relation should therefore read as

$$q_i = \beta p_i + \eta y_i + \lambda z_i + u_i \, . \tag{9.8}$$

As before, lower-case roman letters stand for deviations from the mean of logarithms, so that the parameters are elasticities; y is income and z is any other factor making for demand shifts, such as the supply of substitute commodities, depending upon the product under review.

The complement of the demand equation is not a supply equation but the statement

q is predetermined .

It follows at once that in writing down (9.8) we have erred in treating q_i as a dependent (and thereby stochastic) variable; the only dependent variable of this single equation model is p_i and the demand curve should have been written as

$$q_i = \beta \underline{p}_i + \eta y_i + \lambda z_i + u_i \ ^\dagger. \tag{9.9}$$

Transferring $\underline{p}_i$ to the left-hand side we obtain the reduced form

$$\underline{p}_i = \pi_1 q_i + \pi_2 y_i + \pi_3 z_i + \underline{v}_i \tag{9.10}$$

with

$$\pi_1 = 1/\beta, \quad \pi_2 = -\eta/\beta, \quad \pi_3 = -\lambda/\beta, \quad \underline{v}_i = -\underline{u}_i/\beta \, .$$

Since all variables on the right of (9.10) are predetermined, the reduced form parameters π can be estimated by least-squares regression; moreover it is clear that identification is no problem and that the corresponding structural estimates are readily derived.

In economics the situation of the present model is of course known as a market that operates by price adjustment as opposed to the case where the

---

† If the reader has difficulty in accepting this he may find it helpful to retrace the argument on the basis of an initial distinction between quantity demanded and quantity supplied which is eliminated by the introduction of market equilibrium, as in section 82.

price is set and quantity varies. The reduced-form coefficient π_1 is indeed so familiar that it is known by a name of its own as the *price flexibility of demand*.

175 The estimation of the demand elasticity β by taking the inverse of the estimated price flexibility is of course tantamount to the use of the second regression in a simple two-variable analysis of price and quantity data alone. Temporarily reverting to the earlier model of (9.1) to (9.3), the second regression coefficient would be

$$\underline{b}_2 = \frac{\Sigma q^2}{\Sigma \underline{pq}} \; ;$$

upon substitution of (9.3), and making use of the independence of $\underline{u}$ and $\underline{v}$, we find

$$\text{Plim}(\underline{b}_2) = \frac{\gamma^2 \sigma_u^2 + \beta^2 \sigma_v^2}{\gamma \sigma_u^2 + \beta \sigma_v^2} \; . \tag{9.11}$$

The present situation of perfectly inelastic supply corresponds to the special case $\gamma = 0$, and upon substitution of this value it follows that

$$\text{Plim}(\underline{b}_2) = \beta \; . \tag{9.12}$$

•This vindicates the earlier argument in favour of the indirect estimation of β from the corresponding price flexibility. The reader may note that (9.12) holds irrespective of the relative magnitude of the variances σ_u^2 and σ_v^2, so that the explicit introduction of demand shift factors into the demand equation is not needed for the reduction of bias, as in Schultz's case. In fact y serves to obtain an estimate of the income elasticity of demand, and both y and z contribute to the precision of the estimates by reducing residual variation (see 77).

176 In his actual analyses of U.S. time series for the period 1922–1941 Fox takes first differences of (the logarithms of) the data in order to eliminate the effects of serial correlation of the disturbances; since he does retain a constant term in the regressions this is equivalent to the use of a time trend variable in the original equation[†]. For present purposes we may regard this as just another demand shift variable like z.

Some of Fox's results are shown in table 22. The main empirical result is

---

[†] See section 69.

TABLE 22

Fox's estimates of price and income elasticities of demand (United States, 1922–1941).

commodity	price elasticity	income elasticity
pork	−.65	1.06
beef	−.84	1.07
veal	−1.22	1.59
lamb	−.67	.73
chicken	−1.61	1.71
turkey	−.83	.88
eggs	−.34	.49
fluid milk	−.67	.50
apples	−1.27	1.32
oranges	−.62	.83
grapefruit	−.57	.73
lemons	−.59	.46
potatoes	−.28	.34
sweet potatoes	−1.30	1.15
onions	−.44	.44
watermelons	−1.00	1.06

For notes see appendix A.

that quantity demand for many farm products is rather inelastic in respect of price as well as of income. Very broadly the price elasticities are in line with those obtained by Schultz, although they are slightly higher insofar as Fox studies specific commodities rather than the large staple products analysed by Schultz; equally broadly, the income elasticities are in line with the low values for foodstuffs obtained from budget survey data in ch. 7. We note that exceptions go together in the sense that commodities that are price-elastic (and therefore presumably have easy substitutes) tend to have high income elasticities as well, so that they would rank as luxuries. We must add, however, that there is no evidence that this is a general connection which would hold also for other commodities outside the group of farm products.

Single-commodity studies: concluding remarks

177 The low quantity demand elasticities of many farm products have important consequences. In high-income countries like the United States or Western Europe demand for staple foodstuffs has ceased to increase with further rises in income; the increase in expenditure is confined to a shift towards the higher-priced varieties. This is of course the same phenomenon as the quality elasticity of expenditure in budget surveys discussed in section 129. But the shift towards higher-priced products that takes place over time allows for reactions by suppliers, and as a matter of fact only part of it is a benefit to the agricultural sector since much is taken up by increased processing and packing of the products concerned. If these two elements could be distinguished we.would observe the same low income elasticity of quantity demand as before with a high elasticity (and consequently a steep increase in consumption) of the services that go with the products as they are sold at the retail level.

An attempt to give substance to this interpretation has been made by DALY (1958), who determines the income elasticity of demand for the total volume of farm products by a time-series analysis for the period 1929–1956. He estimates separate income (and price) elasticities for two distinct measurements of the volume of agricultural production, one being based on an evaluation at farm prices and the other on retail prices. The latter can be regarded as the sum of the former and the packing and processing services included in the final product; its elasticities can then be interpreted as a weighted average of the demand elasticities of each of these two components. In this manner Daly arrives at an income elasticity of .18 for agricultural products at the farmers' gate, and of .83 for the processing services; on the average these parts make up 40% and 60% of the value of the finished product, which has an income elasticity of .57 [†].

178   The main result of the low elasticities of quantity demand for agricultural products is of course that the income of the agricultural sector tends to lag behind. By the low income elasticity the general rise in real income does not result in an appreciable upward shift of the demand schedule, and the low price elasticity means that increases in productivity will lead to a reduction of total revenue. These are of course the reasons why in most developed countries agricultural markets are no longer left to themselves and all sorts of farm support schemes are imposed. These regulations may affect prices or production directly or indirectly; we mention their existence

---

[†] $.57 = .4 \times .18 + .6 \times .83$. The interest of Daly's work lies in the empirical results but not in his method of estimation; indeed his use of a regression of volume on price and income cannot be justified by the sort of argument we have applied to the analyses of Schultz and Fox.

here because they have very largely destroyed the perfect inelasticity of agricultural supply, as they were of course meant to do. Hence the scope of the simple methods of analysis we have discussed has been very much reduced, and they certainly cannot be applied blindly to present-day agricultural markets. But their principles are sound, and they still serve to show how the simultaneous equation difficulty can at times be turned quite easily.

179   One case where the justification of single-equation analyses as used by Fox continues to apply is the demand for public utilities. We have already indicated that this is one of the few industrial products for which reliable price and quantity data are available; we can now add that the particular market conditions favour the use of a simple regression of quantity on price and income. The reason is that prices are largely set by public regulation and governed by policies as to what is in the public interest rather than by cost or supply considerations. As a result price may be regarded as a predetermined variable, at any rate in the short run of annual data, and the argument of section 174 applies *mutatis mutandis* to justify a single-equation analysis with quantity as the dependent variable. As examples we may mention the analyses of electricity demand by FISHER and KAYSEN (1964), and the studies of demand for public transport by DE WOLFF (1937) and FASE (1968).

180   In conclusion we stress once more that the simple methods we have described are applicable in special cases only. In general the determination of demand elasticities (or supply elasticities) will call for a full simultaneous model that is carefully designed to meet the specific conditions of the market under review. We cannot do justice here to such highly specialized studies and refer the reader for examples to the analysis of the watermelon market by SUITS (1957) or of the poultry industry by FISHER (1958). When in doubt this is the course to adopt; it may of course happen that upon application of the simultaneous equations model the situation turns out to be in fact amenable to simpler methods of analysis. A good example of the exploratory use of a simultaneous equations model is the study of the butter market by GOLLNICK (1957).

Complete demand systems

181 We now turn to an altogether different approach to demand analysis which pays much less attention to the particular characteristics of a given market and much more to the theoretical prerequisites of a complete and consistent description of consumer demand for an exhaustive set of distinct commodities. These models, or *complete demand systems*, start from the general theoretical proposition that consumer demand for any one commodity is determined by income and by the prices of *all* commodities. Apart from income and own price all other prices are therefore introduced in the demand functions as a matter of principle. Since the available data are insufficient for the estimation of so many coefficients, they are strengthened by imposing various theoretical restrictions, and this cannot be done effectively unless all demand functions are assembled into a coherent system that is considered as a whole. In practice the emphasis is on the theoretical requirements, and statistical considerations or a careful evaluation of the process whereby the observations have been generated usually take second place. It should however be understood that these models have not been prompted by pedantic concern with abstruse theorems but by the very practical problem of how to provide full and coherent projections in the face of insufficient data.

182 We distinguish k commodities. Consumer demand for any commodity is a function of income and of all k prices, so that we have k equations, say

$$Q_j = \phi_j(Y, P_1, P_2, ..., P_k, U_j) \qquad \text{for } j = 1, 2, ..., k . \qquad (9.13)$$

As before, Q_j stands for the quantity and P_j for the price of the jth commodity. The applications however invariably refer to composite commodity groups for which these variables are not defined; in practice, therefore, P_j is the price index of the jth commodity group and Q_j is the volume of demand for the commodities concerned[†]. The use of volume variables has the advantage that "quality" shifts towards higher-priced varieties are

---

[†] These volume series are constructed by evaluating the quantities of the constituent commodities at some constant base year prices, and the price index is often obtained by dividing this series into demand at current prices. This ensures that the resulting series pass the factor test (price times volume equals value), as they must do for the budget restriction introduced below to make sense.

shown as an increase in demand. The variable Y represents income, which is equated to total expenditure; as in the case of the family budget studies of section 122, income and/or the k commodity groups are defined in such a way that the observations identically satisfy the budget restriction,

$$\sum_j P_{ji} Q_{ji} = Y_i \qquad \text{for } i = 1, 2, ..., n .\tag{9.14}$$

Finally we take it for granted that the Q_j and Y are expressed on a per capita basis and that P_j and Y are real variables whenever it is felt that variations in population or in the general price level should be eliminated.

The variable $\underline{U}_j$ appears in (9.13) as a reminder that at some stage disturbances will have to be taken into account; as a matter of fact they are often omitted altogether in the construction of the demand system and introduced only after the equations have been specified in the light of theoretical considerations. This disregard of statistical questions extends to the neglect of any simultaneous equations problem that may arise. None of the complete demand models add further equations to the system (9.13); Y and the P_j are treated as predetermined variables, and all feedback relations, from demand to price or from expenditure to income, are ignored. There appears to be no justification for this neglect apart from the fact that the models are already quite complicated without such further additions. Since Y_i is regarded as a predetermined variable, it must be independent of the $\underline{U}_{ji}$ and is best considered as a nonrandom constant[†]. Equation (9.14) then implies a side relation among the k disturbances $\underline{U}_{ji}$, $j = 1, 2, ..., k$. By (9.13) we have, from (9.14),

$$\sum_j P_{ji} \underline{Q}_{ji} = \sum_j P_{ji} \phi_j (Y_i, P_{1i}, P_{2i}, ..., P_{ki}, \underline{U}_{ji}) = Y_i$$

or, upon rearrangement, say

$$\psi (Y_i, P_{1i}, P_{2i}, ..., P_{ki}, \underline{U}_{1i}, \underline{U}_{2i}, ..., \underline{U}_{ki}) = 0 \text{ for } i = 1, 2, ..., n .\tag{9.15}$$

183 All complete demand models impose five restrictions on the system (9.13).

The first of these is that the k demand functions ϕ_j have the same mathematical form and differ at most in the values of the parameters involved. This is a matter of convenience, or, to put it more kindly, of symmetry: in the absence of strong arguments to the contrary all commodities should be

---

[†]   The alternative is to regard Y_i as a random variable that is independent of all $\underline{U}_{ji}$; this makes no material difference beyond complicating the discussion.

treated alike. This simplification is hardly debatable since it is hard to see what alternative can reasonably be put forward.

The issue is ostensibly evaded by omitting any explicit specification of the demand functions in an analysis of their behaviour at a given point, as has been done by FRISCH (1959). In this case it is sufficient to consider (i) the level of the k demand surfaces and (ii) their slopes in respect of income and of all k prices, all at some selected point[†]. This makes for a total of $k(k+2)$ coefficients, and this is indeed the minimum number of parameters required for an adequate description of the system. Since it is impossible to estimate so many coefficients from the data normally available, the number of independent parameters is reduced by additional assumptions.

These additional restrictions can at will be expressed in quantities, expenditures or budget coefficients, in derivatives or elasticities. If the demand functions are fully specified, as in the models of STONE (1954b), SOMERMEIJER (1961) and BARTEN (1964), the restrictions follow implicitly from the specification adopted. We shall here give a general formulation in terms of quantities and of derivatives of the demand functions.

184   The restrictions invariably refer to the "theoretical" demand functions that are obtained by setting all disturbances equal to their expected value which is zero. Instead of (9.13) we therefore consider the *expected demand* Q_j^*, defined as

$$Q_j^* = \phi_j(Y, P_1, P_2, ..., P_k, 0) \qquad \text{for } j = 1, 2, ..., k . \tag{9.16}$$

The first condition is that expected demand, like observed demand, must identically satisfy the budget restriction, so that

$$\sum_j P_j Q_j^* = Y \tag{9.17}$$

and also

$$\sum_j P_j \frac{\partial \phi_j}{\partial Y} = 1 . \tag{9.18}$$

These are properties of the functions ϕ_j, and as such they do not follow from the budget restriction (9.14) which holds for the data these functions must

---

[†] The application of these coefficients beyond the point of departure is of course equivalent to the specification of linear or iso-elastic demand surfaces, depending on the nature of the slope coefficients (derivatives or elasticities). But the restrictions on the coefficients which we are about to discuss will hold at the selected point only.

describe, but represent strictly independent restrictions[†]. If we think of our earlier count of the number of parameters it is seen that two side relations are introduced; (9.17) restricts the k demand levels, and (9.18) the k demand slopes in respect of income.

The next condition is that aggregate demand is as impervious to the money illusion as the individual consumer was already earlier assumed to be (see section 142). This means that equal proportionate changes in income and all prices must leave expected demand unchanged, i.e. that the demand functions must be homogeneous of degree zero in income and all prices. The derivatives must therefore satisfy

$$Y \frac{\partial \phi_j}{\partial Y} + \sum_i P_i \frac{\partial \phi_j}{\partial P_i} = 0 \qquad \text{for } j = 1, 2, ..., k , \tag{9.19}$$

and this amounts to another k restrictions on the slope coefficients of the demand system.

The two restrictions introduced above have been presented as assumptions about the behaviour of aggregate demand, but if this is of any help they can be easily derived from the corresponding properties of the individual consumer's behaviour. Thus (9.17) can be obtained at once by summation over individuals, and (9.19) follows from the simple argument that if individual demand is invariant under equiproportionate changes of income and of all prices, total demand must be invariant too.

Restrictions from utility theory

185   The next two constraints are not so easily justified. They are drawn from rather sophisticated results of the classical utility theory of individual consumer behaviour, and their application to aggregate demand functions is a matter of unsupported analogy. The theory of consumer behaviour derives certain properties of individual demand from the constrained maximization of a given (but quite general) individual utility function that is a nondecreasing function of the quantities of all k commodities. To ascribe these properties to market demand is to assume that the aggregate demand structure behaves as if it were the outcome of the same maximizing process.

[†] They do affect (and usually simplify) the side relation (9.15) among the disturbances U_{ji}, $j = 1, 2, ..., k$, which by (9.16) and (9.17) is now seen to be satisfied by their zero expected values.

I can think of no argument in favour of this assumption[†]. On this view the origins of the constraints in utility theory do not strengthen their plausibility, and they must be judged by their implications for aggregate demand and, eventually, by their performance in fitting the observed data. For this reason, and also because a review of utility theory is beyond our scope, we shall not show the derivation of these restrictions; the reader must take the theoretical background to which we have alluded on trust [††].

186 The first restrictions derived from utility theory are the *Slutsky relations* which express a rather complex form of symmetry between pairs of demand functions. We define the substitution effect Π_{ji} for the jth commodity in respect of the ith price as

$$\Pi_{ji} = \frac{\partial \phi_j}{\partial P_i} + Q_i^* \frac{\partial \phi_j}{\partial Y} ; \tag{9.20}$$

the Slutsky relations then read as

$$\Pi_{ji} = \Pi_{ij} \qquad \text{for all } i, j = 1, 2, ..., k. \tag{9.21}$$

These relations follow quite generally from the theory of consumer behaviour and call for no particular assumptions about the utility function involved. Equation (9.21) holds for all i and j, but it is of course trivial for $i = j$, and the $k(k-1)$ relations for $i \neq j$ are pairwise identical by their very symmetry. The Slutsky relations therefore amount to $\frac{1}{2}k(k-1)$ independent restrictions.

187 At this stage the general results of the theory of consumer behaviour are exhausted. The initial number of $k(k+2)$ coefficients has successively been reduced by 2 (budget restriction), by k (absence of money illusion) and by $\frac{1}{2}k(k-1)$ (Slutsky relations), so that $(\frac{1}{2}k+2)(k-1)$ independent parameters remain. Although the initial number has nearly been halved, estimation usually requires that it is still further reduced, and as the general properties from utility theory have already been used one must turn to specific and somewhat arbitrary additional assumptions. The obvious choice is to restrict the interrelations between commodity groups, and at

---

[†] The reader may well take a more sympathetic view of the matter upon reading the elegant and persuasive representations put forward by HOUTHAKKER (1960).
[††] The mathematical analysis of the utility theory of consumer behaviour is due to SLUTSKY (1915) and to ALLEN and HICKS (1934). A thorough treatise is that of WOLD and JUREEN (1953); my own favourite exposé is the mathematical appendix of HICKS (1957).

first sight the simplest proposal along these lines is to set all cross-price derivatives $\partial \phi_j/\partial P_i$ for $i \neq j$ equal to zero. To do so is to abandon all pretence at a complete demand system, and to return to the simple demand functions in terms of income and own price alone; unless the coefficients are quite severely restricted they will moreover fail to meet the general theoretical requirements that we have discussed. Hence complete demand systems are based on more sophisticated assumptions that equally qualify the inter-action between commodities, so that their plausibility is often (quite spe-culatively) related to the actual demarcation of the commodity groups under consideration.

188 The first assumption of this kind is that of *want independence* or *direct additivity*. In terms of the classical utility function this means that the marginal utility of any one commodity is a function of its own quantity alone and is thus independent of the quantities of all other goods. In con-junction with the earlier theoretical requirements this assumption can be shown to give

$$\frac{\partial \phi_j/\partial P_h}{\partial \phi_i/\partial P_h} = -\frac{\partial \phi_j/\partial Y}{\partial \phi_i/\partial Y} \qquad \text{for all } i, j \neq h, \qquad (9.22)$$

which is perhaps the most telling demonstration of its implications since it refers directly to the slopes of the demand surfaces[†]. In order to appreciate the reduction of the number of coefficients we quote an equivalent relation by which for all $i \neq j$ the substitution effect of (9.20) can be expressed in income derivatives, viz.

$$\Pi_{ji} = \lambda \frac{\partial \phi_j}{\partial Y} \frac{\partial \phi_i}{\partial Y} \qquad \text{for all } i \neq j. \qquad (9.23)$$

This takes care of the Π_{ji} with $j \neq i$, or, by (9.21), of $\frac{1}{2}k(k-1)$ parameters, at the cost of one new parameter λ which is an arbitrary (generally positive) constant. As a result the final number of independent parameters is $(2k-1)$.

Another, somewhat less tractable assumption is that of *indirect additivity*. We merely mention that this restricts the derivatives of the demand func-tions by

$$\frac{\partial \phi_j/\partial P_h}{\partial \phi_i/\partial P_h} = \frac{Q_j^*}{Q_i^*} \qquad \text{for all } i, j \neq h, \qquad (9.24)$$

[†]   In this section we draw freely on the analysis of HOUTHAKKER (1960).

so that the cross-price elasticities in respect of any given price are the same for all (alien) commodities. Upon combining (9.24) with the earlier restrictions we can once more express the substitution effect Π_{ji} of (9.20) in terms of other parameters at the cost of introducing one new parameter; we find

$$\Pi_{ji} = \mu Q_j^* Q_i^* + Q_j^* \frac{\partial \phi_i}{\partial Y} + Q_i^* \frac{\partial \phi_j}{\partial Y} \qquad \text{for all } i \neq j. \tag{9.25}$$

As in the case of (9.23) this can be seen to reduce the number of independent parameters of the demand system to $(2k-1)$.

Examples

189 We have already hinted that the applications of complete demand models are seldom distinguished by the sophisticated statistical techniques that would be appropriate. Even with perfunctory methods of estimation the computations soon become laborious, and for this reason the number of commodity groups is usually quite small. Some authors think that there is an advantage in the use of a few vast commodity groups since the assumption of independence (however defined) is more likely to apply to categories like "food" and "transport" than to single commodities within such groups. The point is discussed at some length by PEARCE (1964) and by FRISCH (1959). Both authors are more interested in the theoretical properties of the system than in statistical estimation, and neither specifies the demand functions ϕ_j, let alone the disturbances involved. In these conditions there can be no question of fitting the system to observed series. Pearce's illustration of his model for 18 commodity groups is by his own admission lacking in statistical expertise; Frisch proposes the computation of the full array of demand derivatives or elasticities at a given point from the estimates of $(2k-1)$ of them which are taken from some other study and treated as given constants. This precept has been carried out by JOHANSEN (1960) for a model with 18 commodity groups.

The applications of STONE (1954b), HOUTHAKKER (1960), LESER (1960) and BARTEN (1964) belong to a second category[†]. In these cases the demand functions ϕ_j are fully specified and the coefficients are estimated by fitting the system to observed series, usually by an extension of the principle of least squares. Since this method is seldom explicitly related to assumed

---

[†] For further work along the same lines by Stone see STONE, BROWN and ROWE (1963).

properties of the disturbance terms it is not clear what desirable properties the estimates possess. Now the system must be fitted as a whole, bearing in mind a number of intricate side relations between the coefficients, and at times these coefficients are moreover allowed to show a trend-like variation over time; it may thus be too much to ask for a method of estimation that is adequate if not optimal from the viewpoint of statistical methodology. Even on more modest requirements, the computational burden soon becomes very heavy indeed, so that the application is restricted to a limited number of commodity groups. Of the authors cited above Stone distinguishes six or eight commodity groups, Leser nine and Houthakker only five.

The work of Barten (1964) is an exception in that it is based on a properly specified statistical model, and also in the use of no less than fourteen distinct commodity groups. The latter feature requires the estimation of so many coefficients (a considerable number of restrictions notwithstanding) that Barten is led to strengthen the available data by the introduction of additional a priori information. We cannot do justice here to the delicate intricacies of Barten's analysis, and must be content to draw the reader's attention to it.

All the empirical work named in this brief review employs the direct additivity assumption (9.22) or some variant thereof; the indirect additivity restriction of (9.24) has found less favour[†]. The statistical basis of its empirical applications are equally weak.

190   Of the four material assumptions involved in complete demand systems the budget restriction is automatically satisfied because the data are made to meet it, and the absence of a money illusion is such an obvious requirement that it can be imposed as a matter of course. But the application of the Slutsky relations to aggregate demand functions and the further additivity restrictions are highly speculative, and statistical tests of these hypotheses would seem to be in order. So far, however, all we can report in this respect is a study by Barten (1967). Barten considers aggregate demand for four commodity groups (that together exhaust total consumer expenditure) in Holland over the years 1922–1939 and 1949–1961, and he concludes that its behaviour does not contradict the symmetry conditions of (9.21) that we have here called the Slutsky relations[††]. This is a considerable achievement. We must all the same point out that the symmetry conditions are not

---

[†] Houthakker (1960) gives parallel illustrative applications of both assumptions; indirect additivity has also been used by Leser (1942) and Somermeijer (1960).
[††] Barten uses a slightly different terminology.

confirmed in the sense that the alternative hypothesis is found to be significantly at variance with the evidence at hand. With the economic observations at present available it is unreasonable to ask for such confirmation;
yet this is what the hypothesis would require.

The further additivity restrictions have not been submitted to statistical
tests. In several instances, however, constants like λ of (9.23) or μ of (9.25) are
evaluated by alternative routes, and some comfort is derived from their
agreement.

191 We conclude the discussion of complete demand systems by presenting
two examples. Although we have discussed the properties of these systems in
terms of derivatives of the demand functions ϕ_j we now revert to elasticities
since these are easier assessed. Tables 23 and 24 therefore show estimates of
the income elasticities

$$\eta_j = \frac{\partial \log Q_j^*}{\partial \log Y}$$

and of complete sets of price elasticities

$$\sigma_{ji} = \frac{\partial \log Q_j^*}{\partial \log P_i}.$$

The first example, given in table 23, is taken from BARTEN (1967) to which
we have already referred above. Apart from the budget restriction that is
identically satisfied by the data, no restrictions at all are imposed on the
estimates for this modest four-commodity demand system. The result is

TABLE 23

Barten's estimates of a complete set of demand elasticities (Holland, 1922–1961).

commodity group	elasticity of demand in respect of				
	income	price of commodity group			
		1	2	3	4
1. food	.55	−.54	−.10	−.01	.26
2. pleasure goods	.85	−.00	−.31	−.22	−.20
3. durables	1.89	−.29	−.42	−.72	−.60
4. other	.71	−.12	.19	−.15	−.68

For notes see appendix A.

a quite well-behaved set of elasticities, which confirms that with such vast
aggregate commodity groups the own-price elasticities predominate and

cross-price elasticities largely reflect the income effect rather than the substitution effect of a price change. The second example, shown in table 24, is taken from a much more ambitious analysis by STONE et al. (1963). The number of commodity groups is double that of Barten, but the number of coefficients is not correspondingly larger since all the restrictions that we have discussed are simultaneously imposed; moreover these authors have longer time-series at their disposal than has Barten. The results are not

TABLE 24

Stone's estimates of a complete set of demand elasticities (Great Britain, 1900–1960).

commodity group		elasticity of demand in respect of							
	income	price of commodity							
		nr. 1	nr. 2	nr. 3	nr. 4	nr. 5	nr. 6	nr. 7	nr. 8
1. food	.26	−.11	−.02	−.05	−.00	−.02	−.03	−.01	−.02
2. clothing	1.57	−.47	−.32	−.29	−.01	−.11	−.19	−.06	−.13
3. household	1.08	−.32	−.09	−.33	−.01	−.08	−.13	−.04	−.09
4. communications	.29	−.09	−.02	−.05	−.04	−.02	−.03	−.01	−.02
5. transport	2.37	−.71	−.19	−.43	−.02	−.45	−.28	−.09	−.19
6. drink & tobacco	.72	−.22	−.06	−.13	−.01	−.05	−.17	−.03	−.06
7. entertainment	−.41	+.12	+.03	+.07	+.00	+.03	+.05	+.07	+.03
8. other	2.04	−.61	−.16	−.37	−.02	−.14	−.25	−.08	−.42

For notes see appendix A.

altogether satisfactory and their systematic traits (like the opposite signs of income and price elasticities for the same commodity) reflect properties of the demand system specification rather than empirical evidence. Many of the price elasticities are virtually zero, and contrary to what one would expect the own-price elasticities do not systematically surpass the cross-price elasticities. As before there is no evidence of strong substitution effects among the latter, but this again is due to the specification of the model rather than to the data at hand.

CHAPTER 10

The production function

Introduction

192   The production function is a highly abstract concept that has evolved in connection with specific problems of economic theory, and before we can turn to its empirical investigation we must first discuss at some length the role that it is meant to fulfil.

Basically, the production function is a technical relation between the quantities of various factors of production or inputs on the one hand and the amount of product or output which they yield on the other. These terms suggest that production is a physical process whereby inputs are transformed into outputs; the production function is however not restricted to the variations that are possible within a single technical production process but it covers the full range of all conceivable methods of production. The traditional example is that of roadworks being performed by different methods –many men with shovels, fewer men with wheelbarrows, one man with a bulldozer[†]. If we were to describe these variations by a production function with quantities of homogeneous inputs as its arguments, the latter variables would each in turn assume nonzero values as we move from one process to another. Economic theory is however concerned with quite abstract factors of production like labour and capital, and the example that we have just

---

[†] This is not as fanciful as it may seem. ZIMMERMAN (1959) quotes a study by Ritter of performing the groundworks for the German autobahnen by nine alternative methods that vary precisely in this manner.

quoted is indeed intended to demonstrate the variation of the amounts of these inputs, not of their composition. This can only be done if the quantities of various homogeneous inputs are aggregated into volume variables for the heterogeneous categories at issue, and output, which so often is heterogeneous too, can be treated in the same way[†]. Once this step has been taken the production function is easily extended beyond a single production line to cover a plant, a firm, an industry, or even industry as a whole. We thus arrive at the macro-economic production function that appears in the theory of distributive shares and more recently in the theory of growth; the national product is output, and the labour force and the stock of capital are the factors of production. This highly abstract concept is far removed from the simple roadworks that we have viewed above, but in the end it still reflects the technical properties of the processes of production. The aggregation involved is however rather obscure, if only because of the difficulties of definition and of measurement of such variables as the total labour force.

193   Given the technical possibilities that are set by the production function the choice of the method of production that is actually employed is a matter of economic considerations; the production function summarizes the technical constraints that restrict economic behaviour in, say, varying the relative proportions of various inputs. Now the main interest of the economic theories that we have named is precisely in this variation, i.e. in the substitution of one factor of production for another. We refer to the rate of substitution between labour and capital in particular, and also to the elasticity of substitution which brings out how their relative proportions vary in response to a change in their relative prices. We raise this point here because it explains why in the present chapter the production function must be understood to cover all conceivable modes of production so that in principle it allows for a wide variation in the proportions of the various inputs.

   This is by no means self-evident; one may well envisage a production function that permits no substitution at all, so that the quantities of all inputs are proportional to the level of output. This assumption is indeed employed in several models designed for other ends than the theories to which we have already referred. Thus in *input-output analysis* separate production functions with such fixed proportions are attributed to a number of industries or productive sectors; in each of these the inputs required for a given output are proportional to the latter by constant "technical coefficients". The main

---

[†] We came across the same problem in section 182.

object of this analysis is to bring out the interrelations that arise because the inputs of one sector are part of the output of another sector. A second example of fixed proportions is the theory of the *accelerator* which (at least in its primitive form) assumes that there is a fixed relation between an increase in production and the increase in capital or investment required. In these instances output or production is taken as the independent variable, and inputs or investment follows suit; the opposite point of view is taken in the discussion of *capital-output ratios*, which relate an (incremental) amount of capital to the production that it will bring forth. Similar views for labour instead of capital are at the basis of many studies of labour productivity and of manpower requirements. In the further development of these studies the simple assumption of constant coefficients (whether "average" or "marginal") has been considerably modified. But even so they do not from the very outset explicitly allow for the substitution between several factors of production as do the production functions with which we are here concerned.

The economic model[†]

194 We consider the production function

$$X = \Phi(V_1, V_2, ..., V_k),$$
(10.1)

where X is the volume of output and the V_j, $j = 1, 2, ..., k$, denote quantities or volumina of various factors of production. At this stage we do not specify the form of the production function nor do we yet introduce a disturbance term[††]. We also ignore all problems of definition and measurement by taking it for granted that we have sufficient observations of X and the V_j as well as of the corresponding prices which we denote by P, P_j. For the moment these observations are taken to pertain to production at the plant level and to show sufficient variation for our purposes; it is immaterial whether this variation has been brought about by the passage of time or by cross-section differences.

[†] We have tried to restrict the discussion to those points that are relevant to the empirical determination of the production function. For a fuller treatment of the general economic theory see SAMUELSON (1948), ch. 4.

[††] In practice this will almost invariably be equivalent to equating the disturbance term to its zero expected value, as in section 184. But see below, section 199.

The first point we wish to make is that it would be a mistake to read (10.1) as if the V_j were independent, exogenous variables that determine X. Production is not spontaneous, and it certainly does not consist of bringing together some arbitrarily given inputs and then patiently awaiting the result. On the contrary, the joint determination of the V_j, and thereby of X, is governed by economic considerations, and we should incorporate these into the model. This will lead to a system of simultaneous equations[†]. The standard approach is to assume that the producer determines the V_j so as to maximize profits W, defined by

$$W = PX - \sum_j P_j V_j,$$

(10.2)

and that he operates in conditions of perfect competition both on output and on factor markets. This means that prices P, P_j are not affected by his choice in the matter, in other words that they are predetermined variables. If a definite maximum of W exists the inputs V_j will be set by the producer at values that satisfy the maximum conditions

$$\frac{\partial W}{\partial V_j} = 0 \qquad \text{for } j = 1, 2, ..., k,$$

(10.3)

and these values (and thereby the value of X) are determined by the solution of this system of k simultaneous equations. Upon substitution of (10.1) in (10.2) these equations read

$$P\frac{\partial \Phi}{\partial V_j} = P_j \qquad \text{for } j = 1, 2, ..., k ;$$

(10.4)

in this form they are known as the marginal productivity conditions. To bring out still more clearly the simultaneous equations character of the model we may rearrange (10.1) and (10.4) into a system of $(k+1)$ equations relating the $(k+1)$ endogenous variables X, V_j to the predetermined prices, viz.

$$\frac{\partial \Phi}{\partial V_j}(V_1, V_2, ..., V_k) = P_j/P \qquad \text{for } j = 1, 2, ..., k,$$

$$X - \Phi(V_1, V_2, ..., V_k) = 0.$$

(10.5)

[†] This was first recognized by MARSCHAK and ANDREWS (1944) who put forward the general line of argument followed below.

195   The marginal productivity conditions (10.4) are here used to determine the quantities of the input as a function of given prices, not the other way round. In economic theory the same relations are however at times invoked to explain the pricing of the factors of production, and in this connection there arises the vexed question whether or not the rewards of the factors of production together exhaust (i.e. equal) the total proceeds from output. Clearly they must do so or there will be pure losses or profits. In theory this can be ruled out by the assumption of free entry of new firms to the industry; losses and profits will then be zero in the equilibrium situation.

For empirical work this is of little help for it is improbable that any set of data reflect such an equilibrium. Yet the equality at issue,

$$\sum_j P_{ji} V_{ji} = P_i X_i \quad \text{for all observations } i,$$

is often tacitly implied. This is because the rewards of the production factor capital, say $P_{ki} V_{ki}$, are treated as a residual item: while the inputs V_{ki} can be observed (if only by heroic simplification), independent measurement of the price of capital P_{ki} is virtually impossible.

As given above this is a harmless convention. But with cross-section data the economic model implies that all firms face the same prices, and we should therefore omit the index i from these and write (upon arrangement)

$$P_k V_{ki} = P X_i - \sum_{j \neq k} P_j V_{ji} \quad \text{for all } i. \tag{10.6}$$

This means that the residual rewards are strictly proportional to the observed capital inputs V_{ki}. In view of the measures of V_k employed this is a very strong assumption.

Complications

196   The model that we have briefly sketched above is of no avail unless the extremum conditions (10.4) have a single determinate solution for non-negative values of the V_j and unless this extremum corresponds to a maximum. The latter requirement implies that profits W must decrease for any finite variation of the inputs; in particular, since prices are given, equal proportional increases of all inputs must lead to a smaller proportional increase of output, i.e. there must be decreasing returns to scale. Hence the special interest accorded in economic theory to the cases of constant and increasing returns to scale, which are incompatible with the model given above; if the production function is of either type, the hypothesis of profit maximization under conditions of perfect competition is insufficient to determine inputs and output.

In economic theory this situation is met by the introduction of additional assumptions. The general view is that, as technical characteristics of the productive process, constant or increasing returns to scale cannot be ruled out by assumption. But indeterminacy of the V_j and X is inadmissible since it is patently unrealistic; in actual fact these variables take definite values and there must be an explanation for it. This explanation is found by relaxing the assumption of perfect elasticity of input supply and of output demand, i.e. of perfectly competitive conditions where all prices are given constants and inputs and output can be varied at will by the producer.

197 Although we cannot discuss these matters fully we shall take the argument a little further for the particular case of a linearly homogeneous production function. In this case

$$\Phi(\gamma V_1, \gamma V_2, ..., \gamma V_k) = \gamma \Phi(V_1, V_2, ..., V_k) \tag{10.7}$$

for any combination of inputs V_j and any γ. Hence there are constant returns to scale at all points of the production function. If a combination V_j^0 would yield a positive profit W^0, actual profit is proportional to the scale of operations γ, as substitution of (10.7) in (10.1) and (10.2) will show; at given prices, profit maximization does not determine the levels of inputs and output.

In terms of the model given above, the system of k equations (10.4) fails to provide a determinate solution, since by Euler's theorem the partial derivatives of the linearly homogeneous production function will satisfy

$$\sum_j \frac{\partial \Phi}{\partial V_j} V_j = X . \tag{10.8}$$

If the k equations of (10.4) can be put into linear form – as is the case for the common Cobb-Douglas specification of Φ – they are by (10.8) no longer independent, and their coefficient matrix will be singular. In the general simultaneous equations model of ch. 6 this is B, the coefficient matrix of the jointly dependent variables in the structural relations.

This, then, is the case to which we have alluded in section 89 where we dismissed the possibility of B being singular on the grounds that economic theory would guard against it. Economic theory does so because its object is to show how economic variables are determined. In the present instance there are alternative remedies; in the case of imperfect competition one or more prices may be turned into endogenous variables, in other situations some input or output can be regarded as predetermined. In either case the maximum profit conditions must be reformulated. We shall discuss the case of predetermined output, but not because it offers a way out in the case of constant returns; the interest of this model for empirical work is that it is often realistic.

An alternative model

198 As we have earlier pointed out in connection with demand analysis –in section 178–public utilities and regulated industries generally are often singled out for econometric studies because the relevant data are somewhat more easily accessible. Railroads or electricity generating firms cannot however vary their output at will; they are usually under some compulsion to meet demand. Output is therefore no longer endogenous but a predetermined variable representing the given volume of production that the firm must provide.

The general view is that no other changes in the situation previously considered are required, and that all prices continue to be predetermined. For the input prices P_j this can be justified by reference to the competitive character of the factor markets, but for the output price P this argument clearly will not do. This price is therefore taken to be predetermined on the grounds that the regulations governing the industry concerned usually severely limit or preclude price adjustments, at least at short notice. Finally the equality

$$PX = \sum_j P_j V_j \qquad\qquad (10.9)$$

is again often assumed. Most of section 195 applies, but instead of free entry we can here use the stronger theoretical argument that the ubiquitous regulations will not permit nonzero profits to arise.

For the individual producer output X as well as all prices P, P_j are now given constants, and the maximization of profit W still given by (10.2),

$$W = PX - \sum_j P_j V_j,$$

is equivalent to the minimization of costs $\Sigma_j P_j V_j$. To this end the producer proceeds to vary inputs V_j subject to the constraint

$$\Phi(V_1, V_2, ..., V_k) = X .$$

Using Lagrange's method for the determination of a constrained extremum we form the expression

$$\psi = \sum_j P_j V_j - \lambda(\Phi(V_1, V_2, ..., V_k) - X) \tag{10.10}$$

and obtain the appropriate minimum conditions by equating the partial derivatives in respect of λ and of all V_j to zero. This yields a system of $(k+1)$ equations which are easily arranged in the form

$$\frac{\partial \Phi}{\partial V_j}(V_1, V_2, ..., V_k) = P_j/\lambda \qquad \text{for } j = 1, 2, ..., k ,$$

$$\Phi(V_1, V_2, ..., V_k) = X . \tag{10.11}$$

This system of $(k+1)$ simultaneous equations in $(k+1)$ unknowns – viz. the V_j and λ – bears a strong resemblance to (10.5). They can even be made to look exactly alike if we consider the special case of constant returns to scale. As we have seen above in (10.8) this implies

$$\sum_j \frac{\partial \Phi}{\partial V_j} V_j = X ,$$

or, upon substitution from (10.11),

$$\frac{1}{\lambda} \sum_j P_j V_j = X .$$

Insofar as (10.9) applies we must therefore have

$$\lambda = P ,$$

and if this is substituted into (10.11) the latter system is apparently identical with (10.5). The difference is however that in (10.5) X is one of the unknowns of the system while in (10.11) it is a given constant; (10.11) consists of $(k+1)$ equations in k unknowns, but then these equations are not independent because of (10.8).

The reader should note that the last paragraph refers to a special case, and that in the general model for a regulated industry we have made no assumption about the presence or otherwise of constant returns to scale. The last addendum is merely intended to show that the model under discussion is capable of dealing with this complication, unlike the earlier one.

The statistical model

199 By now we have obtained two alternative systems of simultaneous equations (10.5) and (10.11). In any empirical application we must of course specify the form of these equations as well as the properties of the random disturbance terms that must be added to allow for the effect of all variables ignored in the analysis.

In the present instance the separate equations of either model cannot be taken one by one, and in fact they lack the autonomous character of structural relations to which we have referred in section 87. Thus the specification of the production function also determines the form of its derivatives that enter into the marginal productivity conditions. What is worse (because it is more difficult to handle) is the fact that in principle the disturbances of the separate equations are similarly interdependent.

We need hardly recall from ch. 5 that the disturbance term is a representation, adopted by the investigator, of effective yet neglected factors that have contributed to the observed values. Since the production function describes technical possibilities that are open to all firms or the same for all periods or all regions, whatever is appropriate to the data at hand, its disturbance term U_i represents technical factors that are unique to the ith observation. Similarly the optimum conditions that complete the model have disturbances which reflect deviations from the maximum profit situation.

In the case of a cross-section analysis where the data refer to individual firms further inspection quickly leads to quite involved arguments. The disturbance of the production function corresponds to individual differences in *technical efficiency*, such as technical know-how or advantages of location. This raises the delicate question whether or not this technical efficiency affects the optimum conditions, i.e. whether the individual producer allows for the value of his disturbance in maximizing profits. If he does so the disturbance of the production function will in some way or other be transmitted to the partial derivatives that enter into the optimum condition equations. Again the disturbances that these equations already have of their own now represent the firm's *commercial efficiency* in realizing the maximum profit conditions by quickly and correctly adjusting its inputs, and it is a matter of speculation whether the technical and commercial achievements (or otherwise) of individual firms are positively correlated or not. It is clear that these considerations can lead to various assumptions that will be reflected in the variance-covariance matrix of the disturbances from the set of simultaneous equations.

Ordinarily estimation can proceed regardless of this variance-covariance matrix, but precisely in the case of a cross-section over individual firms this is not so. The reason is that these firms will as a rule face the same prices, so that the innocuous assumption that the data show sufficient variation which we slipped in section 194 is not met. As a result the coefficients of the simultaneous equation system turn out to be unidentified but for additional restrictions on the variance-covariance matrix. Hence the importance attached to these quite intricate models which are discussed in a substantial literature. The interested reader is referred to the contributions by MARSCHAK and ANDREWS (1944), HOCH (1958), MUNDLAK (1963), MUNDLAK and HOCH (1965) and NERLOVE (1965); here we shall not pursue the matter further. So far these models have not been widely applied, and we shall be content to keep to the much simpler models used in the practical studies to which we now turn.

Douglas' investigations

200 Until recently studies were exclusively based on the Cobb-Douglas production function, and this specification still largely dominates the field. As a rule only two distinct inputs are considered, viz. labour (V_l) and capital (V_k), and output X is equated to value added[†]. The Cobb-Douglas function then reads

$$X = A V_l^{\alpha} V_k^{\beta} \tag{10.12}$$

where A, α and β are positive constants.

This specification combines simplicity with some attractive theoretical properties which we shall note as we go along; it also owes its widespread acceptance to the impressive results obtained by its originator since its first

---

[†] Apparently the possibility of substitution between these factors of production and inputs like raw materials, fuel and the like are ignored. These inputs presumably vary in fixed proportion with gross output or production, so that it is legitimate to measure the latter by its value added component alone.

presentation by Cobb and Douglas (1928). We shall therefore briefly review one of these studies.

201   The example is taken from Douglas (1948) and consists of parallel analyses of time-series and cross-section data. The former refer to annual data for the aggregate United States manufacturing industry for the period 1899–1922, and the latter consist of a cross-section of industries (not firms) from the American census of 1919[†].

Douglas first takes logarithms of the three volume variables X, V_l and V_k and adds a disturbance term to the ensuing form of (10.12) so that he obtains the regression equation

$$\underline{\log X} = \log A + \alpha \log V_l + \beta \log V_k + \underline{U} . \tag{10.13}$$

Least-squares estimation then yields the estimates of α and β shown in the top half of table 25.

TABLE 25

Production function estimates by Douglas (United States, all manufacturing industry).

	time series	cross-section
unrestricted estimates of (10.13)		
a	.73 (.12)	.76 (.02)
b	.25 (.05)	.25 (.02)
constant returns to scale, (10.15)		
a	.76 (.04)	.75 (.02)

For notes see appendix A.

These results show a very good agreement between the estimates from time series and from cross-section data, and this in itself is confirmation of the model employed. The estimates also come close to the condition

$$\alpha + \beta = 1 , \tag{10.14}$$

and in the specification adopted this is equivalent to constant returns to scale.

[†] While this is a fair example of Douglas' methods, its outcome represents his views of 1928 rather than of 1948; in the latter year he finally concludes from a number of similar analyses that in the case under review (i.e. U.S.A., early 20th century) α equals about two-thirds, and not .75 as in the example given here. See Douglas (1948), p. 14.

Douglas proceeds to impose (10.14) and rewrites (10.13) as

$$\underline{\log X = \log A + \alpha \log V_l + (1-\alpha) \log V_k + U}$$

(10.15)

or

$$\underline{\log (X/V_k) = \log A + \alpha \log (V_l/V_k) + U}.$$

The latter reformulation permits the estimation of α by simple regression and has the added advantage of removing some multicollinearity between V_l and V_k in the time series data; the precision of the estimate concerned is therefore somewhat improved, as can be seen in the second part of table 25. The estimates themselves are of course very much the same as before.

202 Douglas goes on to consider the marginal productivity condition for profit maximization which we have already met in (10.4), i.c.

$$\frac{\partial \Phi}{\partial V_l} = \frac{P_l}{P}.$$

In the present instance we have, from (10.12),

$$\frac{\partial \Phi}{\partial V_l} = \alpha \frac{X}{V_l},$$

(10.16)

so that the marginal productivity condition is equivalent to

$$\alpha \frac{X}{V_l} = \frac{P_l}{P}, \qquad \alpha = \frac{P_l V_l}{PX}.$$

(10.17)

By the latter formulation α should be equal to the share of wages in the total value of output, here equated (as we may recall) to value added. It turns out that the average share of labour for the years 1909–1918 is .74[†]. This is in excellent agreement with the estimates of α, and thus apparently vindicates marginal productivity theory as well as the Cobb-Douglas production function specification.

Douglas uses (10.17) and its observed counterpart merely as a check on his regression estimates of the input elasticity α. In fact the argument suggests, however, that there is an alternative method of estimating the input elasticities from the relative shares of the production factors concerned in the total proceeds. The point has been taken up by Klein, who argues that the input elasticities should be estimated by taking the geometric sample mean of the observed relative shares, and who has shown that this method is

---

[†] See DOUGLAS (1948), p. 7.

valid in the context of a simultaneous equations model[†]. Below we give an example where Klein applies a variant of this method.

203   Although Douglas' applications refer to aggregate data for all industry or for separate industries, and not to individual firms, our objections to the statistical method employed remain. Even for a whole country the available manpower and capital are not taken as given and put to work to produce output, but they are variable and their actual employment is determined by economic considerations. It is therefore erroneous to treat these inputs as predetermined variables.

Such theoretical strictures are not very convincing in view of the impressive agreement of Douglas' results with economic theory. On closer inspection it appears however that this can at least in part be attributed to a technical characteristic of the data. We shall in fact show that Douglas' results follow easily if the data happen to satisfy (10.6) of section 195, i.e.

$$PX_i = P_l V_{li} + P_k V_{ki} .$$

Since we take it that the same prices apply to all observations i, this is a remarkable property of the data. It can be rewritten as

$$X_i = \frac{P_l}{P} V_{li} + \frac{P_k}{P} V_{ki} \qquad \text{for all } i, \tag{10.18}$$

and it stands to reason that any function fitted to the points (X_i, V_{li}, V_{ki}) will at least approximately respect this relation. This means that when such a function is put into linear form its slope coefficients will reflect the price ratios of (10.18) and its constant term will be zero since it is absent from (10.18).

In order to apply this argument to Douglas' estimates we first rewrite the fitted regression of (10.13) for deviations from the sample mean as

$$\log(X_i/\overline{X}) = a \log(V_{li}/\overline{V_l}) + b \log(V_{ki}/\overline{V_k}) , \tag{10.19}$$

where $\overline{X}$, $\overline{V_l}$ and $\overline{V_k}$ stand for the (geometric) sample mean of the variables concerned. Provided the sample coefficients of variation are not too large we have

$$X_i/\overline{X} \quad \text{close to 1}$$

[†] See KLEIN (1953), p. 193–199.

so that we may reasonably use the linear approximation

$$\log(X_i/\overline{X}) \sim X_i/\overline{X} - 1$$

and similarly for the two other variables[†]. Upon substitution into (10.19) we find that this is equivalent to

$$(X_i/\overline{X} - 1) \sim a(V_{li}/\overline{V}_l - 1) + b(V_{ki}/\overline{V}_k - 1)$$

or, upon rearrangement,

$$X_i \sim a\,\frac{\overline{X}}{\overline{V}_l}\,V_{li} + b\,\frac{\overline{X}}{\overline{V}_k}\,V_{ki} + (1-a-b)\overline{X} . \tag{10.20}$$

We now follow up the argument given above and equate the coefficients of (10.20) to those of (10.18). This leads to three relations, viz.

$$a\,\frac{\overline{X}}{\overline{V}_l} \sim \frac{P_l}{P}, \quad \text{or} \quad a \sim \frac{P_l\overline{V}_l}{P\overline{X}} ;$$

$$b\,\frac{\overline{X}}{\overline{V}_k} \sim \frac{P_k}{P}, \quad \text{or} \quad b \sim \frac{P_k\overline{V}_k}{P\overline{X}} ;$$

$$(1-a-b)\overline{X} \sim 0, \qquad \overline{X} \neq 0, \text{ or} : a+b \sim 1.$$

These conditions faithfully reproduce the main results of Douglas' analysis. The latter may therefore arise because the data happen to satisfy (10.9) or (10.6). As we have pointed out in section 195 this in itself would be quite remarkable; but it vindicates the measurement of inputs and the prevalence of competitive conditions rather than the sophisticated hypotheses of constant returns or of marginal productivity theory.

Klein's analysis of railroad operation

204 An example of the correct statistical treatment of a Cobb-Douglas production function is Klein's ingenious analysis of the production of railway services by some 80 U.S. railway companies in 1936[††]. While the simultaneous equations character of the model is fully recognized, the

---

[†] The use of decimal logarithms instead of natural logarithms in the actual calculations does not affect the argument, since it merely means that all variables used in the regression are changed by the same constant multiplicative factor.

[††] KLEIN (1953), p. 226–236.

Cobb-Douglas specification will be seen to permit estimation by a short-cut method.

In this micro-economic analysis of a single industry the production function is considerably modified to meet the special conditions of railroad operation. To begin with output consists of freight transport (X_g) and passenger transport (X_p), and Klein combines the appropriate physical measures of these two categories into a single output variable by defining the latter as

$$X = X_p X_g^\delta,\qquad (10.21)$$

where δ is a parameter that will in due course be estimated from the data. This is of course much more flexible than the construction of an output volume variable by means of given price weights. In the second place there are three factors of production instead of two, viz. labour (V_l), capital, or rather capital services as measured by train-hours (V_k), and fuel consumption which we denote by V_f. Great use is made of the corresponding factor rewards. Since capital costs are equated to maintenance, there is no residual item and total rewards do not equal proceeds. Finally, Klein allows for shifts of the production function due to the technical characteristics of the transport services provided. These characteristics are represented by the average length of haul (Z_1) and by the proportion of bulk loads, or rather of mineral products, among the freight carried (Z_2). These variables are introduced with unknown exponents μ and ν into the production function which therefore reads

$$X = A V_l^\alpha V_k^\beta V_f^\gamma Z_1^\mu Z_2^\nu.\qquad (10.22)$$

The analysis is based on data for individual firms, and the economic model is therefore dictated by a consideration of the operating conditions of a single railroad company. Since this is a clear example of a publicly regulated industry the model of section 198 applies. It is therefore assumed that each firm minimizes costs by varying the three endogenous input variables V_l, V_k and V_f, subject to the condition that it must meet given transport demand. Thus the total level of output as well as its characteristics are predetermined variables. When we substitute (10.21) into (10.22), add a disturbance term and rearrange the resulting expression we obtain

$$\underline{V}_{li}^\alpha \underline{V}_{ki}^\beta \underline{V}_{fi}^\gamma = A^{-1} X_p X_g^\delta Z_1^{-\mu} Z_2^{-\nu} \exp(\underline{U}_i)\qquad (10.23)$$

or

$$\underline{V}_{li}^\alpha \underline{V}_{ki}^\beta \underline{V}_{fi}^\gamma = \underline{C}_i\qquad (10.24)$$

with
$$\underline{C}_i = A^{-1} X_p X_g^\delta Z_1^{-\mu} Z_2^{-\nu} \exp(\underline{U}_i)$$
for easier reference. For any firm i $\underline{C}_i$ is a given constant, and (10.24) represents the constraint that it must respect in varying its inputs.

As in section 198 input prices are taken as given, too, and cost minimization therefore leads to the same system of equations as in (10.11). In the present instance we substitute the derivatives of the production function (10.24), and upon adding disturbance terms to the minimum cost conditions for each category of input we obtain the system

$$\alpha \underline{C}_i / \underline{V}_{li} = (P_{li}/\lambda_i) \exp(\underline{V}_i)$$
$$\beta \underline{C}_i / \underline{V}_{ki} = (P_{ki}/\lambda_i) \exp(\underline{W}_i)$$
$$\gamma \underline{C}_i / \underline{V}_{fi} = (P_{fi}/\lambda_i) \exp(\underline{Y}_i) \qquad (10.25)$$
$$\underline{V}_{li}^\alpha \underline{V}_{ki}^\beta \underline{V}_{fi}^\gamma - \underline{C}_i = 0$$

where λ is a Langrangean multiplier, and $\underline{V}$, $\underline{W}$ and $\underline{Y}$ are disturbances.

205   At first sight the proper approach to the estimation of α, β and γ would be first to rearrange (10.25) to show the jointly dependent variables $-\lambda_i$, $\underline{V}_{li}$, $\underline{V}_{ki}$, $\underline{V}_{fi}$—as functions of the predetermined variables and the disturbance terms, and to write this reduced form in linear form by taking logarithms of the variables. The identification properties of the system can then be examined and the appropriate estimation method selected. It can already be surmised that in carrying out this programme we would run into serious difficulties because of insufficient variation of observed prices in the cross-section data.

Fortunately there is a much simpler method open to us in the present instance. Klein observes that the first three equations of the system (10.25) can be combined and rearranged to yield

$$\frac{P_{ki} \underline{V}_{ki}}{P_{li} \underline{V}_{li}} = \frac{\beta}{\alpha} \exp(\underline{V}_i - \underline{W}_i),$$

$$\frac{P_{fi} \underline{V}_{fi}}{P_{li} \underline{V}_{li}} = \frac{\gamma}{\alpha} \exp(\underline{V}_i - \underline{Y}_i).$$

Upon further rearrangement and taking logarithms this is equivalent to
$$\log(\beta/\alpha) = \log(P_{ki} \underline{V}_{ki}/P_{li} \underline{V}_{li}) + (\underline{W}_i - \underline{V}_i),$$
$$\log(\gamma/\alpha) = \log(P_{fi} \underline{V}_{fi}/P_{li} \underline{V}_{li}) + (\underline{Y}_i - \underline{V}_i). \qquad (10.26)$$

The unknown parameters on the left-hand side of these expressions can now simply be estimated by taking the sample means of the right-hand sides, i.e. by equating b/a and c/a respectively to the (geometric) sample average of the ratio of the corresponding production factor rewards, or

$$\log\left(\frac{b}{a}\right) = \frac{1}{n}\sum_i \log(P_{ki}V_{ki}/P_{li}V_{li}) \qquad (10.27)$$

and similarly for the other expression.

As we have already noted in section 202 this method is closely related to the estimation of the input elasticities α and β by the relative share of the production factor concerned that was used by Douglas as confirmation of his direct estimates. From the statistical point of view, the main point is of course that by (10.26) and (10.27) both the jointly dependent variables and the disturbance terms enter additively in the estimators. The estimates (10.27) are therefore both unbiased and consistent, even though the terms involved are not independent; but the question of independence does not arise unless we have to consider *products* of random variables, as in the case of regression estimators, and here we consider *sums*.

206   Having obtained the estimates of (10.27), Klein uses the corresponding estimates a/b and a/c in order to obtain the remaining parameters of his model; by this transformation the unbiased character of the estimates is lost, but not so their asymptotic properties. To see how the estimated ratios are used we return to (10.23) and rewrite this upon taking logarithms as

$$\log V_{li} + \frac{\beta}{\alpha}\log V_{ki} + \frac{\gamma}{\alpha}\log V_{fi} =$$
$$- \frac{1}{\alpha}\log A + \frac{1}{\alpha}\log X_{pi} + \frac{\delta}{\alpha}\log X_{gi} - \frac{\mu}{\alpha}\log Z_{1i} - \frac{\nu}{\alpha}\log Z_{2i} + U_i .$$

The left-hand term can now be constructed, rather in the manner of two-stage least squares, by substituting the estimates (b/a) and (c/a) for the corresponding parameter ratios. The difference is that this variable is then used as the *dependent* variable in a least-squares regression on the predetermined variables X_p, X_g, Z_1 and Z_2, all in logarithms. This yields estimates of parameter ratios from which the original parameters are readily identified.

207   The numerical results of Klein's computations are easiest understood if we show them in the original production function as given by (10.21) and (10.22). This reads as

$$X_p X_g^{.16} = 5.26 \, V_l^{.89} V_k^{.28} V_f^{.12} Z_1^{.34} Z_2^{.25} \,.$$

It will be observed that the input elasticities add up to 1.29, and since this exceeds unity the railway companies can be said to operate under conditions of increasing returns. Bearing in mind that output is predetermined, however, it would seem better to reverse the order and to consider the increase in inputs required by a given rise of output rather than the result of applying equal proportionate increases to all inputs. One way of putting the matter is to consider the case of both passenger and freight transport increasing in the same ratio r, $r > 1$. If this happens total output X goes up by a factor

$$r^{1.16} \,,$$

and one way of meeting the increased demand is to increase all inputs in the same proportion. If this is done they must each increase by a factor s such that

$$s^{1.29} = r^{1.16} \,,$$

or

$$s \sim r^{.9} \,.$$

The increasing returns to scale are here brought out by the fact that the required ratio increase of inputs is less than of both output categories.

Estimates of manufacturing production functions by Hildebrand and Liu

208 As a final example of what can be done with a Cobb-Douglas production function we take the analysis of U.S. manfacturing industries by HILDEBRAND and LIU (1965). This is again a study of cross-section data for individual industries, based on average firm data of various states from the U.S. Census of manufactures for 1957; its main interest lies in the treatment of technological advance and in the economic model. It is clear that the regulated industry model will not apply, and that recourse must be had to the general approach of section 194. The authors do however considerably improve on this model by eschewing the simple but unrealistic assumption of perfect competition[†].

[†] Hildebrand and Liu's work is also distinguished by their willingness to examine alternative specifications and methods, and by their painstaking discussion of the economic implications of the results; but here we cannot do justice to these matters.

But for the distinction of production workers (V_p) and nonproduction employees (V_n), the production function is of the common Cobb-Douglas type

$$X = A V_p^{\alpha_1} V_n^{\alpha_2} V_k^{\beta} \tag{10.28}$$

where X stands for value added; at times, when this approach fails to yield satisfactory results, the authors revert to the traditional form

$$X = A V_l^{\alpha} V_k^{\beta} . \tag{10.29}$$

In measuring the input variables some refinements are introduced. Thus V_p is as a rule weighted by an index of the educational level of the adult population in the state concerned. Capital input V_k is equated to the gross book value of equipment and plant at the beginning of the year concerned, usually augmented by the imputed value of rented capital goods; the result is moreover weighted by an index of capital vintage. This is R, the ratio of net to gross book value, expressed as a percentage, which represents the extent of depreciation or age of the capital goods currently used. It enters exponentially in V_k, i.e. if B_k is the gross book value (including the imputed value of rented capital goods) V_k is defined as

$$V_k = B_k^{\log R} . \tag{10.30}$$

This will be found to have some interesting consequences for the interpretation of the results.

209   The economic model is of particular interest. It is firmly based on a full recognition of the simultaneous equations nature of the situation. Since V_k represents capital at the beginning of the year it is a predetermined variable, and in order to describe the joint determination of X, V_p and V_n it is sufficient to add two demand functions for the categories of labour to the production function already given. In deriving these demand functions Hildebrand and Liu allow for several complications. To begin with they reject the easy assumption of perfect competition on the output market and specifically introduce nonzero demand elasticities faced by the individual producer. In the second place it is assumed that the optimum labour input is not simply determined by the ensuing maximum conditions, but that it is moreover affected by the size of the firm, measured by X, and by the appropriate wage rate, P_p or P_n. Finally the producer is not supposed to be capable of instantaneous and perfect adjustment of the labour inputs to their optimum level; instead, an incomplete adjustment mechanism of the type we have already encountered in another context in section 154 is introduced. Naturally this leads again to the introduction of lagged values of the labour input variable into the demand functions for labour. Altogether, the three complicating assumptions yield demand functions for labour inputs in terms of X, representing the firm's size, of the wage rate P_p or P_n and of previous labour input V_{p-1} or V_{n-1}.

Since no perfect competition is assumed, the equality of marginal product value to the wage rate of (10.4) no longer applies, and even with the Cobb-Douglas specification there can be no question of estimating the input elasticities from their relative rewards as in (10.17) or as in the more sophisticated procedure of Klein. Instead we must consider estimation in the context of a system of three simultaneous equations which, upon passing to logarithms, can be put in linear form. These three equations are the production function (10.28) and the two labour demand equations that we have described in general terms only[†] . There are three jointly dependent variables, viz. X, V_p and V_n; V_k is predetermined, as we noted before, and so are P_p and P_n as well as the lagged variables V_{p-1} and V_{n-1}. One way of estimating the production function is to employ two-stage least squares of section 103, and this is what Hildebrand and Liu have done [††].

210 Hildebrand and Liu have made separate analyses of 17 manufacturing industries, and for 15 of these they have obtained results that by their own standards are acceptable. We reproduce the production function estimates in table 26. To begin with this table contains estimates of the labour input elasticities α_1 and α_2 of (10.28) or, alternatively, an estimate of α of (10.29). For each industry there are moreover three distinct elasticity estimates connected with capital input. The first is b, the estimate of the coefficient β as it appears in (10.28) and (10.29). But because of the particular method of constructing V_k from gross book value on the one hand and the ratio of net to gross book values on the other, this coefficient does not correspond to the elasticity of output in respect of capital in the usual sense. In assessing the effect of an increase in capital on output we must indeed on account of (10.30) distinguish between two cases which yield quite different results. The first is that of an increase in the gross book value B_k while the ratio of net to

---

[†] Here as elsewhere we need not spell out what happens if the simpler approach of (10.29) is preferred and production and nonproduction labour are taken together into a single variable.
[††] They have also done a great many other things; in what follows we respect their own choice of preferred estimates from among a variety of results.

TABLE 26

Production function estimates by Hildebrand and Liu (United States, 1957).

industry	N	labour elasticities		capital elasticities			returns to scale
		a_1	a_2	b	b'_1	b'_2	
estimates of equation (10.28)							
food products	35	.32 (.10)	.40 (.08)	.31 (.06)	.53	1.29	2.00
apparel	18	.59 (.13)	.26 (.12)	.11 (.07)	.20	.44	1.28
paper products	28	.55 (.12)	.27 (.11)	.16 (.03)	.28	.65	1.47
chemicals	31	.35 (.21)	.57 (.20)	.16 (.05)	.27	.75	1.66
petroleum and coal prod.	18	.27 (.23)	.50 (.27)	.14 (.16)	.23	.74	1.51
stone, clay, glass	25	.67 (.18)	.30 (.18)	.08 (.04)	.13	.32	1.28
fabricated metal produce	32	.53 (.14)	.34 (.12)	.09 (.04)	.15	.34	1.21
machinery, not electrical	25	.47 (.13)	.27 (.14)	.19 (.04)	.33	.78	1.52
electrical machinery	22	.41 (.13)	.24 (.08)	.17 (.04)	.30	.69	1.34
transport equipment	26	.41 (.24)	.28 (.17)	.19 (.04)	.32	.84	1.53
estimates of equation (10.29)							
lumber & wood products	14		.79 (.34)	.18 (.07)	.31	.63	1.42
rubber and plastics	16		.85 (.10)	.14 (.05)	.23	.72	1.57
leather	15		.85 (.12)	.04 (.04)	.07	.20	1.05
primary metals	28		.96 (.11)	.10 (.05)	.16	.58	1.54
instruments	12		.67 (.12)	.25 (.07)	.44	1.00	1.67

For notes see appendix A.

gross value R remains constant. This may seem pretty unrealistic but it may in fact occur through an increase in rental capital. By (10.28) and (10.30) the elasticity at issue is given by

$$\frac{\partial \log X}{\partial \log B_k} = \beta \log R ,$$

and this is estimated by

$$b'_1 = b \log R$$

where $\log R$ is presumably equated to its sample mean value. Since R is a percentage, not a proper fraction, $\log R$ as a rule exceeds unity and b'_1 is larger than b. The second case is of course the much more realistic one of an increase in capital through new investment. Since this will raise R as well as B_k the effect on output will be greater than in the former case. We shall not go into the algebra of this elasticity; it suffices that its estimate is given as b'_2.

The elasticity b'_2 must exceed b'_1 since they differ by the positive effect on output of an increase in R. In the analyses under review these effects are substantial. If we measure returns to scale by summing the labour elasticities and b_2', as has been done in table 26, we find quite spectacular increasing returns for all industries, and this is indeed largely (if not exclusively) due to the excess of b_2' over b_1'. The interesting thing is of course that this excess brings out how much output is affected by the modernization of plant and equipment, i.e. by technological progress embodied in new capital goods. Unfortunately there is no way of knowing whether the large values obtained by Hildebrand and Liu for this effect are robust empirical results or whether they are to some extent due to the particular specification (10.30) employed.

The elasticity of substitution

211 Insofar as the amounts of various inputs are determined by profit maximization a change in their relative prices will generally lead to an adjustment of the proportions in which they are employed. This effect is measured by the elasticity of substitution, i.e. the elasticity of the relative proportion of a pair of inputs in respect of their price ratio. Thus the elasticity of substitution of labour and capital (by far the most popular pair) is defined as

$$\sigma = \frac{d \log(V_l/V_k)}{d \log(P_l/P_k)} \tag{10.31}$$

where the implied relation of (V_l/V_k) to (P_l/P_k) is understood to follow from strict adherence to the maximum profit conditions[†]. We recall that these conditions can always be written as

$$\frac{\partial \Phi}{\partial V_l} = c_1 P_l, \qquad \frac{\partial \Phi}{\partial V_k} = c_1 P_k, \tag{10.32}$$

provided only that the inputs are in perfectly elastic supply at the given prices, as in the case of perfect competition on the factor markets. The meaning of the constant of proportionality c_1 varies according to the further assumptions of the model. Thus in section 194 we supposed demand for output to be perfectly elastic too and then found c_1 to equal $1/P$, as in (10.5).

[†] In economics the sign of (10.31) is often reverted so that σ is positive. We shall not follow this usage.

In the alternative model for regulated industries of section 198 it is equal to $1/\lambda$, as in (10.11), and upon adding constant returns to scale and the absence of profit this again came out at $1/P$. These examples by no means exhaust the possibilities.

212 If Φ is the Cobb-Douglas function (10.12) the elasticity of substitution is -1. As in (10.16) and (10.17) substitution of the derivatives of Φ in (10.32) yields

$$\alpha \frac{X}{V_l} = c_1 P_l , \qquad \beta \frac{X}{V_k} = c_1 P_k , \tag{10.33}$$

so that the inputs are given by

$$V_l = \alpha \frac{X}{c_1 P_l} , \qquad V_k = \beta \frac{X}{c_1 P_k} . \tag{10.34}$$

It follows at once that

$$\left(\frac{V_l}{V_k} \right) = \frac{\alpha}{\beta} \frac{P_k}{P_l} = \frac{\alpha}{\beta} \left(\frac{P_l}{P_k} \right)^{-1} \tag{10.35}$$

and the elasticity of substitution σ of (10.31) is seen to equal -1.

213 This property is closely related to many other convenient equalities that arise from a Cobb-Douglas production function under maximum profit conditions. Thus (10.34) can be rewritten as

$$P_l V_l = \alpha \frac{X}{c_1} , \qquad P_k V_k = \beta \frac{X}{c_1} ,$$

or again

$$\frac{P_l V_l}{P_k V_k} = \frac{\alpha}{\beta} . \tag{10.36}$$

This equality is at the basis of Klein's variant of the estimation of input elasticities from their relative shares that we discussed in section 205. In economic theory the implications of these equations are that the factor rewards are independent of factor prices, and that their ratio is constant.

Further results follow if this is combined with the additional assumption that the two factors together exhaust total proceeds, or

$$P_l V_l + P_k V_k = PX , \tag{10.37}$$

where X stands for value added. As we have seen in section 195 this equality is often supposed to hold, if only because of the difficulty of otherwise defining the rewards of capital. From (10.36) and (10.37) we have

$$P_l V_l = \left(1 + \frac{\beta}{\alpha} \right)^{-1} PX , \qquad (10.38)$$

and if this is freely transposed to macro-economic aggregates it means that the rewards of labour, or wage income, is a constant proportion of national income. In view of the underlying assumptions this passage to national aggregates would seem a rather wild generalisation of the model, and the controversial question whether it is supported or contradicted by the empirical evidence can hardly be taken seriously[†].

214 We return to the proper province of production function studies, which is an industry or group of industries that is sufficiently homogeneous for a single production function to hold, and we note one further relation for future reference. This is

$$\frac{X}{V_l} = \frac{c_1}{\alpha} P_l$$

or, writing c_2 for another constant,

$$\log(X/V_l) = c_2 + \log P_l \qquad (10.39)$$

which follows at once from (10.33) and is thus independent of the additional macro-economic assumption (10.37). By this relation labour productivity (X/V_l) has unit elasticity in respect of the wage rate, and as we shall see this is related to the fact that the Cobb-Douglas production function has unit elasticity of substitution. The usefulness of (10.39) for empirical research is that it can be investigated without any data on the capital variable, which are always hard to get.

The C.E.S. production function

215 Of late considerable interest has been aroused by an alternative to the Cobb-Douglas specification of the production function. This is the Constant

---

[†] But the interested reader may consult e.g. KRAVIS (1959), SOLOW (1958) or GRANT (1963) on this point.

Elasticity of Substitution or C.E.S. production function[†]. It can be obtained as the general form of a production function that (i) is linearly homogeneous (i.e. has constant returns to scale), and (ii) has a constant (but not necessarily unitary) elasticity of substitution. In the common case of two factors of production, labour and capital, this function is

$$X = A\{V_l^{-\zeta}+\varepsilon V_k^{-\zeta}\}^{-1/\zeta},$$

and this is usually rearranged as

$$X = \gamma\{\delta V_l^{-\zeta}+(1-\delta)V_k^{-\zeta}\}^{-1/\zeta}.\text{[††]} \tag{10.40}$$

The elasticity of substitution σ depends uniquely on the parameter ζ by

$$\sigma = -\frac{1}{1+\zeta}, \tag{10.41}$$

and upon a rather tricky passage to the limit for $\zeta\to 0$, $\sigma\to -1$ the C.E.S. function (10.40) is found to include the linearly homogeneous Cobb-Douglas function

$$X = \gamma V_l^\delta V_k^{(1-\delta)}$$

as a special case. The C.E.S. function has indeed arisen as the natural generalisation of a Cobb-Douglas function with constant returns to scale; it can itself in turn be generalized beyond constant returns by replacing (10.40) by

$$X = \gamma\{\delta V_l^{-\zeta}+(1-\delta)V_k^{-\zeta}\}^{-1/\xi} \tag{10.42}$$

where ξ is not necessarily equal to ζ. This function combines a constant elasticity of substitution, as before determined by ζ according to (10.41), with decreasing, constant or increasing returns to scale as we have $\zeta/\xi < 1$, $\zeta/\xi = 1$ or $\zeta/\xi > 1$ respectively.

216   We have gradually been drawn into mathematical economics rather than econometrics, but having obtained the C.E.S. function we can again concentrate on what is relevant to empirical research. So far empirical work has largely turned on a single derived regression equation. This is obtained by taking the derivative of (10.42),

[†] Also known as the Solow function or the S.M.A.C. function as a tribute to ARROW et al. (1961), but developed independently by BROWN and DE CANI (1963).
[††] The restriction to two inputs is a matter of convenience and can easily be removed.

$$\frac{\partial \Phi}{\partial V_l} = \delta \gamma^{-\xi} \frac{\zeta}{\xi} \frac{X^{(1+\xi)}}{V_l^{(1+\zeta)}}$$

and substituting it into the optimum condition (10.32),

$$\frac{\partial \Phi}{\partial V_l} = c_1 P_l.$$

This yields

$$\frac{X^{(1+\xi)}}{V_l^{(1+\zeta)}} = c_3 P_l.$$

or

$$(X/V_l) = c_4 P_l^{1/(1+\zeta)} X^{(\zeta-\xi)/(1+\zeta)}$$

where c_3, c_4 etc. continue to stand for constants, i.c. combinations of c_1 and the parameters δ, γ, ξ and ζ. Upon taking logarithms we obtain

$$\log(X/V_l) = c_5 - \sigma \log P_l - \sigma(\zeta - \xi) \log X , \tag{10.43}$$

where we introduce σ by substituting (10.41). In the special case of constant returns to scale $\zeta = \xi$ so that (10.43) becomes

$$\log(X/V_l) = c_5 - \sigma \log P_l . \tag{10.44}$$

For contrast we recall that the Cobb-Douglas specification, combined with the same optimum condition, led to (10.39)

$$\log(X/V_l) = c_2 + \log P_l .$$

217 The discovery and further empirical testing of the C.E.S. function largely rest on a comparison of the last two expressions. The main idea is to consider the equation

$$\underline{\log(X/V_l)} = \beta_0 + \beta_1 \log P_l + \underline{U} \tag{10.45}$$

in connection with industry data. The wage rate is regarded as predetermined, as in the other models that we have discussed, and β_0 and β_1 can be estimated by simple least-squares regression. It is then argued that by the Cobb-Douglas specification β_1 must equal 1, and that significant deviations from this value should be taken as evidence in favour of the alternative formula (10.44) and therefore of the C.E.S. function. We have come across another instance of the statistical testing of an economic theory.

The procedure we have indicated provides a valid (if indirect) test of the null hypothesis that the production function is a Cobb-Douglas function of any type, viz. with decreasing, constant or increasing returns to scale. But it seems unduly restrictive to identify the alternative hypothesis with a C.E.S. function with constant returns to scale. Still this is what is being done; the more general equation (10.43) is not considered, nor are other possibilities which might lead to another interesting class of production functions. The last point has been made by Hildebrand and Liu, who relate (X/V_l) to (V_k/V_l) as well as to P_l.[†] By the C.E.S. specification this variable should not affect (X/V_l) at all; in fact however it turns out to have a significant nonzero coefficient for most industries.

218 ARROW, CHENERY, MINHAS and SOLOW (1961) have fitted the regression (10.45) to twenty-four separate industries, using an international cross-section. The data refer to the early 1950's, and the number of countries (i.e. of observations) varies by industry from 10 to 18 out of a total of 19 countries. We reproduce the resulting estimates $\underline{b}_1$ of β_1 together with their standard errors in the first part of table 27. With one exception these estimates are all less than unity, and since this can hardly be accidental it strongly suggests that the elasticity of substitution is less than this value which is prescribed by the Cobb-Douglas production function. On assuming a normal distribution of the disturbances $\underline{U}$ of (10.45) one may moreover test the null hypothesis $\beta_1 = 1$ for each separate industry by the classical t-test. On the assumption just mentioned, the estimates, standardized by their estimated standard error, would follow a t-distribution with $(N-2)$ degrees of freedom, where N is the number of observations. By this test ten out of the twenty-four industries that have been investigated show a significant deviation from the null hypothesis.

These apparently conclusive results have been challenged by FUCHS (1963), who notes that the 19 countries employed in the analysis range from the United States to Iraq and comprise about an equal number of developed and of underdeveloped economies. It is unlikely that the same technical production function holds in both groups, and if there are differences in this respect there will also be differences in the parameters of (10.45). A co-variance analysis confirms that the two categories differ significantly in respect of β_0 but not in respect of β_1; the regression lines have the same slope, but not the same level. Fuchs accordingly fits the equation

$$\log(X/V_l) = \beta_0 + \beta_0' + \beta_1 \log P_l + \underline{U} \tag{10.46}$$

[†] See HILDEBRAND and LIU (1965), p. 33–39.

TABLE 27

Tests of Cobb-Douglas elasticity of substitution by international comparisons
(Arrow et al. and Fuchs).

industry	Arrow et al.: eqn. (10.45)		Fuchs: eqn. (10.46)	
	d.f.	$\underline{b}_1$	d.f.	$\underline{b}_1$
dairy products	14	.721 (.073) **	13	.902 (.080)
fruit & vegetable canning	12	.855 (.075)	11	1.086 (.098)
grain & mill products	14	.909 (.096)	13	1.324 (.167)
bakery products	14	.900 (.065)	13	1.056 (.105)
sugar	11	.781 (.115)	10	.898 (.183)
tobacco	13	.753 (.151)	12	1.215 (.208)
textile spinning & weaving	16	.809 (.068) *	15	.976 (.104)
knitting mills	13	.785 (.064) **	12	.948 (.083)
lumber & wood	16	.860 (.066) *	15	1.083 (.141)
furniture	14	.894 (.042) *	13	1.043 (.090)
pulp & paper	14	.965 (.101)	13	.912 (.175)
printing & publishing	14	.868 (.056) *	13	1.021 (.085)
leather finishing	12	.857 (.062) *	11	.975 (.100)
basic chemicals	14	.831 (.070) *	13	1.113 (.104)
fats & oils	12	.839 (.090)	11	1.058 (.181)
miscellaneous chemicals	14	.895 (.059)	13	1.060 (.088)
clay products	11	.919 (.098)	10	.658 (.197)
glass	11	.999 (.084)	10	1.269 (.096) **
ceramics	10	.901 (.044) *	9	1.078 (.125)
cement	10	.920 (.149)	9	1.308 (.217)
iron and steel	11	.811 (.051) **	10	.756 (.112)
non-ferrous metals	8	1.011 (.120)	7	.935 (.197)
metal products	11	.902 (.088)	10	1.006 (.166)
electrical machinery	12	.870 (.118)	11	1.026 (.214)

Significantly different from 1 : * at .05 significance level, ** at .01 significance level.
For notes see appendix A.

where the differential constant β_0' is estimated for the developed countries
but equated to zero for the other group.

As the second part of table 27 shows this further refinement of the empirical analysis completely alters the picture as far as the estimates $\underline{b}_1$ of β_1 are concerned. These estimates are now evenly spread around the disputed value of 1, and only one of them is significantly different from it. The Cobb-Douglas hypothesis can therefore no longer be rejected on the basis of this evidence.

As for the differential constant β_0', negative estimates of about $-.2$ (not shown in our table) predominate. Fuchs attributes this to an underestimation of the true wage rate by the values reported in underdeveloped countries, but one may equally well account for it by other differences in the constant term or, say, in the measurement of (X/V_l). We shall not pursue the matter further.

219 Another application of the regression equation (10.45) is due to FERGUSON (1965), who has fitted it to time-series of U.S. Census data for 18 industries. Ferguson is mainly concerned with the measurement of technological advance, and this leads him to introduce a trend term which is however suppressed when its regression coefficient turns out to be negative. This is the case for seven industries. Following Ferguson's choice in this matter we may consider his estimates of β_1 and use them to test the Cobb-Douglas hypothesis $\beta_1 = 1$.

These estimates are reproduced in table 28. They offer no grounds for

TABLE 28

Tests of Cobb-Douglas elasticity of substitution by time-series analysis
(United States, 1949–1961; Ferguson).

industry		d.f.	b_1
food & kindred products	(T)	10	.241 (.20) n.s.
tobacco manufactures	(T)	10	1.183 (.46)
textile mill products	(T)	10	1.104 (.44)
apparel	(T)	10	1.084 (.16)
lumber & wood		11	.905 (.067)
furniture & fixtures		11	1.123 (.045) *
paper & allied products		11	1.016 (.060)
printing & publishing	(T)	10	1.147 (.31)
chemicals		11	1.248 (.072) **
petroleum & coal		11	1.300 (.149)
rubber & plastic	(T)	7	.759 (.56) n.s.
leather & leather products	(T)	10	.856 (.14)
stone, clay & glass	(T)	7	.666 (.47)
primary metals		8	1.200 (.105)
fabricated metal products	(T)	10	.926 (.26)
machinery, not electrical		11	1.041 (.041)
electrical machinery	(T)	10	.643 (.36)
transportation equipment	(T)	10	.237 (.56) n.s.
instruments	(T)	10	.763 (.29)

n.s. not significantly different from zero.

* significantly different from 1 at .05 significance level.

** significantly different from 1 at .01 significance level.

For notes see appendix A.

rejecting the Cobb-Douglas hypothesis of unitary elasticity. They are about evenly spread around this value, and while two of them significantly exceed unity three are not even significantly different from zero.

220   The C.E.S. production function has attracted an almost exaggerated amount of interest as an alternative to the Cobb-Douglas specification. Since it is a more general specification (provided the restriction to constant returns to scale is lifted) we shall not dispute its theoretical superiority. But there is no evidence that it is a better description of reality. We have argued in section 217 that the alternative to the null hypothesis of the Cobb-Douglas function need not be the C.E.S. function; moreover the null hypothesis cannot be rejected, as we have seen since. In fairness it must be said that the general impression from the tables 27 and 28 is the lack of precision of the estimates, due no doubt to the small numbers of observations on which they are based. In these conditions the evidence is bound to be inconclusive. It is.

Notes to the tables

Table 1

The basic data consist of the numbers of ships of various nationalities arriving at the Port of Amsterdam on each day of the year 1963. These figures were collected from the records by courtesy of the *Havenmeester van Amsterdam.*

Table 2

Same basic data as table 1. The observed relative frequencies refer to 365 daily records for the year 1963; the theoretical values were computed from the Poisson density (2.6) with λ equal to the observed mean arrival rate of 1.22.

Table 3

Data from *Leergang besliskunde*, Amsterdam: Mathematisch Centrum, 1963, vol. 1, p. 34.

Table 4

Some basic data as table 3, rearranged as explained in the text. Theoretical relative frequencies computed from the Poisson density (2.6) with λ equal to the observed mean number of customers per day of .683.

Table 5

Except for the two values of (1) these estimates were obtained by the graphical method of section 31 from the data indicated below.

(1) Maximum likelihood estimates; motoring is defined as the use of motor vehicles as indicated by expenditure on petrol, oil, etc. See J. S. Cramer, Private motoring and the demand for petrol, *Journal of the Royal Statistical Society, series A*, **122** (1959), p. 334–337. The first estimate is based on the same data as figs. 8 and 9, and the second on those of fig. 11.

(2) Data from the 1959 Survey of Consumer Finances; see *Federal Reserve Bulletin*, 1959, July, p. 700–723, in particular table 9 on p. 717. The same data appear in fig. 9.

(3) Data from the 1953 Oxford Savings Survey. Ownership rates from L. R. Klein, Major consumer expenditure and ownership of consumer durable goods, *Bulletin of the Oxford Institute of Statistics*, **17** (1955), p. 387–414, in particular p. 410. The two lower income classes have been omitted and the four highest income classes have been combined into two classes; the weights for the latter operation were taken from T. P. Hill, L. R. Klein and K. H. Straw, The Savings Survey 1953, *Bulletin of the Oxford Institute of Statistics*, **17** (1955), p. 89–128, notably p. 89.

(4) Data from the *Family expenditure report 1964* of the Ministry of Labour, London: H.M.S.O., 1966.

(5) See H. Faure, Un modèle prospectif du marché de l'automobile, *Consommation*, 1959, nr. 4, p. 3–32, in particular p. 13.

(6) Data from H. Faure, Une enquête par sondage sur l'utilisation des voitures particulières et commerciales, *Consommation*, 1963, nr. 1, p. 3–84, in particular p. 46.

(7) Data from A. van der Zwan, Het bezit van duurzame consumptiegoederen, *Economisch-Statistische Berichten*, **49** (1965), p. 644–647.

(8) Data from the *N.I.P.O. Media-onderzoek 1965–1966*.

(9) Data for 476 nonfarm wage-earned and employee households from *Huishoudrekeningen van 598 gezinnen ... in 1935–1936*, Den Haag: Rijksuitgeverij, 1937. The attribute of butter consumption is defined as nonnegligible expenditure on butter over a full year. Fig. 10 is based on the same data.

Table 6

The elasticities have been obtained by evaluating the right-hand side of (3.13) for values of the standard normal deviate t that correspond to $\bar{Q}$ according to (3.13); the multiplicative factor involved in (3.13) is equated to .8 and .95 respectively by the argument of section 34.

Table 7

Except for the values of (3) these estimates have been obtained by the graphical method of section 31 from the data indicated below.

(1) Highly approximate values from rearrangements of the data reported by E. A. Pessemier, *Experimental methods of analyzing demand for branded consumer goods*, Pullman: Washington State University Press, 1963, p. 47–48 and p. 116.

(2) Data from D. Adam, *Les réactions de consommateur devant les prix*, Paris: S.E.D.E.S., 1958, p. 41 and following. The refrigerator data are the same as in fig. 13.

(3) Variance of logarithms of quoted rents and purchase prices reported by E. Salembien, Une méthode pour étudier la solvabilité de la demande des logements, *Consommation*, 1966, nr. 4, p. 3–58, on p. 22.

Table 8

These elasticities have been obtained by evaluating the right-hand side of (3.17) for values of the standard normal deviate v that correspond to Q (p) according to

$$Q(p) = N\ (v;\ 0, 1)$$

which follows from (3.16) in conjunction with (3.18), the multiplicative constant in (3.17) following from the values indicated in the column headings.

Table 9

But for typographical changes this is the same table as that given on p. 325 of D.G. Champernowne, A model of income distribution, *Economic Journal*, **63** (1953), p. 318–351.

Table 10

Except for (4) all estimates of this table are either direct quotations or they have been read off from graphical representations of the lognormal and Pareto type. In any case the model adopted in the source indicated below has been preserved, so that the values of σ come from applications of the lognormal model and the values of α from applications of Pareto's law.

(1) From V. Pareto, *Cours d'économie politique*, reprinted by Droz, Geneva, 1964, pt. II, p. 311.

(2) From R. S. Tucker, The distribution of income among income tax payers in the United States, 1863–1935, *Quarterly Journal of Economics*, **52** (1938), p. 547–587, especially p. 562–563.

(3) See D. H. MacGregor, Pareto's law, *Economic Journal*, **46** (1936), p. 80–87, for the 1867 data from Baxter and their usage.

(4) Based on data from *National income of India*, Bombay: Indian Merchant's Chamber, 1963, p. 244.

(5) From J. Aitchison and J. A. C. Brown, *The lognormal distribution*, Cambridge: Cambridge University Press, 1957, p. 117.

(6) From Recente ontwikkelingen in de inkomensverdeling van Nederland en enkele andere landen, *Statistische en Econometrische Onderzoekingen*, 1960, nr. 2, p. 57.

(7) See Centraal Bureau voor de Statistiek, *Maandstatistiek van het financiewezen*, maart 1962, p. 100–102.

(8) From J. Steindl, *Random processes and the growth of firms*, London: Griffin, 1965, p. 190, 192, 195, 199 and 217.

(9) From R. Gibrat, *Les inégalités économiques*, Paris: Sirey, 1931, p. 181.

(10) See P. E. Hart and S. J. Prais, The analysis of business concentration, *Journal of the Royal Statistical Society, series A*, **119** (1956), p. 150–181, especially p. 154.

Table 12

The basic data of the analysis reported in this table consist of 189 household expenditure records for October or November 1962 from the German 1962–1963 Survey, kindly provided by the Statistisches Bundesamt, Wiesbaden. These records refer to selected households that consist of a couple with two children; the head of household is a wage-earner or employee, not engaged in agriculture; his wife is not working. For the present analysis 16 of the 189 records were laid aside because they contained zero entries for one or more of the seven commodities under consideration; these zeros would complicate matters when fitting double-logarithmic functions to the individual data. All entries in table 12 thus refer to the same 173 household records; they are fully comparable.

The 173 individual expenditure records have been grouped by income (i.e. total expenditure), first into 29 and then into 7 income classes; and group means of income and of expenditure on seven commodities have been determined. We have then for each commodity fitted three Engel functions each in turn to three arrangements of the same basic data. The three Engel functions were:

(1) the linear function;
(2) the iso-elastic or double-logarithmic function;
(3) the semi-logarithmic form;

and the three representations of the data were:

(a) 173 individual data;
(b) 29 income class means, duly weighted;
(c) 7 income class means, duly weighted.

For the linear and semi-logarithmic functions the income elasticities shown in the table have been evaluated at the sample mean income, and the standard errors of these estimates have been obtained by the approximation of section 75.

Table 13

All the estimates in this table refer to expenditure elasticities of nonfarm households, the worst effects of family size differences having been eliminated either by restricting the sample to households of roughly the same composition or by the use of equivalent adult scales. The sources of the quoted estimates are:

Germany 1950–1951: H. Gollnick, *Ausgaben und Verbrauch in Abhängigkeit von Einkommen und Haushaltsstruktur*, Hannover: Strothe, 1959, p. 235 and following.

United States 1955: G. R. Rockwell, *Income and household size, their effect on food consumption*, Washington: U.S. Department of Agriculture, 1959, p. 8.

France 1956: G. Rottier, Niveau de vie et consommation de la population non-agricole, *Consommation*, 1959, nr. 3, p. 13–39, especially p. 38.

Great Britain 1958: *Domestic food consumption and expenditure 1958*, London: H.M.S.O., 1960, p. 36–37.

Table 14

The entries in this table were obtained by combining various results from Gollnick's analysis of data for households consisting of a couple with two children from the German 1950–1951 survey. See H. Gollnick, *Ausgaben und Verbrauch in Abhängigkeit von Einkommen und Haushaltsstruktur*, Hannover: Strothe, 1959, in particular p. 232, 235, 252 and p. 175, 179. The expenditures and quantities shown are per annum household averages in DM and kg respectively.

Table 15

This table lists only a few of the many equivalent adult scales that have been invented; the publication *Inkomsten, uitgaven en verbruik ... van 184 gezinnen*, Amsterdam: Bureau van Statistiek, 1941, lists 37 different scales in a historical survey covering the period from 1882 to 1936, and R. M. Woodbury, *Méthodes d'enquête sur les conditions de vie des familles*, Geneva: I.L.O., 1941, records 14 different scales used in the years 1925–1937.

League of Nations scale: established by an international comittee of experts in the 1930's and adopted in surveys held in Estonia and South Africa. See Woodbury, op.cit., p. 164.

Amsterdam scale: established in 1917 at the Bureau van Statistiek of Amsterdam and used in most Dutch surveys up to the 1950's, at least for expenditure and consumption of food. See e.g. *Nationaal Budgetonderzoek 1950, methodologische inleiding*, Utrecht: De Haan. 1953, p. 42. I.N.S.E.E.–C.R.E.D.O.C. scale: employed in the first large-scale French survey of 1956; see La consommation des ménages Français en 1956, *Consommation*, 1960, nr. 2, p. 24. This particular scale enables one, for any reasonable family size, to infer the households' composition from its number of equivalent adults. For obscure reasons, which I have been unable to trace, the scale is known in France as the Oxford scale.

Table 16

The contents of this table have been derived from the Engel curve estimates based on the British Ministry of Labour 1953–1954 household expenditure enquiry of F. G. Forsyth, The relationship between family size and family expenditure, *Journal of the Royal Statistical Society, series A*, **132** (1960), p. 367–397. In applying the method described in section 138 we have taken the estimates of the common income elasticity for all household size groups from Forsyth's table 1 (p. 374), and subsequently evaluated the differences between the intercepts for different household sizes from the mean expenditures given in Forsyth's table 2 (p. 380). All values refer to the comparison of households consisting of a couple and *k* children with households consisting of a couple only.

Table 17

This table contains a selection from the evidence collected and discussed by M. Friedman, *A theory of the consumption function*, Princeton: Princeton University Press, 1957. The values of *E* are estimates of the income elasticity of measured consumption in respect of measured income. Most of these estimates have been taken by Friedman from other studies; we do not quote these sources at one remove but refer the reader to Friedman. The examples copied in table 17 are taken from Friedman as follows: (1), (2) both from table 1, p. 44, (3) from table 3, p. 62 and table 5, p. 71.

Table 21

These estimates have been taken from H. Schultz, *The theory and measurement of demand*, Chicago: Chicago University Press, 1938, p. 548, table 48, column 4; they refer to simple least-squares regressions of logarithms of quantity on logarithms of price, both variables being represented by deviations from a fitted trend. We have rearranged the commodities roughly in ascending order of the elasticities. For a few commodities the exact delimitation of the three periods differs somewhat from the years indicated in the table.

Table 22

The elasticities of this table are based on the analyses of K. A. Fox, *Econometric analysis for public policy*, Ames: Iowa State College Press, 1958; we have used results from table 4.3 on p. 78 (livestock) and from table 5.1 on p. 120 (crops). Fox has estimated flexibilities by a regression of farm price on quantity (usually production) and income, all variables being represented by first differences of logarithms. We have converted these estimates into the corresponding elasticities, but we have been unable to evaluate the standard errors of these transformed estimates; Fox duly reports the variances (standard errors) of his estimates, but he does not show their covariances, and this precludes the use of the approximation of section 75.

Table 23

The elasticities of this table are based on table 1 of A. P. Barten, Evidence on the Slutsky conditions for demand equations, *Review of Economics and Statistics*, **49** (1967), p. 77–84. Barten fits demand equations to Dutch data for the years 1922–1939, 1949–1961, and the resulting coefficients can be converted into elasticities at the 1961 level of the variables concerned with the help of additional information from Barten's text. The results suffer from accumulated rounding; the values shown in table 23 are however free from this defect, for they were revised by Barten (private correspondence) on the basis of the original calculations.

Table 24

The elasticities of this table are based on R. Stone, J. A. C. Brown and D. A. Rowe, Demand analysis and projections for Britain 1900–1970, p. 200–225 of *Europe's future consumption*, edited by J. Sandee, Amsterdam: North-Holland, 1963. This study provides estimates of a linear expenditure system for the period 1900–1960, and we have converted these estimates into elasticities at the 1960 level of all variables. This conversion is not straightforward. Briefly, the elasticities can be obtained from equation (3.1) of Stone, Brown and Rowe in terms of the parameters b_i and c_i and of the variables μ, p_i and q_i, and the corresponding values can be found in various tables. Thus q_i and c_i come from table 1, μ from table 4, the $(p_i q_i)$ from the percentages of table 9 and the knowledge of μ, and the q_i from table 6. Since many of these values are rounded and since the elasticities of table 24 have been built up by several consecutive computations, the latter may suffer from an accumulation of rounding errors; the second decimal shown is of very doubtful precision.

Table 25

These estimates have been taken from P. H. Douglas, Are there laws of production?, *American Economic Review*, **38** (1948), p. 1–49; the time-series estimates are from the third line and the cross-section estimates from the tenth line of table 1, p. 12.

Table 26

All the entries in this table are from G. H. Hildebrand and T. C. Liu, *Manufacturing production functions in the United States, 1957*, Ithaca: New York State School of Industrial and Labor Relations, 1965. N is the number of observations of each analysis, i.e. the number of states with sufficient establishments of the industry concerned to be included in the calculations; these numbers have been taken from the state surveys on p. 143–145 and p. 150. But for rounding to two decimals the values of a_1, a_2, a and b come from table 2 on p. 104. The values of b'_1 and b'_2 (no standard errors available) are from table 3 on p. 107, and the returns to scale from table 5, p. 110. The latter values may differ from the sum of the a's and b'_2 because of rounding.

Table 27

This table summarizes two analyses of the same data, viz. figures on labour productivity and the wage rate of various industries in 19 countries for various years circa 1950–1956. These figures were collected by B. S. Minhas and they have been reproduced on p. 248–250 of K. J. Arrow, H. B. Chenery, B. S. Minhas and R. M. Solow, Capital-labor substitution and economic efficiency, *Review of Economics and Statistics*, **43** (1961), p. 225–250. The estimates and numbers of degrees of freedom of the first column are from table 2, p. 227 of the paper, and the second set of estimates has been taken from V. R. Fuchs, Capital-labor substitution, a note, *Review of Economics and Statistics*, **45** (1963), p. 436–438.

Table 28

Results from C. E. Ferguson, Time-series production functions and technological progress in American manufacturing industry, *Journal of Political Economy*, **73** (1965), p. 135–147. The estimates are from tables 1 and 2 on p. 140–141, (T) indicating industries for which a time trend was retained in the regression analysis. The numbers of degrees of freedom follow from Ferguson's remarks on p. 147; the significance levels, established according to the t-distribution, slightly differ from those given by Ferguson.

Notes to the figures

Figure 1

The data refer to the intervals between successive requests for landing clearance to traffic control at Schiphol airport, observed on weekday afternoons during January and February 1950 by the *Rijksluchtvaartdienst*.

Figure 2

The basic data consist of the numbers of ships of various flags arriving at the Port of Amsterdam on each day of the year 1963. These figures were collected from the records by courtesy of the *Havenmeester van Amsterdam*.

Figure 4

Data taken from table 1, p. 29 of A. S. C. Ehrenberg, The pattern of consumer purchases, *Applied Statistics*, **8** (1959), p. 26–41.

Figure 5

A reproduction of fig. 2, p. 36 of A. S. C. Ehrenberg, The pattern of consumer purchases, *Applied Statistics*, **8** (1959), p. 26–41.

Figure 8

Data from the Ministry of Labour *Household expenditure survey*, 1953; motoring defined as the use of motor vehicles as indicated by expenditure on petrol, oil, etc. The parameters of the fitted lognormal curve have been estimated by the principle of maximum likelihood; see J. S. Cramer, Private motoring and the demand for petrol, *Journal of the Royal Statistical Society, series A*, **122** (1959), p. 334–337.

Figure 9

British data as in fig. 8; U.S. data from the 1959 Survey of Consumer Finances, *Federal Reserve Bulletin*, 1959, July, p. 700–723, in particular table 9 on p. 717.

Figure 10

Data for 476 nonfarm households of wage-earners and employees from *Huishoudrekeningen van 598 gezinnen ... in 1935–1936*, Den Haag: Rijksuitgeverij, 1937. The attribute of butter consumption is defined as nonnegligible expenditure on butter over a full year.

Figure 11

Data from the Cambridgeshire survey of 1954; motoring defined as motor vehicle use as indicated by expenditure on petrol, oil, etc. For further details see J. S. Cramer, Private motoring and the demand for petrol, *Journal of the Royal Statistical Society, series A*, **122** (1959), p. 334–337.

Figure 13

Data from D. Adam, *Les réactions du consommateur devant les prix*, Paris: S.E.D.E.S., 1958, p. 48–49.

Figures 14 and 15

Data from Centraal Bureau voor de Statistiek, *Inkomensverdeling 1959 en vermogensverdeling 1960*, Zeist: De Haan, 1963. The distribution of all incomes of fig. 14 is taken from table 1, p. 37 and the separation into two age-groups from table 2, p. 38. The data of fig. 15 are taken from table 5, p. 47.

Figures 16 and 17

Data from H. P. Miller, *Income of the American people*, New York: Wiley, 1955. Fig. 16 is based on table 39, p. 83, and fig. 17 on table C2, p. 178.

Figure 23

Based on unpublished sales records of all 58 cigarette brands (including imported brands) sold by the French state tobacco monopoly S.E.I.T.A. in 1958.

Figure 24

Data for 65 nonfarm households of wage-earners and employees consisting of a couple with one child from *Huishoudrekeningen van 598 gezinnen ... in 1935–1936*, Den Haag: Rijksuitgeverij, 1937.

Figure 27

Fig. 27a is identical with fig. 24; fig. 27b represents the same data after grouping into 5 income groups with income class limits of 1250, 2000, 3000 and 4500 guilders per annum.

Figure 28

Three iso-elastic curves $C_j = AX^2$ and three semi-logarithmic curves $C_j = \beta_0 + \beta_1 \log X$ have been constructed so that they all pass through the same point $X = 5$, $C_j = 3$. The three iso-elastic curves have elasticities η of .8, 1.2 and 1.6 respectively, and the semi-log curves have elasticities of .4, .8 and 1.2 at the common point.

Figure 29

Data for households of wage-earners and employees from Centraal Bureau voor de Statistiek, *Spaaronderzoek 1960*, part II, Zeist: De Haan, 1963, table 2A, p. 44–45.

References

ADAM, D. (1958). *Les réactions du consommateur devant les prix*. Paris: S.E.D.E.S.

AITCHISON, J., and J. A. C. BROWN (1957). *The lognormal distribution*. Cambridge: Cambridge University Press.

ALLEN, R. G. D. (1937). *Mathematical analysis for economists*. London: Macmillan.

ALLEN, R. G. D., and A. L. BOWLEY (1935). *Family expenditure*. London: London School of Economics.

ALLEN, R. G. D., and J. R. HICKS (1934). A reconsideration of the theory of value, I and II. *Economica, new series*, 1, p. 52–75 and p. 196–219.

ALT, F. L. (1942). Distributed lags. *Econometrica*, 10, p. 113–129.

ANDERSON, T. W. and H. RUBIN (1949). Estimation of the parameters of a single equation in a complete system of stochastic equations. *Annals of Mathematical Statistics*, 20, p. 46–63.

ARROW, K. J., H. B. CHENERY, B. S. MINHAS and R. M. SOLOW (1961). Capital-labor substitution and economic efficiency. *Review of Economics and Statistics*, 43, p. 225–250.

BARTEN, A. P. (1964). Consumer demand functions under conditions of almost additive preferences. *Econometrica*, 32, p. 1–38.

BARTEN, A. P. (1967). Evidence on the Slutsky conditions for demand equations. *Review of Economics and Statistics*, 49, p. 77–84.

BAYES, T. (1763). An essay towards solving a problem in the doctrine of chances. *Philosophical Transactions*, 53, p. 376–398.

BERNOULLI, D. (1738). Specimen theoriae novae de mensura sortis. *Commentarii Academiae Scientiarum Imperialis Petropolitanae*, 5, p. 175–192. English translation in *Econometrica*, 22 (1954), p. 23–36.

BODKIN, R. (1959). Windfall income and consumption. *American Economic Review*, 49, p. 602–614.

BOWEN, E. G., and T. PEARCY (1948). Delays in the flow of air traffic. *Journal of the Royal Aeronautical Society*, **52**, p. 251–258.

BROCKMEYER, E., H. L. HOLSTRØM and A. JENSEN (1948). *The life and works of A. K. Erlang.* Copenhagen: Copenhagen Telephone Cy.

BROWN, M., and J. S. DE CANI (1963). Technological change and the distribution of income. *International Economic Review.*

BROWN, T. M. (1952). Habit persistence and lags in consumer behaviour. *Econometrica*, **20**, p. 355–371.

CHAMPERNOWNE, D. G. (1953). A model of income distribution. *Economic Journal*, **63**, p. 318–351.

CHATFIELD, C., A. S. C. EHRENBERG and G. J. GOODHARDT (1966). Progress on a simplified model of stationary purchasing behaviour. *Journal of the Royal Statistical Society*, A, **129**, p. 317–360.

CLARK, C. (1951). *The conditions of economic progress* (2nd ed.). London: Macmillan.

COBB, C. W., and P. H. DOUGLAS (1928). A theory of production. *American Economic Review*, **18**, *supplement*, p. 139–165.

CRAMÈR, H. (1945). *Mathematical methods of statistics.* Princeton: Princeton University Press.

CRAMER, J. S. (1964). Efficient grouping, regression and correlation in Engel curve analysis. *Journal of the American Statistical Association*, **59**, p. 233–250.

DALY, R. F. (1958). Demand for farm products at retail and the farm level. *Journal of the American Statistical Association*, **53**, p. 656–668.

DAVIS, T. E. (1952). The consumption function as a tool for prediction. *Review of Economics and Statistics*, **34**, p. 270–277.

DE WOLFF, P. (1938). De vraag naar vervoer per tram. *De Nederlandse Conjunctuur*, p. 12–28.

DOUGLAS, P. H. (1948). Are there laws of production? *American Economic Review*, **38**, p. 1–41.

DUESENBERRY, J. S. (1952). *Income, saving and the theory of consumer behaviour.* Harvard: Harvard University Press.

DURBIN, J., and G. S. WATSON (1950, 1951). Testing for serial correlation in least squares regression, I and II. *Biometrika*, **37**, p. 409–428, and **38**, p. 159–178.

EHRENBERG, A. S. C. (1959). The pattern of consumer purchases. *Applied Statistics*, **8**, p. 26–41.

ENGEL, E. (1857). Die Produktions- und Consumtionsverhältnisse des Königreichs Sachsen. *Zeitschrift des Statistischen Büreaus des Königlich Sächsischen Ministerium des Innern*, 22 November 1857. Reprinted in 1895 as appendix to E. Engel, Die Lebenskosten belgischer Arbeiter-Familien früher und jetzt. *Bulletin de l'Institut International de Statistique*, **9**, p. 1–124.

EZEKIEL, M. (1938). The cobweb theorem. *Quarterly Journal of Economics*, **20**, p. 255–280. Reprinted in 1944 in *Readings in business cycle theory*, edited by G. Haberler, p. 422–442, Philadelphia: Blakiston.

FASE, M. M. G. (1968). De vraag naar openbaar vervoer in de drie grote steden. *De Economist*, **116**, p. 619–639.

FELLER, W. (1966). *An introduction to probability theory and its applications, vol. II.* New York: Wiley.

FERGUSON, C. E. (1965). Time-series production functions and technological progress in American manufacturing industry. *Journal of Political Economy*, **73**, p. 135–147.

Fisher, F. M. (1966). *The identification problem in econometrics.* New York: McGraw-Hill.

Fisher, F. M., and C. Kaysen (1962). *The demand for electricity in the United States.* Amsterdam: North-Holland.

Fisher, M. R. (1958). A sector model–the poultry industry in the U.S.A. *Econometrica*, **26**, p. 37–66.

Fisher, R. A. (1935). *The design of experiments.* Edinburgh: Oliver and Boyd.

Forsyth, F. G. (1960). The relationship between family size and family expenditure. *Journal of the Royal Statistical Society, A*, **123**, p. 367–397.

Fox, K. A.(1958). *Econometric analysis for public policy.* Ames: Iowa State College Press.

Friedman, M. (1957). *A theory of the consumption function.* Princeton: Princeton University Press.

Frisch, R. (1959). A complete scheme for computing all direct and cross demand elasticities in a model with many sectors. *Econometrica*, **27**, p. 177–196.

Frisch, R., and F. V. Waugh (1933). Partial time regressions as compared with individual trends. *Econometrica*, **1**, p. 387–401.

Fuchs, V. R. (1963). Capital-labor substitution: a note. *Review of Economics and Statistics*, **45**, p. 436–438.

Gibrat, R. (1931). *Les inégalités économiques.* Paris: Sirey.

Golberger, A. S. (1964). *Econometric theory.* New York: Wiley.

Gollnick, H. (1957). Demand structure and inventories on the butter market. *Econometrica*, **25**, p. 393–422.

Grant, A. (1963). Issues in distribution theory: the measurement of labor's relative share, 1899–1929. *Review of Economics and Statistics*, **45**, p. 273–279.

Greenwood, M. and G. U. Yule (1820). An inquiry into the nature of frequency distributions representative of multiple happenings. *Journal of the Royal Statistical Society*, **83**, p. 255–279.

Griliches, Z. (1967). Distributed lags: a survey. *Econometrica*, **35**, p. 16–49.

Griliches, Z., G. S. Maddala, R. Lucas and N. Wallace (1962). Notes on estimated aggregate quarterly consumption functions. *Econometrica*, **30**, p. 491–499.

Haavelmo, T. (1944). The probability approach in econometrics. *Econometrica*, **12**, supplement.

Hemelrijk, J. (1966). Underlining random variables. *Statistica Neerlandica*, **20**, p. 1–8.

Hicks, J. R. (1939). *Value and capital.* Oxford: Clarendon.

Hildebrand, G. H., and Ta Chung Liu (1965). *Manufacturing production functions in the United States, 1957.* Ithaca: New York State School of Industrial and Labor Relations.

Hoch, I. (1958). Simultaneous equation bias in the context of the Cobb-Douglas production function. *Econometrica*, **26**, p. 566–578.

Hoel, P. G. (1947). *Introduction to mathematical statistics.* New York: Wiley.

Houthakker, H. S. (1953). La forme des courbes d'Engel. *Cahiers du Séminaire d'Econométrie*, p. 59–66.

Houthakker, H. S. (1957). An international comparison of household expenditure patterns. *Econometrica*, **25**, p. 532–552.

Houthakker, H. S. (1960). Additive preferences. *Econometrica*, **28**, p. 244–257.

Houthakker, H. S., and L. D. Taylor (1966). *Consumer demand in the United States, 1929–1970.* Harvard: Harvard University Press.

Huishoudrekeningen van 598 gezinnen ... (1937). Den Haag: Rijksuitgeverij.

IJIRI, Y., and H. A. SIMON (1964). Business firm growth and size. *American Economic Review*, **54**, p. 77–89.

JOHANSEN, L. (1960). *A multi-sectoral study of economic growth*. Amsterdam: North-Holland.
JOHNSTON, J. (1963). *Econometric methods*. New York: McGraw-Hill.

KALECKI, M. (1945). On the Gibrat distribution. *Econometrica*, **13**, p. 161–170.
KEYNES, J. M. (1936). *The general theory of employment, interest and money*. London: Macmillan.
KLEIN, L. R. (1950). *Economic fluctuations in the United States, 1921–1941*. New York: Wiley.
KLEIN, L. R. (1953). *A textbook of econometrics*. Evanston: Row, Peterson.
KLEIN, L. R. (1958). The estimation of distributed lags. *Econometrica*, **26**, p. 553–565.
KLEIN, L. R. (1962). *Introduction to econometrics*. Englewood Cliffs: Prentice Hall.
KOOPMANS, T. C., H. RUBIN and R. B. LEIPNIK (1950). Measuring the equation systems of dynamic economics. In: *Statistical inference in dynamic economic models*, edited by T. C. Koopmans, p. 53–237. New York: Wiley.
KOOPMANS, T. C., and W. C. HOOD (1953). The estimation of simultaneous linear relationships. In: *Studies in econometric method*, edited by T. C. Koopmans and W. C. Hood, p. 112–199. New York: Wiley.
KOYCK, L. M. (1954). *Distributed lags and investment analysis*. Amsterdam: North-Holland.
KRAVIS, I. B. (1959). Relative income shares in fact and theory. *American Economic Review*, **49**, p. 917–949.

Leergang besliskunde (1963). Amsterdam: Mathematisch Centrum.
LESER, C. E. V. (1940). Family budget data and price elasticities of demand. *Review of Economic Studies*, **9**, p. 40–57.
LESER, C. E. V. (1960). Demand functions for nine commodity groups in Australia. *Australian Journal of Statistics*, **2**, p. 102–113.
LESER, C. E. V. (1963). Forms of Engel functions. *Econometrica*, **31**, p. 694–703.
LÉVY, P. (1925). *Calcul des probabilités*. Paris: Gauthier-Villars.
LÉVY, P. (1937). *Théorie de l'addition des variables aléatoires*. Paris: Gauthier-Villars.
LIU, TA CHUNG (1960). Underidentification, structural estimation and forecasting. *Econometrica*, **28**, p. 855–865.
LIVIATAN, N. (1961). Errors in variables and Engel curve analysis. *Econometrica*, **29**, p. 336–362.

MACK, R. P. (1948). The direction of change in income and the consumption function. *Review of Economics and Statistics*, **30**, p. 239–258.
MALINVAUD, E. (1966). *Statistical methods of econometrics*. Amsterdam: North-Holland.
MANDELBROT, B. (1960). The Pareto-Lévy law and the distribution of income. *International Economic Review*, **1**, p. 79–106.
MANDELBROT, B. (1961). Stable Paretian random functions and the multiplicative variation of income. *Econometrica*, **29**, p. 517–543.
MARSCHAK, J. (1953). Economic measurements for policy and prediction. In: *Studies in econometric method*, edited by T. C. Koopmans and W. C. Hood, p. 1–26. New York: Wiley.
MARSCHAK, J., and W. H. ANDREWS (1944). Random simultaneous equations and the theory of production. *Econometrica*, **12**, p. 143–205.
MARSHALL, A. (1890). *Principles of economics*. London: Macmillan.

MILLER, H. P. (1955). *Income of the American people*. New York: Wiley.

MILLER, H. P. (1966). *Income distribution in the United States*. Washington: U.S. Department of Commerce.

MODIGLIANI, F. (1949). Fluctuations in the saving-income ratio: a problem in economic forecasting. In: *Studies in Income and Wealth*, vol. 11, p. 371–443. New York: National Bureau of Economic Research.

MODIGLIANI, F., and R.˙E. BRUMBERG (1954). Utility analysis and the consumption function: an interpretation of cross-section data. In: *Post-Keynesian economics*, edited by K. K. Kurihara, p. 388–436. New Brunswick: Rutgers University Press, 1954.

MOORE, H. L. (1914). *Economic cycles: their law and cause*. New York: Macmillan.

MUNDLAK, Y. (1963). Estimation of production and behavioral functions from a combination of cross-section and time-series data. In: *Measurement in economics*, by C. F. Christ and others, p. 138–166. Stanford: Stanford University Press.

MUNDLAK, Y., and I. HOCH (1965). Consequences of alternative specifications in estimation of Cobb-Douglas production functions. *Econometrica*, **33**, p. 814–828.

NERLOVE, M. (1958). *Distributed lags and demand analysis for agricultural and other commodities*. Agriculture Handbook nr. 141. Washington: U.S. Department of Agriculture.

NERLOVE, M. (1965). *Estimation and identification of Cobb-Douglas production functions*. Amsterdam: North-Holland.

NICHOLSON, J. L. (1949). Variations in working class family expenditure. *Journal of the Royal Statistical Society*, A, **112**, p. 359–411.

NICHOLSON, J. L. (1957). The general form of the adding-up criterion. *Journal of the Royal Statistical Society*, A, **120**, p. 84–85.

ORCUTT, G. H. (1948). A study of the autoregressive nature of the time series used for Tinbergen's model of the economic system of the United States. *Journal of the Royal Statistical Society, Supplement*, **10**, p. 1–53.

PARETO, V. (1896). La courbe de la répartition de la richesse. In: *Recueil publié par la Faculté de Droit à l'occasion de l'exposition nationale Suisse*, p. 373–387. Lausanne: Université de Lausanne. Reprinted in 1965 in V. Pareto, *Ecrits sur la courbe de la répartition de la richesse*, edited by G. Busino. Genève: Droz.

PEARCE, I. F. (1964). *A contribution to demand analysis*. Oxford: Clarendon.

PESSEMIER, E. A. (1963). *Experimental methods of analyzing demand for branded consumer goods*. Pullman: Washington State University Press.

PRAIS, S. J., and J. AITCHISON (1954). The grouping of observations in regression analysis. *Review of the International Statistical Institute*, **22**, p. 1–22.

PRAIS, S. J., and H. S. HOUTHAKKER (1955). *The analysis of family budgets*. Cambridge: Cambridge University Press.

QUENOUILLE, M. H. (1949). A relation between the logarithmic, Poisson and negative binomial series. *Biometrics*, **5**, p. 162–164.

RUTHERFORD, G. S. (1955). Income distributions: a new model. *Econometrica*, **23**, p. 277–294.

SAMUELSON, P. A. (1948). *Foundations of economic analysis*. Cambridge: Harvard University Press.

SCHULTZ, H. (1938). *The theory and measurement of demand*. Chicago: University of Chicago Press.

SIMON, H. A. (1955). On a class of skew distribution functions. *Biometrika*, **42**, p. 425–440. Also in: H. A. SIMON, *Models of man*. New York: Wiley, 1957.

SIMON, H. A., and C. P. BONINI (1958). The size distribution of business firms. *American Economic Review*, **48**, p. 607–617.

SLUTSKY, E. (1915). Sulla teoria del biancio del consommatore. *Giornale degli Economisti*, **51**, p. 1–26. English translation in: *Readings in price theory*, edited by G. J. STIGLER and K. BOULDING, p. 26–56. Homewood: American Economic Association, Irwin, 1952.

SOLOW, R. M. (1958). A sceptical note on the constancy of relative shares. *American Economic Review*, **48**, p. 618–631.

SOMERMEIJER, W. H., J. G. M. HILHORST and J. W. W. A. WIT (1962). A method for estimating price and income elasticities from time series and its application to consumers' expenditures in the Netherlands, 1949–1959. *Statistical Studies of the Netherlands Central Bureau of Statistics*, nr. 13, p. 30–53.

STEINDL, J. (1965). *Random processes and the growth of firms*. London: Griffin.

STONE, R. (1947). On the interdependence of blocks of transactions. *Journal of the Royal Statistical Society, Supplement*, **9**, p. 1–45.

STONE, R. (1954a). *The measurement of consumers' expenditure and behaviour in the United Kingdom, 1920–1938, vol. I*. Cambridge: Cambridge University Press.

STONE, R. (1954b). Linear expenditure systems and demand analysis. *Economic Journal*, **64**, p. 511–527.

STONE, R., J. A. C. BROWN and D. A. ROWE (1964). Demand analysis and projections for Britain: 1900–1970. In: *Europe's future consumption*, edited by J. SANDEE, p. 200–225. Amsterdam: North-Holland.

SUITS, D. B. (1955). An econometric model of the watermelon market. *Journal of Farm Economics*, **37**, p. 237–251.

SYDENSTRICKER, E., and W. L. KING (1921). The measurement of the economic status of families. *Quarterly Publications of the American Statistical Association*, **17**, p. 842–857.

THEIL, H. (1954). *Linear aggregation of economic relations*. Amsterdam: North-Holland.

THEIL, H. (1958). *Economic forecasts and policy*. Amsterdam: North-Holland.

THEIL, H., and A. L. NAGAR (1961). Testing the independence of regression disturbances. *Journal of the American Statistical Association*, **56**, p. 793–806.

THEIL, H., J. C. G. BOOT and T. KLOEK (1965). *Operations research and quantitative economics*. New York: McGraw-Hill.

THEIL, H. (forthcoming). Introduction to econometrics. New York: Wiley.

TINBERGEN, J. (1939). *Statistical testing of business cycle theories, vol. II: Business cycles in the U.S.A., 1919–1932*. Geneva: League of Nations.

TINBERGEN, J. (1951). *Econometrics*. London: Allen and Unwin.

VAN DE WOESTIJNE, W. (1953). *Een algemene vorm van de vraagfunktie*. Leiden: Stenfert Kroese.

WILLIAMSON, E., and M. H. BRETHERTON (1964). Tables of the logarithmic series distribution. *Annals of Mathematical Statistics*, **35**, p. 284–297.

WILKS, S. S. (1962). *Mathematical statistics*. New York: Wiley.

WOLD, H., and L. JUREEN (1953). *Demand analysis*. New York: Wiley.

WOLD, H. O. A., and P. WHITTLE (1957). A model explaining the Pareto distribution of wealth. *Econometrica*, **25**, p. 591–595.

WORKING, E. J. (1927). What do statistical 'demand curves' show? *Quarterly Journal of Economics*, **41**, p. 212–235. Reprinted in 1953 in: *Readings in price theory*, edited by G. J. STIGLER and K. J. BOULDING, p. 97–115. Homewood: American Economic Association, Irwin.
WORSWICK, G. O. N., and D. G. CHAMPERNOWNE (1954). Notes on the adding-up criterion. *Review of Economic Studies*, **22**, p. 57–60.

ZELLNER, A. (1957). The short-run consumption function. *Econometrica*, **25**, p. 552–567.
ZELLNER, A., D. S. HUANG and L. C. CHAU (1965). Further analysis of the short-run consumption function with emphasis on the role of liquid assets. *Econometrica*, **33**, p. 574–581.
ZIMMERMAN, L. J. (1957). *Arme en rijke landen*. Den Haag: Albani.

Index of names

Index of subjects